Torn Trousers

Andrew St.Pierre White

Gwynn White

Published by 4xOverland LTD

Thurlby, Lincolnshire
England
+44 (0) 7946 650541
www.4xoverland.com
Publishing enquiries: support@4xforum.com

First published in 2015

ISBN-13:978-1506099323

TO

Jenny, Tony and Woodie

Andrew   Gwynn

AUTHOR'S NOTES

A sub-title for this book could be 'A Year in Wonderland,' for as hackneyed as it may sound, it is precisely what the events in *Torn Trousers* depict. Way back in the nineties, we ditched our frenetic Johannesburg business routine and, travelling light, opted for a life of adventure in one of the most idyllic spots on Earth: the Okavango Delta in Botswana, southern Africa.

As woefully inexperienced managers of a high-class tourist lodge, our triumphs and defeats were jointly shared — there was no avoiding it — and virtually interchangeable, too. Just like the writing of this book. So, although the story is written in first person, some liberties have been taken. Parts of the book are written from Andrew's perspective, others from Gwynn's. We hope this binocular view gives you as much pleasure in reading it as we had in living it, and now, after more years than we care to recall, finally writing it.

The Botswana we write about is not the Botswana you'd find if you were to land at the new Maun International Airport today. The airbase where bush pilots swaggered is long gone. A string of high-gloss chain stores, selling everything from Beluga caviar to Prada shoes, have replaced the two dusty wholesalers that struggled valiantly — and often failing just as valiantly — to keep us and our guests fed. The Internet and mobile phones now compete with the VHF radios we used to communicate with the world. Yes, things have definitely changed over the years, but we write about the way it was. Still, if you go to the camp we managed you'd find the hospitality and the glory of the Okavango unchanged. We've been back, so we know.

All of the people you'll meet in this book are real but some names have been changed. If you recognise yourself, then thank you for playing your part in the cast who made our *Torn Trousers* experience unforgettable.

This book is written in British English, not American, so some of the spellings may be unfamiliar to American readers.

Andrew and Gwynn

CHAPTER 1

There was a place so tranquil that angels went there to rest. It was a place of such singular beauty, even the lilies dressed for dinner. Yet the ebb and flow of its life-giving water was determined by a climate a thousand miles away. The water level was high during times of drought and low in times of rain. At its heart ran a river that sought the sea but never found it. Instead, it spilled onto a plateau of sand, spreading like an Eden across the desert until at last it vanished into the dust.

Animals, great and small, followed the river, each in pursuit of happiness. When they found it, they stayed. Fish swam in quiet eddies. There were birds so varied in hue they confused the rainbows. Vast herds of elephant, buffalo, and antelope made homes here, and behind them carnivores trod. Trees offered shelter to snakes and comfort to travellers.

This was where my heart lay, in the Okavango Delta in northern Botswana.

But instead, I lived in Johannesburg, a sprawling, crime-ridden city in South Africa, Botswana's southern neighbour.

Here, chrome and glass shopping malls selling designer western must-haves jostled side-by-side with shantytowns. Known as squatter camps, the residents of these homes—corrugated iron, plastic bags, and gum poles tacked together with nails—considered themselves lucky if they had one meal a day.

Back on the asphalt streets in the "real" town, motorists jumped the red traffic lights at night, too scared to stop in case they were hijacked at gunpoint. The police turned a blind eye to such infringements.

Glue-sniffing children begged at car windows, fighting for elbowroom amongst vendors selling everything from sunglasses to cold

1

Cokes. It was a world where crime and poverty, abundance and luxury coexisted in mutual discomfort.

All I wanted was to get out.

But, I was trapped; a slave to my career, my mortgage, my car payments, and my keeping up with the Joneses. I think they're the folks who lived next door, but who could tell in suburban Johannesburg, hidden behind six-foot walls, razor-wire, and armed response companies? Perhaps life in Johannesburg wasn't that different to most cities in the developing world, but I'd had enough.

And one day it came to a head.

Snarled in the traffic on the lemming-run to work, I allowed my mind to slip away.

I was a kid again, growing beans between layers of soggy cotton wool. After a week, the upper layer bulged. Soon, thin dark tendrils appeared, pushing their way through the gaps into the daylight. That's what the city resembled on this smoggy morning. Smoke from thousands of paraffin and wood fires burning in the squatter camps curled into the air, trapped by the winter inversion layer. Like the cotton wool, the smog settled between the buildings, stretching skyward, as if reaching for fresh air.

I was the bean.

Except, instead of grasping bravely into a new world, I was slowly dying. Melodramatic, perhaps, but that's how it felt as I edged my way through the traffic toward my office.

Once there, I'd spend most of my daylight hours in a dark room staring at a moving screen. I worked with images, each stylised in a long, monotonous line of hand-crafted performances, where perfect people live in a perfect world. Where all girls are slim, all men are tall, all cars are shiny, and all food looks too good to eat. I edited television commercials, and nothing I helped create bore any resemblance to the world outside my editing room door.

I sighed, pulled my eyes away from the traffic, and stroked my car's steering wheel—caressed it, actually, because it was the only bright star in this otherwise gloomy scene.

I loved Darien—that was my Land Rover—because she gave me a safari feeling, even in the rush hour. The environment of painted steel, whirring gears, and the occasional sulfurous whiff of gearbox oil triggered thoughts that took me away, back to the Okavango.

In the end, the day turned out well.

I was fired.

It wasn't as dramatic as it sounds because I fired myself.

I'd spent eight hours with Jane Michaelino, a short-skirted, short-tempered film producer in her mid-thirties. Her husband, Jack, was a talented director who charged big bucks. With neither talent nor manners, Jane lived off of his energy, and everyone else's, creating an edgy atmosphere. By four o'clock, my fragile nerves shattered. I asked them to take their film rolls out of my cutting room and never come back. Jane was outraged. In my madness, I was calm and adamant.

They had to go. Now.

Once Jane's expletives and cigarette smoke cleared, I sat in the dark, the only light coming from the screen, absorbing what I'd done. The Michaelinos accounted for two-thirds of my income.

I wish I could say fear or regret gripped me. They didn't. My only emotion was relief.

I refused to be a bean any longer.

The only trouble was, I had no idea how to replace the Michaelinos. But right then I didn't care.

* * *

Gwynn was already home from work when I pulled into the drive. Tension pulled her usually smiling face taut. She grunted a greeting. Unfortunately, she had the disadvantage of a mere five minutes in her car to get home from her clients. It wasn't nearly long enough for her to cool down, so it wasn't unusual for her to vent her day's frustrations on me.

But I wasn't letting her get the jump on me today.

"Sit," I said as I walked into our lounge.

Gwynn moved Woodie, our Siamese cat, off the chair and sat. Both Woodie and Gwynn glared at me.

"You had a lousy day, yes?" I asked.

"If I ever have to write another word about air-conditioner compressors, I'll launch—"

"I fired Jack and Jane," I said, ignoring her attempt to grab my stage.

Gwynn stared at me, her green eyes wide, her mouth gaping in dumbfounded astonishment.

Expecting an outburst of rage to equal Jane's, I mustered my courage, and with false bravado, added, "Yup. Told them to go forth and multiply."

Gwynn did something very unexpected. She grabbed my shoulders, pulled me toward her, and smacked her lips on mine.

A bucket load of tension evaporated. "I was scared you'd be miffed."

"Not when I fired Grab 'n Cough today. No more boring copy for me." Grab 'n Cough was the name we had given to the supermarket chain for which Gwynn did research and wrote training manuals. They accounted for two-thirds of her income.

I cracked a smile.

Gwynn smiled back. "It seems destiny has taken a hand in our affairs. Let's go live in Botswana."

Afraid of the glint in her eye, I cautioned, "Nice idea. But the TV industry's not very big in Botswana."

"Please, no more commercials!" Gwynn wailed, both hands clutching at her unruly hair. "The last thing I want is to live through another one of your bad moods as you edit pointless adverts."

"Then what? We have to eat." Maybe I was being dense, but I just couldn't see what she was driving at. Work had kept me away from home for a while, and we hadn't been talking much. It showed.

"Yes, we need to eat. But how about getting someone else to buy lunch? And breakfast. Dinner, too."

I frowned. "Gwynn—"

"Let's manage a tourist lodge in Botswana."

Now my mouth gaped. I snapped it closed. "Manage a tourist lodge? With what experience?"

Gwynn brushed my incredulity aside as if I hadn't spoken. "C'mon, Droon, let's just sell everything and go." She quickly added, "Except for Darien, of course. And Woodie. We're keeping them." A quick dig in her handbag, and she pulled out our well-worn Botswana travel guide. "I've been dreaming about this for weeks now. Plotting actually, to be more precise."

She wasn't kidding—the book fell open onto a page listing the names and contact numbers of twenty tourist camps and lodges in Botswana. I wondered if she'd already selected the agent to sell our house. Probably. I have to admit to being hurt that she hadn't confided her escape plan to me earlier.

But then, Gwynn and I were very different when it came to life-changing concepts. She fluttered around, throwing ideas at me, expecting me to catch them, polish them, and chuck them straight back. Instead, I caught them, held them, thought hard and clearly about how to polish them, and only then did I roll them back to her.

This time was different. I caught her ball, saw only its shiny side, and, without a second thought, tossed it straight back.

"Come with me," I said, sprinting to the study.

Gwynn scooped up Woodie and followed, saying, "I hope these lodges welcome Siamese cats and Land Rovers."

"Any other day, that would be a problem," I declared over my shoulder. "But not today, because the four of us are invincible!"

CHAPTER 2

One press of the keyboard and the Apple Mac went ping! A blank screen stared back at me, cursor flashing expectantly. My stomach knotted, even though I'd planned this moment for weeks.

"Now what?" I asked Andrew.

He cracked his knuckles. "Leave it to me." A minute later, he had a letter that read:

My name is Andrew, and I'm a film editor with over 13 years experience in the film industry. During this time, I have successfully run my own business. Gwynn, my wife, manages her own company in the marketing and training fields.

We have both travelled extensively throughout Southern Africa - especially in the more remote parts of the Kalahari. We want to settle in Botswana and work in the tourism industry. We take the liberty of requesting consideration for any available posts at your camp.

It may appear that neither film editing nor marketing/training are suitable qualifications for running a game lodge; however, both are service industries. We have sound managerial and people skills.

I think saying we had sound managerial and people skills was a bit of a stretch, but then, job-seeking letters weren't written under oath, were they? Trembling with hope and excitement, I licked the stamps. Twenty letters went off in the morning post, and I settled down to wait.

And wait.

To keep the bills paid, I wrote low-key advertising copy, while Andrew took on a few low-budget corporate videos. How long we would survive with our colossal mortgage and car payments, only the angels knew.

Like most nineties yuppies, in our stupidity, Andrew and I had amassed three cars (between two people), two houses (one to live in, one for Andrew's business), an airplane (Andrew flies for a hobby), and a bunch of high-end computers. Just about all of it came with a monthly bill in the post.

In my weaker moments, I mused that perhaps we should have sent the job begging letters *before* firing our clients, but it was too late now.

After a month of suspense, three envelopes dropped into my post box.

None offered a job. One writer did, however, say that the life was wonderful. With seventeen replies still outstanding, my hopes remained high.

Another month went by with no further missives from Botswana. Andrew's heart began to fail him, and I heard occasional mutters of, "This is a waste of time." I ignored him openly, while inwardly my heart quailed, too.

Then, one bright morning, I trudged down to the gate to check the post box.

A buff-coloured envelope, nibbled by slugs and snails that prowled my garden, waited for me. I grabbed it, knocked off a disgruntled mollusc, and charged into the garage, where Andrew tinkered on Darien.

"This is it!" I crowed, waving the letter around.

The spanner Andrew poked into Darien's engine bay dropped with a clang. "Fantastic! Which camp is it?"

"How must I know? I haven't opened the letter."

"Then how do you know it's the one?"

"I just do."

I started tearing the envelope open but he grabbed it from me. The cheek! He was the one whose heart had failed. And then he had the temerity to dawdle over reading the letter. I reached out to snatch it back when he finally plucked up the courage and read out loud: "Thank you for your letter. I will be in Johannesburg at the end of November and would like to meet with you then. S. Pieters. Tau Camp."

I threw my head back and screamed with sheer joy.

Andrew tugged at his scraggly red beard, a sure sign that he was going to overthink this. "It doesn't mean he has a job for us."

"Of course it does," I said. "How can you be so negative? He needs someone to manage his lodge. Where's Tau Camp?" I rushed to a map of southern Africa mounted on the garage wall. Strung with red tape, it highlighted our travels. I had Tau Camp—meaning Lion Camp in Setswana—pinpointed in seconds.

Andrew gasped and his eyes lit up. "I visited there when I went to the Okavango."

"No way!" I slumped down on a pile of Darien's old tires. "Tell. Everything. Now."

"I stayed at her sister camp, an el-cheapo lodge called Scops

Camp. Tau was at the other end of the island. It's called Noga Island, by the way." He eyeballed me. "That means snake."

"You can't scare me," I said with a flippancy that was hard to match. "So what's Tau Camp like?"

"Maybe 'visited' is a bit of an exaggeration. My guide said it was a no-go area to Scops Camp visitors. Very classy. Definitely not friendly to uninvited guests."

Disappointed at his lack of info, I chewed the inside of my mouth, my tell that I was beginning to overthink things. "An island in the middle of a delta? I wonder how we'll get the Landy there?"

Andrew's jaw set into a hard line. "I refuse to even think about that hurdle."

* * *

For the next two weeks, the ringing phone caused agony, equalled only by a medieval torture rack. Despite my jitters, no one by the name of S. Pieters called. I had almost stopped flinching at the sound when, on an ordinary Wednesday morning, the pesky thing rang.

Andrew answered. I poked my head around the door to listen. He wasn't giving away any clues, so I mouthed, "Who's it?"

He ignored me, chatted some more, and then hung up.

"So, don't keep me in suspense. Who was it?"

"Sean." Andrew grinned. I frowned, trying to think of a Sean we knew. When I shrugged, he taunted, "We're meeting him today at Hyde Park. For lunch."

My impatience got the better of me. "Sean who?"

"Pieters," Andrew added with a serenity that could calm an ocean. "We have a job interview."

My heart threatened to chisel its way straight through my chest. "What? You're joking?"

"No. He wants to meet us today."

I succumbed to panic. "We need to dress up. Tie. Nice shoes." I started throwing wardrobes open, snatching at dresses when Andrew grabbed my arm.

"It's an interview for a bush lodge, not a bank."

He was right. My blood slowed to a manageable rush. We agreed on smart casual attire and arrived in the restaurant parking lot an hour later, just a tad nervous.

Okay, very nervous.

Andrew turned to me, his blue eyes dark and serious. "I think I'll leave my cigarettes in the car." He wasn't a heavy smoker but liked one after a meal. Going without them was out of character.

We walked into the swanky establishment, not knowing what to expect. Barely ten seconds later, a dark-haired man ambled in. He looked us over and announced in a clipped tone, "Andrew. Gwynn."

I didn't realise I was wearing a sign. But regardless of how distinctive we appeared, we were no match for Sean Pieters.

He stood six-foot-five inches in his bare feet. Yes, Sean was bare-footed. And Hyde Park in Johannesburg is not unlike, well, Hyde Park in London. I tried not to blink, focusing instead on the rest of him.

Reed-thin, he wore a baggy, once-white T-shirt and ragged jeans.

Not what I expected.

Not even close.

Even the *maître d'* looked startled. For a moment there, I thought we'd be refused service. But, seemingly oblivious to all reaction, Sean pushed past the disapproving door guard and headed for a table with a reserved sign. We followed.

Sean fired his first question before we even sat. "Why do you want to live in the bush?"

"We hate Johannesburg and love Botswana," Andrew said.

From then, I don't remember anything else Sean asked. But Andrew and I had tons of questions: the staff, the guests, the pay, the leave, all of which Sean answered with brevity. Finally, the deal breakers: the Land Rover and our small, bad-tempered Siamese cat.

Coward that I am, I let Andrew raise the subject of Darien before I mentioned Woodie.

It turned out Sean's eccentricity went beyond the superficial. The word Luddite springs to mind. I mention this because, apart from airplanes to ferry guests and food into the camp, plus a couple of water pumps, Sean was virulently against anything with an engine or wheels on his island. Gas, muscles, and sunlight powered technology on Noga Island.

Darien would have to stay in Johannesburg.

Glumness passed like a summer cloud across Andrew's face. He soon brightened as Sean launched into an explanation of runway maintenance, a crucial part of the manager's duties. As a pilot with his own airplane, keeping the dirt strip in tip-top condition, along with chatting to bush pilots, would be Andrew's version of heaven.

Darien's fate was sealed. Andrew agreed to mothball her while we were at Tau Camp.

If we got the job, of course.

Now it was my turn to ask about Woodie. Because mothballing wasn't an option, I dug my fingernails into Andrew's thigh as I waited for Sean's answer. He didn't seem to mind. Much.

Sean's answer was quick but curt. "There's already a cat there.

Tom. I employ him to catch rats. You can bring yours, too. Plenty of work to go round."

I almost gave a whoop but restrained myself. Sean probably wouldn't appreciate a manager who shrieked at meal times.

As we drained the last dregs of our Cokes, Andrew and I made plans with Sean to visit the camp in December. That was one month away.

"An LSD trip," Sean called it. "Look. See. Decide."

For me, it was pretty much a done deal. I leaned back in my chair with a triumphant sigh. Then, I saw Andrew reach for a cigarette.

Sean's eyes widened. "You guys don't smoke, do you? I can't have camp managers who smoke."

"No." Andrew lied, dropping his hand onto his lap.

I didn't say a word.

CHAPTER 3

Maun, in northern Botswana, had been known to register the highest temperatures on Earth. As impressive as that sounds, it paled into insignificance when stacked against Maun's other great accolade: it was the gateway to the Okavango Delta, a UNESCO World Heritage site of note. Ask any of the locals, and they would tell you that Maun's real *raison d'être* was to provide clientele for The Duck Inn.

Ah. . .The Duck Inn.

Many of Africa's great white hunters have drank there. Many fell over there, too. But before I wax lyrical on that honey trap, let me hasten to tell you about Maun's two other high spots: the airport and the shopping mall.

The airport was little more than a mismatched collection of prefabricated boxes dumped in the desert. Here, uniformed men and women sat around in the shade, engaged in desultory conversation, swatting flies. They only moved about four times a day, when a plane arrived. With the setting of the sun, they'd wait for one of the pilots to say, "I'm off to The Duck Inn." Then, with an alacrity that belied their almost moribund state, they'd leap to their feet and vanish off to the shopping mall.

Maun's mall was unique amongst malls. Women had to remove their shoes to walk through it because their high heels sunk deep into the thick sand between the shops.

As for the shops. . .

For the most part, they were little more than outdoor vendors selling anything from freshly slaughtered meat—blood and guts attracting flies in a bucket behind the plank that served as a counter—to dried mopane worm, a local, but quite revolting, delicacy. Visiting was a real treat—unless you were hungry.

But none of these attractions brought Gwynn and me to Maun on New Year's Eve. We were here for our LSD trip.

Sean told us to meet him at his office. Two hours earlier, we'd parked outside the building in the diminutive shade of a scrawny thorn tree.

He was late. Very late.

After driving two days to get here, one spent almost breaking our teeth as we rattled across one of the worst roads in southern Africa, we were not happy. Then, just as I thought we were victims of a cruel practical joke, we heard a vehicle grinding towards us.

It was Sean.

Gwynn and I exchanged looks mingled with relief, frustration, and trepidation.

His vehicle pulled up next to us, and he hopped out of it without a word of apology. He wore an almost white T-shirt, a faded kikoy, and bare feet. For those who don't follow traditional African fashions, a kikoy is colourful, striped cotton sarong, worn like a skirt by both men and women in East Africa. Somehow, the fashion had wowed the Maun fraternity, who now also sported kikoys.

I shook my head in wonder. Sean and his beat-up, colourless Ford four-wheel-drive pickup were a perfect match. Both looked as if they had endured way too many miles. A thirty-something woman climbed out of the other side of the truck. Although probably once attractive, her face was etched with dissatisfaction. She wore an almost white T-shirt, a faded kikoy, and bare feet.

Sean introduced us. "Sandy. Wife and business partner."

I stuck out my hand while Gwynn grinned. Sandy looked at my offering as if it held mopane worms. I was about to drop my hand to my side when she gave it a limp shake. Her lips cracked a smile but neglected to tell her eyes to join in.

"Come." Sean gestured to a building bearing a faded sign: *Okavango Safaris*, the headquarters of their empire, I guessed.

By Maun's standards, their offices were large and plush. Three of the four walls had deep cracks, and a tidemark ran two feet above the floor around the reception. Pretending not to notice, enjoying the *Africanness* of it all, I sat on a rickety chair in Sean's private office. Gwynn sank into an armchair that threatened to swallow her whole.

"We had a flood. Almost took the building away," Sean said, gesturing to the stains on the walls. I think he was about to make more apologies when Sandy cut in.

"I'm sure they want to get into camp and see their new home."

Despite being an LSD trip, it sounded like we'd got the job. I shot Gwynn a happy look, only to see her grinning wildly.

Sandy's next comment confirmed my suspicions. "I'm counting on you to do a better job than Barbara and Rodney."

I was so excited, I barely noticed Sandy's nose puckering as if a nasty smell had wafted into the room.

"Barbara and Rodney? The current managers, I assume," Gwynn replied.

"Managers?" Sandy spat with startling venom. "Managers manage! They don't. All they do is complain. Sean, tell them about the oven."

With an air of tiredness, Sean obeyed. "Rodney can't fix a damn thing. My camp is falling to pieces."

"And Barbara never cleans anything, so now *my* camp is filthy," Sandy interrupted. "She had just put the turkey into the oven on Christmas morning when the door fell off. We were unwrapping presents with our kids when we got these frantic radio calls. What the hell were we to do, miles away in Maun?"

"So I told them to barbecue the damn thing," Sean added to what was supposed to be his story to tell.

"Just what our English guests don't want. Barbecued Christmas," Sandy interrupted again, almost drowning him out. "And then the stupid woman tried to blame us. She said it was our fault because the oven was old."

More looks passed between Gwynn and me. Troubled ones this time. Trashing the old help in front of the new help didn't sound like a productive management technique to me. I wondered what Sean and Sandy would say about us when we resigned from Tau Camp.

That's if we even took the job.

Who was I kidding? Even if Sean and Sandy were the worst bosses in the world, nothing would stop me claiming this prize. All I wanted now was to get the preliminaries over and to move onto the camp.

An hour later, with holes drilled through my ears from more horror stories featuring Barbara and Rodney, Sean stood and grabbed his car keys. "Come. Plane's waiting."

Sandy grabbed my arm as we followed him from the office. "I know Barbara gossips about us, but I don't know exactly what she says. Keep your ears open so you can report back to me after your visit."

Yeah, right. Like I'm in the espionage business. The minute we left the office, I flushed her order from my mind.

A six-seat Cessna 206 waited on the tarmac at the airport. A crowd of people ringed it, the most conspicuous being a rotund black woman with a cheery face. Amid much laughter and cackling in Setswana, the local language I didn't understand, she supervised a young lad loading bags of toilet paper, a pallet of bread flour, stacks of canned goods, some tired vegetables, and half a dozen trays of eggs into a pod under the fuselage.

Sean didn't bother introducing us.

Pod bulging, the pilot slammed the hatch, flatly refusing to allow another tin can on board, much to the lady's consternation. He gestured to Gwynn and me, his only passengers, to climb on.

"Name's Mick," he drawled in an American accent as grizzled as his face. "Fifteen minutes, and I'll have you at Tau Camp." He guided Gwynn into the backseat.

I hopped into the prime spot next to him as I introduced myself.

Mick whipped through his cockpit checks, crackled into the mic, and we were soon airborne over Maun.

Gwynn let rip with a wild whoop, loud enough to be heard above the roar of the engine. Mick smiled at me, a conciliatory one, as if he sympathised with my plight. I grinned back and settled into my seat to soak up the view.

From the air, Maun looked even dustier than it did on the ground. Its sprawling suburbs consisted primarily of tin shacks, many with brand new cars glinting in their yards. Hundreds of vehicle tracks weaved across the flat desertscape, going nowhere in particular. Soon the commuter belt (if you could call a drive into Maun a "commute") gave way to gray patchwork, dotted with tiny mud and grass huts. Thorn bushes, stripped from the over-grazed desert, surrounded each hut.

Long before I got bored watching tiny cattle and goats drifting aimlessly across the drab landscape, we reached the Buffalo Fence. This controversial barrier ran the length of the southern perimeter of the Okavango, dividing the burning drylands of the south from paradise in the north.

It was a paradoxical blessing.

These few strands of wire had singlehandedly protected that wonderland from the exploitation and destruction so evident everywhere in Botswana. But the price was high.

Designed to keep foot-and-mouth from spreading from the game to the cattle, it prevented cattle herders turning avaricious eyes to the lush green of the delta. The flip side was the game's traditional migratory routes were cut off, locking the wildlife into a vast, almost artificial game reserve in northern Botswana.

Beyond the fence, the view changed again, revealing shimmering water, grassland, and bush in opal-like greens, yellows, and blues.

Water only covered the southern expanse of the Okavango during winter, when the flood was at its highest. Now, in midsummer, thousands of small islands, some no larger than anthills, rose from the grassy floodplains. Like spider webs, animal tracks trailed through the grass and reeds onto each island, where stately palms stood sentinel.

Another five minutes, and we soared over the deeper waters of the permanent swamp. In the deeper channels, the water was a midnight blue. Lilies threw an emerald mantle across the shallows and lagoons. Pink and blue flowers trailed like streamers in the wake of passing hippo and elephant.

It was truly breathtaking.

The Cessna's engine changed tempo.

"There it is. Tau Camp airstrip," Mick shouted above the roar.

Something kicked in my chest. Fear? Maybe. Excitement? Definitely. I peered out the window to spot the strip. All I saw was ubiquitous water, bush, palm trees, and tiny islands. I frowned, staring harder at the scenery. The runway had to be somewhere, but for the life of me, I couldn't see it.

That was embarrassing.

I suppose I could have asked Mick, but pilots don't like letting other pilots know they're lost. It just isn't cool.

Mick babbled into his microphone, announcing to the regional air traffic that he was starting down. My ears popped, and I still couldn't make out where he intended to land.

Then I saw a streak of white sand in the bush. I immediately thought of a cricket pitch.

"You mean that pitch down there?" I asked, half-seriously.

"Yes," Mick replied, pushing a small lever. He studied the ground ahead as the flaps on the wings dropped.

I appreciated his concentration as we plummeted on a collision course to where the cricket stumps and the game umpire would stand—a distance, in the cricketing world, of about twenty-two yards.

Mick cut the throttle and pulled back on the stick. The Cessna hit hard, bouncing once before settling.

"Kilo, Yankee, Bouncer," Mick shouted as my head hit the roof, despite my seatbelt.

Since Bouncer wasn't a call-sign I'd ever heard of, I asked, "Sorry, what was that?"

"K. Y. B. The plane's registration. We nickname it the 'Bouncer' because it was in an accident."

Bemused, I watched him coerce the Cessna into a straight line as it clattered along the strip.

"It was fixed, but has never been the same since. Just flying this thing is a challenge. Landing is like trying to train a rabid Doberman. One slip, and it jumps up and bites you."

I'd wanted bush planes and pilots. Now I had them. A grin spread across my face—one that definitely reached my eyes.

We rolled toward a clump of tall trees. A group of about twenty people stood on a giant anthill, easily six foot high, hogging the shade.

"Landing reception committee ahead," I shouted to Gwynn.

Mick kicked full rudder and opened the throttle. In response, the Cessna flicked its tail out and spun, covering the waiting throng in a cloud of dust and leaves. They turned in unison, shielding their faces.

Pilots obviously did this a lot.

The aircraft came to a stop, now facing down the strip from where we had come. Mick uncoupled his seatbelt and opened the door, letting in a draft of the sweetest smelling air I'd ever gulped.

My first encounter with Tau Camp—and I would never forget it as long as I lived.

CHAPTER 4

I pushed out of my seat, only to be pulled back by the fastened seat belt. Once freed, I stepped onto the runway. A dozen smiling faces surged forward to greet us.

None of them looked anything like a camp manager to me. Disappointed, I walked to the other side of the plane to find Gwynn and to retrieve our luggage. A middle-aged black man, dressed in crisp khakis, hefted our two bags. He said something to me, but I didn't understand a word. He could have been asking who owned the bags or just as easily could have been selling them to the highest bidder. A Germanic-looking chap strode up to him, holding out a fifty dollar bill.

"Excuse me," I said, pointing at my bags riding on his khaki-clad shoulder. "But I think those are mine."

The luggage handler looked me over. "You? Tau Camp?" I nodded. A clipped bow later, he added, "My name is Karomona, *Rra*. I'm guide. I carry bags."

"*Rra*", I knew meant "sir" in Setswana.

Despite his deference, Karomona turned back to the cash-wielding German. They spoke loudly in pidgin English, and the cash vanished into Karomona's pocket. Fifty dollars richer, he gave me a brown-toothed smile.

It was my move, so I introduced myself. He offered his hand, and I couldn't help noticing that all his fingers were deformed.

"We wait," Karomona commanded, standing at attention next to our bags, as if someone might sneak up and filch them.

I watched the busyness. Smiling staff, dressed in kikoys and Tau Camp t-shirts emblazoned with palm trees and a garish sunset, picked up the stock and food items. People boarded the aircraft, engaging in intense conversations and brief good-byes. Then I came back to Earth and looked around. Who were these people? Surely not the camp managers we'd come to replace?

An out-of-breath voice called from across the strip, answering my unspoken question. "Hello, I'm Barbara. Sorry I wasn't here to see you off the plane. I left the camp a bit late. Anyway, welcome, welcome." A sixty-something woman bounded over to join me. Rudely cheerful was how I would describe her face.

"How far is the camp?" Gwynn asked.

I expected a long hike given Barbara's breathless excuses.

"Just through the trees," she said, gesturing to the heavily-shaded grove behind her. She pivoted around, headed to said trees.

The crowd, portering the stock, followed her amid cheerful laughter and banter, none of which I understood. Learning Setswana was rapidly becoming a priority. I grabbed Gwynn's hand, and we joined the procession. We had not gone more than five paces when we entered the camp.

From what I could see, the entire place had been built using reeds and poles gleaned from the very spot upon which the buildings stood. Living tree trunks, bent and twisted like old men, propped up faded gold reed walls. The leafy canopy, jutting out of roofs, cast a soft green glow over everything. A multitude of birds chirped, filling the warm air with song.

In that instant, I fell in love with Tau Camp.

The wonder of the scenery, however, seemed lost on Barbara, who led us at a fast trot along a freshly swept path between the trees.

Too soon, we arrived at a spacious reed building at the opposite end of the camp. A portly man dressed in a blue stiff-collared shirt, red cravat, beige linen trousers, and brown flannel slippers, awaited us. His top half looked like a bank manager, and his bottom half like an English out-of-work stock clerk at home watching the football.

"I'm Rodney, the camp manager," he said, contradicting me with a stiff upper lip. "I have some forms for you." He flipped opened a huge ledger on the counter and handed us each a sheet of paper, black with type. "You can use this pen."

"They're indemnities," Barbara explained, probably seeing our startled expressions.

"In case you get eaten by a crocodile. Ha-ha." No guessing that Rodney had used that joke a thousand times before. Even he sounded bored with it. "Do you have travel vouchers?"

"No, we're guests of Sean," Gwynn said, fanning herself with her indemnity against the late afternoon heat.

"I see." Rodney slammed his big file shut and exchanged a grimace with Barbara. "Yet another bunch of bloody free-loaders."

Barbara nodded in agreement and then said sharply to us, "Number two is yours. Karomona will carry your bags." She marched off towards a reed cottage a little to the left of reception.

I looked at Gwynn, who shrugged her shoulders, her face perplexed. With no explanation for this strange welcome—how would Sean's and Sandy's friends visiting the camp affect Barbara and Rodney?—we followed her and Karomona along another swept path to our cottage.

I took a moment to study the camp. Four reed cottages huddled discreetly in a rough semi-circle under the shady trees and bushes. A large reed-fenced enclosure in the centre of the camp blocked the view of the far end. From it, I heard snatches of Setswana interspersed with laughter and surmised that the off-duty staff hung out there. I longed to ditch Barbara to go exploring, but I curtailed the urge.

From the runway, I had spotted another couple of reed huts, hidden now by the staff area. Sean had mentioned eight guest cottages, housing seventeen people when the camp was full. I stopped on the pathway outside an intriguing cottage. Different than the others, it had a staircase leading to a private lookout post.

"What's that?" I asked Barbara with some envy, wishing we were camped there.

"Number one. The honeymoon suite," came the cold reply as Barbara powered down the path to the next cottage. Number two, I guessed.

Not willing to be rushed, I took a moment to admire the clear water in the channel in front of number one. A lanky-legged bird, an Africa jacana, strode across the lily pads, oblivious of me and my frosty welcome to its world. When it disappeared into the reeds towards its nest, I headed for my new home.

By the time I got inside, a lecture about camp routine had begun. I hardly heard a word because the room blew me away.

In the centre of the polished ochre-coloured floor stood a king-sized bed, draped in a colourful African-print bedspread. A mosquito net, hung from a frame suspended from the reed roof, surrounded the bed, turning it into a sparkling white cocoon.

With no glass, the front expanse was open to the elements, with just a low reed wall dividing it from a small garden of cut grass and the reed-lined riverbank. I caught a glimpse of the river as it swallowed and reflected light. As odd as Sean and Sandy were, they really had something special in this camp.

18

Tired of Barbara's monologue, I said, "I want a drink. I assume the tap water comes out of—"

"The river? Yes," Barbara said, looking somewhat offended at having her prepared speech interrupted. "Pumped straight out into a tank and then to the tap. Try some."

Thanks to thousands of miles of filtering reeds and sand, the waters of the Okavango were amongst the purest in the world and I had no hesitation in drinking it straight from the source.

I pushed through a curtain of reed beads screening the bathroom. The word "bathroom" in this context is a bit of a misnomer, for there was no bath, merely a shower sans curtain, a basin, and a toilet. Undeterred, I turned on a creaky tap above the stained porcelain basin and poked my face under the gushing water.

Ever so slightly green tasting, it took me straight back to my youth when, as boy of twelve, I had first sampled this water. Back then, I had been made a promise, which, time proved, had come true. I stuck my head through the reeds and said to Gwynn, "Have you ever heard the Okavango promise?"

She shook her mass of dark curls. "Nope. I've had tons of other people promise me things, but never the Okavango. What can I look forward to?"

Even Barbara leaned in to listen to my reply.

"Those who partake of the waters of the Okavango are destined to return."

With a giddy laugh, Gwynn joined me in the bathroom.

It was a tight squeeze.

Gwynn manoeuvred herself around me and the toilet, and then plunged her hand under the stream of water. I watched her take a deep gulp. Lips smacking—probably for Barbara's benefit—she declared, "Best water I've ever had. I'll definitely be back." She took my hand, dragging me into the bedroom to face Barbara.

Tongue clicking her disgust—probably at our goofing around during her speech—Barbara turned to leave. I shot Gwynn a look, getting her silent approval to let our hostess know the real reason for us being here. Barbara was already at the door when I said, "We're your replacements, come to look at the camp before we take over."

"Typical," Barbara spat, vying with Sandy for the title of Venom Queen. "Just like them not to let us know. What? Were you supposed to spy on us? Let them know how much we talk about them and their horrible children?"

"I'm not sure that's quite what they had in mind," Gwynn said with a deadpan face.

Barbara wasn't fooled. "Huh. You don't know them like I do." Head shaking, she flounced off, leaving me feeling like an unwelcome intruder. Again.

I shrugged off my dismay as Gwynn gave me a quick hug. She flopped onto the bed. "Why should I care about their petty squabbles?" she asked, rolling back and forth across the covers.

She was right, I hoped.

I lay down next to her, letting my hand trail playfully across her stomach. "I'm here on a desert island with a beautiful woman. Isn't that every bloke's dream?"

"And you're going to get paid to stick around," Gwynn answered, clearly ignoring the suggestion in my tone. "It doesn't get better than that." She leapt up, tangled into the mosquito net, swore, clawed free, and raced to the door before I'd even registered she'd moved.

"Where are you going?" I demanded.

"The kitchen. Time to find out if my culinary skills are up to the task of running Tau Camp."

CHAPTER 5

Andrew and I had not gone far down the path when Barbara intercepted us.

"We're tracking down the place you make the grub," I said, embarrassed that we had been caught snooping.

"Oh, I don't lift a spoon. That's the chefs' job," Barbara said, with a marked softening of tone. Perhaps she had gotten over her fit of pique. "Come meet them."

Rodney grabbed Andrew's arm as we passed reception. "You don't want to join the ladies, do you? Come, have a G&T."

Gin and tonic was the last drink on Earth that would tempt Andrew, so I wasn't surprised when his eyes darted after Barbara and me. We were headed towards a reed-and-chicken-mesh building. Cheerful chatter and laughter spilled forth, presumably coming from the staff.

"Um. . .maybe later," Andrew said, edging away from Rodney.

"Don't say I didn't offer." With a loud harumph, Rodney went back to doing whatever it was he had been doing.

"The staff sound happy," Andrew said, catching up as Barbara and I crossed an area of swept sand between the kitchen and reception.

"It's New Year's Eve. They're anticipating a big bash in the staff village tonight. We're having a bit of a party as well. Special meal. Champagne. Maybe we'll even get you and the other guests singing *Auld Lang Syne.*"

Champaign or not, I would sing, no problem. Andrew, not so much. Still, it seemed appropriate to be in Tau Camp on New Year's Eve, with all the changes we were anticipating in our lives.

We reached the kitchen. Barbara stepped through the door into the dimly lit room.

The staff's cheerful banter froze into silence.

"I told them you're the new managers," Barbara said, pointing to

21

the six pairs of watching eyes. "So now they have gone all shy on us."

Shyness wasn't how I described the intense scrutiny with which we were greeted.

No one said a word.

I blasted them with my friendliest smile and stole a look around. A gas oven gaped at me from a corner of the room. I knew I was being evil, but I couldn't resist pointing at it. "I believe you had a disaster on Christmas day. Sandy told us the door fell off."

Barbara jerked back as if I had hit her. "That silly cow! Did she also tell you she and her dreadful family are the main reasons Rodney and I are leaving?"

I shrank, regretting opening my mouth.

It didn't deter Barbara, who, now in full diatribe, shouted, "Sandy is a spoilt brat. Stand on your head. Do backflips. Makes no difference. Nothing satisfies her. She'll send notice that she and her horrible children are coming, and we'll spend two days scrubbing the camp. Then, the first thing she does is to walk into the kitchen and announce it's filthy." Six heads nodded sagely, as if the kitchen staff agreed with every word. "Then we have to start cleaning again."

"How often does she visit?" I asked, the first signs of nervousness creeping into my voice.

"Too damn often. Even the guests don't like her—and I can prove that." Barbara opened her arms and, brooking no argument, swept Andrew and me out of the kitchen before her. "Take a seat in the lounge behind reception, and I'll be right with you."

Like scolded children, Andrew and I obeyed.

I entered the open-air lounge and stopped short, enthralled by a bay of sparkling water in front of the camp. The size of a large swimming pool, it was partially protected from the swirling river by a diminutive island of reeds. Half a dozen *mekoro*, wooden dugout canoes, lay like giant toothpicks on the grassy bank that rolled down to the crystal water. In the shallows, a pair of Jacana scurried over lily pads.

On the bank, the harsh, grating call of a black crake sounded from a clump of papyrus that bobbed in the gentle breeze. A small, black water bird with an insanely luminous yellow beak and bright red legs, the crake was elusive and shy. I had always wanted to see one but had never gotten that lucky. Now, it seemed, one lived on my future doorstep.

"Tau Camp promises to be a bird paradise," I said to Andrew in awe.

"Wish I brought my binos out with me." Andrew glared playfully at me. "But someone was in a bit of a rush to leave the cottage."

I grinned. "Sex isn't everything, you know. Have some self-control."

"Why on Earth would I want to do that?"

Laughing, I changed the subject. "Apart from the war going on between owners and minions, this place is idyllic."

Andrew nodded. "But nothing is ever perfect, is it?"

"Wouldn't be my life if it was."

"You must be the new managers."

I turned to see a middle-aged couple standing behind us. The woman waved her hand to encompass herself and the earthy-looking man standing next to her. "Bonnie, and this is Chuck. We're potato farmers from Idaho, come for a safari in Africa."

"How nice for you," I murmured, turning back to enjoy the view. Then a thought struck. I was supposed to be a camp manger in training. My guests would expect me to be interested in sharing banalities with them. I turned back and smiled. "Andrew and I are admiring the real estate that comes with our new home and office."

Bonnie and Chuck settled in a wicker sofa in the lounge, and she beckoned us over to join them. Again, like lambs, Andrew and I obeyed, sitting opposite them.

"I heard Barbara say something about the owner's wife." When I nodded, Bonnie added, "She hasn't stopped talking about her since we got here two days ago."

"Getting mighty tiresome, too," Chuck drawled, filling his pipe with tobacco.

"But we grin and bear it," Bonnie said, just as Barbara strode into the lounge, holding a sheet of paper.

"Bonnie. Chuck. Welcome," Barbara said. "I've been filling Gwynn and Andrew in on how terrible Sandy and Sean are."

"Please, no." Chuck moaned, looking pained. "We're not going to read the guest report again, are we?" He'd obviously had enough.

Barbara ignored him. "I have it here. Okavango Safaris sends each guest who visits the camp an assessment sheet to complete once they're home. When Rodney and I took our break in September, Sandy came to manage the camp. Of course, she brought her two young sons with her." With nary a pause for breath, she gushed, "Now, we all know children can be difficult, but these two are, without question, the most obnoxious monsters in Africa. The baboons make less mess." She waved around the well-thumbed sheet of paper. "And the guests agreed, because this is what one wrote: 'My stay at Camp Delta was severely marred by the noise and general bad behaviour of the owner's children. To make matters worse, the advanced stage of his wife's pregnancy clearly affected her disposition. She was rude, ungracious, and most unpleasant

23

to be with.'" Barbara turned to Andrew and me in triumph. "So you see, it isn't just us who think she's terrible. And when you take over, you'll have her baby to contend with, as well."

"I'm surprised they sent it to you." I reached for the sheet to check its authenticity.

Barbara clutched it tighter to her chest. "Those clots in the Maun office sent it here by mistake. But I'm hanging on to it, and when we leave, I'm going to rub Sean's nose in it."

I shot another glance at Andrew to see how he was taking this avalanche of bad news. He was leaning back in his chair, tugging on his beard, a sure sign of serious rumination. It was time for us to talk before he let his rational side derail this for us.

I stood. "Well, Barbara, you've certainly given us something to think about." My eyebrow raised in Andrew's direction was enough to get him on his feet.

We padded silently along the sandy path towards our cottage. I resisted the urge to stop and watch a flock of white-rumped babblers cackling in the thorny scrub near our front door. There would be plenty of time for bird-watching in the future—if I managed to placate Andrew.

Once in our cottage, I asked, "Do you want to take the job and run the risk of having problems with Sandy?" My stomach clenched with anxiety.

Despite Andrew's usual, infuriating caution, his answer was quick in coming. "What's life, if one doesn't take a few risks?"

Heart chirping, I dragged my boy into the bathroom—the only room without a view—and made love to him on three-square-feet of ochre-coloured concrete floor.

* * *

It was nearing six o'clock, the perfect time for a sundowner. With a glow any honeymooner would envy, Andrew and I headed for the lounge—and, hopefully, something to eat. My stomach growled like a lion whose last meal had been a predawn bowl of cereal. Lions don't fancy cereal.

A vivid pink and orange sunset competed for oohs and aahs with a crackling campfire, blazing in a hollow in the middle of a sandy sitting area in front of the lounge. A circle of director-style wooden chairs invited us in to enjoy the show.

It was lost on me. All I saw were two plates of snacks waiting on tables made from palm trunks.

Before I could nab a morsel, Andrew made a dash for an oyster wrapped in bacon, gulping it down as if he were a bass, taking live bait.

Not to be out done, I gobbled a couple, too, and then sighed with relief. "Devil-on-horseback. No better than mine. Thank goodness." I slapped my lips, relishing the tangy aftertaste of smoke oysters fried in bacon.

We cleaned the plate.

I dropped it back onto the table just as Bonnie and Chuck appeared, dressed for dinner. It turned out they were the only other guests in camp this New Year's Eve.

Andrew grinned sheepishly. "Sorry, we polished off the grub. Put it down to intense hunger brought on by excessive travel."

"Never mind the eats," Bonnie tittered, sitting next to me. "I'm more interested in you two crazies. Now that you've been warned about the owner's wicked wife, are you still considering taking the job?"

"It seems the feeling is mutual," I said with a wolfish grin. "The owner's wicked wife doesn't like Barbara much, either."

"I'm not surprised, given the way Barbara and Rodney bad-mouth her to the guests." Bonnie leaned in for what promised to be an extended camp manager bashing session. "They really are poor managers. Resigned. Lost the passion. Disinterested, if you know what I—"

Chuck nudged her in the ribs, looking pointedly over his shoulder.

The subjects of our gossip had arrived.

Bonnie blushed scarlet.

I stammered, "Barbara, the. . .the river on the other side of the bay. . .what's it called?"

"What's it called!" Barbara threw her hands up and sighed. "Brace yourself. You'll be asked that question a thousand times." Still standing, as if she meant to bolt at any second, she added, "It's the Boro, the major waterway dissecting this portion of the delta. It's quite substantial upstream, but here, it narrows into that channel." She pointed vaguely across the bay. "The main feature here is the reed floodplain, but the water level is low at the moment, so the *mekoro* are rather limited in where they can go, as you will see tomorrow, when you go on your outing with Karomona."

Rodney shook his head tiredly and then called Andrew over to a fridge in the corner of the lounge.

"The bar," I heard him say. "Drinks are included in the bill you won't be paying." He and Barbara turned to leave. "We'll be back for dinner at seven-thirty. Sharp."

Forget a banker. The top half of Rodney was an accountant, through and through.

I joined Andrew at the bar. He opened the chest fridge and said unnecessarily, "Beers, cold drinks, white wine." He brushed the row of cans with his fingertips and grinned. "Gwynn, what freezing, close-to-ice, just-the-way-I-like-it beverage can I get you?"

"They aren't cold, are they?" I asked, eyeing the drinks as if they would bite me.

"Nope. What do you want?"

"Coke. Why aren't they cold?"

"You really are labouring the point, you know."

"Meaning?"

"They're not cold because the fridge obviously needs fixing."

* * *

Seven-thirty sharp found us in the dining room—a charming reed structure built around a giant Knobthorn acacia tree. The windowless front wall was low, giving us an uninterrupted view across the floodplain and the river. At the back of the room was a small atrium, filled with lush palms, animal skulls, and time-sculpted chunks of leadwood. (Just as an aside: leadwood is a tall, long-lived tree with wood as heavy as. . .well, lead. Slow-burning, it makes great campfires.)

As enchanting as the dining room was, the focal point had to be the gleaming, wine-red, baronial dining table. It could easily seat seventeen guests and two managers with elbowroom to spare.

Always the gentleman, Andrew pulled out my chair, and then huffed, "Crikey. What are these made from? Leadwood?"

An eye roll from Barbara. She turned to Rodney. "You're the one keeping tally. How many times have we've been asked that question?"

"Three thousand, seven-hundred and twenty-seven."

I believed him. He was anal enough to have counted. It did, however, warn me that running a camp was not all scintillating conversation.

Never one to miss an opportunity to stir trouble, Andrew looked innocently at Barbara. "So what answer did you give to the three thousand, seven-hundred and twenty-six previous enquirers?"

Chuck snorted a laugh. "I was one of them, but I won't steal Barbara's thunder."

Barbara had the grace to smile. "Sit, and I will reveal all."

Chairs clattering, Andrew and I sat opposite Chuck and Bonnie while our hosts took a double throne at the head of the table.

"We didn't know the answer to that question, either," Barbara said. "Not until a retired Canadian wood expert booked in a few months ago. He identified the table and chairs as a mixture of Rhodesian teak and Australian jarrah." Her smile broadened. "Now, Andrew, you who are young, know as much as I, who am old."

Regardless of the hygiene in her kitchen, or the temperature of her drinks, I decided I liked Barbara. She was certainly more personable than

Sandy.

Rodney appeared at my shoulder with a bottle of red wine in one hand and bottle of white in the other. I nodded to the red. While he poured, I asked a question that had played all day on my mind. "I believe you have a cat here?"

"Ah, Big Tom," Rodney crooned, filling my glass with an excellent South African pinotage. "He'll be around to filch tidbits before long."

As if choreographed, a grey and white tabby jumped up onto the bench next to Barbara. A small tank, he was about four times the size of Woodie. Large yellow eyes surveyed the table. Still, he seemed friendly enough, given that his purrs competed in loudness and intensity with the calls of the painted reed frogs over in the bay. I opened my mouth to say I intended bringing a cat but was stopped by waiters bearing bowls of soup.

The moment of culinary truth had come. Despite having three camp chefs at my disposal, would my skills be equal to the cuisine served at this luxury lodge, where guests paid hundreds of U.S. dollars a night to sup? (Thousands, by today's standards)

I took a deep breath and stared down at my bowl. And then stared some more. The soup looked. . .nondescript. Although steaming, no piquant aroma wafted up to aid in its identity. I would have to rely on taste.

Mushroom. As insipid as it appeared. If this was Barbara's idea of a celebratory meal, then she and I saw parties very differently. Still, my heart did a little drum roll. My cooking was definitely in the game if this was the soup of the day. After spicing it up with more salt and pepper than was good for me, I ate it because I was ravenous. Still famished, I eagerly awaited the mains.

"Coq au vin," Barbara announced as the waiters slid plates decked with healthy servings of chicken and veg in front of Chuck and Bonnie. I noticed some raised eyebrows and wondered what was wrong.

Then, my plate arrived—now my little old heart pounded out a joyful rat-a-tat-tat, and I only just managed to resist doing a victory dance. Before me floundered an intoxicated piece of chicken in a flood of red wine sauce. Worse, it smelled as if the wine had been sloshed over the plate moments before leaving the kitchen.

Tom, waiting anxiously for his treat, puckered his nose against the acrid stench, hopped off his chair, and slunk out into the night. I made him a silent promise: the food would improve, but treats would only be forthcoming if he promised to play nicely with Woodie, the new kitty on his beat.

Reluctantly, I picked up my knife and fork and, delaying this culinary nightmare for as long as possible, glanced at Andrew. He was doing an excellent landscaping job on his plate, moving drowned vegetables and chicken around the slowly congealing blood-red gravy. I leaned over and whispered, "Still hungry?"

I saw him swallow his laughter. I guess a guy has to eat something.

The waiters hauled almost full plates of food back to the kitchen. I sat back in my chair, holding out no hope for dessert—the best meal of the day, in my opinion.

But I was wrong, as I so often am.

The crème caramel placed in front of me was the finest I had ever tasted. I even went back for seconds. As I relaxed in my jarrah wood chair, allowing the creamy sweetness to melt in my mouth, I knew I could do this. I could run Tau Camp's kitchen. Glowing with quiet confidence, I smiled at Andrew. He looked more relaxed than I'd seen him in years.

Once the last strains of *Auld Lang Syne*, sung to bid farewell to the old and to welcome in the New Year, had drifted into the night, Andrew and I excused ourselves from the table. Like a velvet mantle, the night air wrapped around me as we made our way by torchlight down the sandy path to our cottage.

"This is our year," I said to Andrew.

His grip on my arm tightened, and I heard the smile in his voice. "You say that every year."

"This time, I mean it."

That night, I slept peacefully under my mosquito net, and instead of worrying about cats and food—more especially whether my cat would become someone else's meal—I dreamt of Karomona and his deformed fingers, and the excursion he was taking us on in the morning.

CHAPTER 6

My dawn wake-up call came from somewhere outside our cottage. In my grogginess, I heard someone shout my name. Jarred awake, I wondered where I was. It all rushed back. I was in paradise. Sighing with delight, I nestled into my pillow and listened to the chorus of bird song, blissfully aware that I'd never heard any of these singers in my Johannesburg garden. In fact, I didn't recognise several of the calls. That reminded me we were going out into the delta today with Karomona.

Excitement flooded though me, washing away my reverie. I nudged Gwynn, sprawled out next to me. "Wake up. Adventure time."

She groaned, so I prodded again. Somewhere in her sleep-addled brain, she must have recalled what was happening because she bolted upright, grinning.

Minutes later, we were dressed and in the dining room with Bonnie and Chuck, eating an excellent fruity rusk and drinking coffee. A rusk is a South African biscuity-thing designed for dunking. Chunky and oblong, they're usually as unpalatable as dried toast. But these had the texture of light fruitcake. Delicious. Fortifying, too, as Barbara said we would not return to camp much before nine-thirty. That's a long time to wait for food after a three hour walk.

In the morning chill, Karomona and another guide waited by their *mekoro*.

Finished snacking, Gwynn and I walked down to the water's edge to join them. Back straight as a board, Karomona still somehow managed to bow, then gestured to his *mokoro*.

Mekoro, plural, or *mokoro*, singular, are long, narrow canoes dug out of tall trees that the local people—the Bayei—use for transport on the delta. With a low freeboard, they usually have water slopping about in the bowels. Today, small mattresses shoved into moulded plastic, legless chairs guaranteed our comfort.

Gwynn stepped on board and claimed the front seat.

A sudden rush of *déjà vu* had me grinning. The front seat of a *mokoro* was not always a good idea. Overnight, spiders spun webs across the channels and the person in front had the sticky job of breaking them and dislodging the owners.

Gwynn, I must tell you, was not great with insects. She could out stare a snake without raising a sweat, but the tiniest bug really got her going.

Expecting panicked shrieks, I let her sit in front. Then I asked innocently, "You happy there?"

"Oh yes. Very," came the reply. "We should do this every day. Me in front in the morning and you in front in the afternoon."

"It's a deal." I knew she'd kill me later.

Karomona took up his position at the back, pole held upright, poised for action. Barbara pushed us off, and we headed out of the bay into the main channel. But instead of relaxing into the rocking rhythm as Karomona propelled us upstream, I waited for Gwynn's reaction to the spiders.

So mesmerised by the motion, the rising sun shining on the waters, and the scrape of dew-covered reeds (often razor-sharp, I must add) against our arms and faces, she didn't seem to notice the arachnoids. But it was when a frog hopped onto her knee that I knew my joke had fizzled. She cooed in delight, picked it up, and popped it back on the reeds.

It's amazing what the Okavango could do to a city girl.

"Painted reed frog," Karomona said.

I turned to look at him, surprised he'd even spotted the quiet visitation.

Another flood of memories hit me. When I was twelve, my parents gave me one of the most treasured gifts of my life. They brought me to the Okavango and introduced me to the painted reed frogs. Every evening, probably since time began, the frogs have gathered in their hundreds to create a symphony of tinkling notes, rather like a massed orchestra of tiny wooden xylophones. When I first heard them, I recorded the sound and narrated what I saw. My childish voice echoed the deep impact the scene had on my soul: *"The sky is very dark, and bright stars appear, and the horizon is much lighter. I can just see the outline of the trees. And the outline of the grass. And shining waters."*

"Look." Karomona's voice cut my musings. "Picnic duck." He pointed to a pair of birds floating a few yards away. One was drab grey and brown, the other, bright green and yellow. They were perfectly camouflaged against the lilies.

"Picnic duck?" Gwynn reached for the bird book she'd toted along. "Never heard of it. Nothing in the index, either."

Karomona stopped the boat.

Gwynn and I studied the water bird pages, finally identifying the very beautiful ducks as pygmy geese.

I held the book up to show him the picture. "That one?" I asked.

He nodded his agreement, studied the page, and then mouthed, "Pygmy goose."

According to Barbara, Karomona was the best tracker in the delta. His bird knowledge sure needed some attention. Maybe instead of a fifty buck tip, that German guy should have gifted him a bird book. Even better, I'd leave our *Newman's* with him when we left.

The *mokoro* ride ended when Karomona ran us aground on the sandy bank of an island at the edge of a small lagoon. "Now we walk." Karomona set off at a brisk pace into the bush.

I exchanged a childlike grin with Gwynn. Lion, elephant, hyena, buffalo, leopard, wild dog; the list of game we could run into seemed endless and thrilling. I couldn't wait to get started.

Karomona, it turned out, had a quaint fixation with sun-dried excrement. It soon became apparent that a major part of the walk was to be devoted to the study of animal droppings. But, after a couple of hours, the poop he showed us, while initially fascinating, began to lose its savour.

Every few yards, he'd stop to admire impala, zebra, wildebeest, and buffalo dung. His face glowed at clumps of small black pellets or, even better, the larger, rounded chunks with tapered ends. Given his waving arms and eagerly prodding fingers, his personal favourite was undoubtedly buffalo chips—splats of runny green mush.

I was beginning to despair of ever meeting the perpetrators when Karomona stopped, holding up his hands to silence us. "Wildebeest." He pointed at an open plain beyond a deep thicket.

I scanned the horizon, finally spotting a small herd of wildebeest grazing in the distance. "You see it?" I asked Gwynn.

She shook her head, so I pointed her in the right direction. She chuckled, and then hopped up and down. I guessed she'd seen them, too.

"We go closer," Karomona said. He turned ninety degrees. We followed, struggling for about five hundred yards through dense shrub. He stopped us about a hundred yards from the herd.

Not my favourite animals. Wildebeests' sloping backs, low haunches, and scraggly whiskers always reminded me of old men with bad posture, desperately in need of a shave.

Then I saw something interesting.

Nudging Gwynn in the ribs, I whispered, making sure Karomona didn't hear, "The one on the far left is dropping some stuff for Karomona. No doubt he'll show it to us tomorrow, if we come back here."

"Isn't it great seeing them on foot, instead of from the inside a vehicle? It's so exciting," Gwynn replied, missing the joke.

I sighed, becoming serious, because she was right. Game viewing on foot *was* an indescribable, almost primordial experience—even if it was just wildebeest we were looking at.

When the wildebeest wandered off across the plain, Karomona continued walking. I think he'd seen our disapproval of his picnic duck identification because he stayed away from mentioning birds, although birds of every hue and description scuttled and chirped enticingly in the trees around us. It was therefore with some surprise that I heard him announce, "Saddle-billed stork."

Doubt besieged me. Those large black and white storks with distinctive red and yellow bands across their bills are quite uncommon. I craned to see where he was pointing—a marshy patch of grass ahead of us. No bird, large or small, jumped into view. When the naked eye failed, I turned to my binoculars.

There, as Karomona promised, stood two saddle-billed storks in knee-deep water surrounded by tall reeds. His eyesight and ability to spot game went up a thousand percent in my estimation.

"Yes, Karomona. Those are saddle-billed stork. Are they common here?" Gwynn asked. Seems this time she'd been looking in the right place.

"They are plenty, and when the sun is low, you can see them fly." He grinned, showing his discoloured teeth, clearly delighted to have redeemed himself.

At this point, we had been walking for almost two and a half hours. The sun that had started the day off mild and pleasant was beginning to punish me. Hungry and thirsty, I was about to suggest to Karomona that we turn back when I realised we'd swung around and were now heading in the direction of the *mokoro*.

At the same moment, Gwynn mopped her brow, saying, "Droon, I think we should ask Karomona if we can head back. It's got to be close to breakfast time."

"I think we've already turned," I replied, somewhat smugly. Direction finding wasn't easy here, but I watched the sun's position. Gwynn always trounced me when it came to finding places in the city. She was always telling me to stop and ask for directions—like I ever would—so it was good to finally prove my manliness.

"You are right, *Rra*," Karomona said, looking both surprised and pleased at my deduction.

Gwynn looked puzzled. "But everything looks the same."

That's how it felt in the city for me. "Wanna ask for directions?" I asked, grinning.

She stuck her tongue out and flounced off after Karomona.

Longing to see the river again, I was somewhat irritated when Karomona knelt in the grass for what had to be another turd. When I didn't quicken my pace, he waved furiously at me.

Gwynn, walking in front of me, stopped for me to catch up. "I've done my bit for animal ablutions," she muttered under her breath.

Not wanting to dampen Karomona's enthusiasm, I grabbed her hand and dragged her over to join him.

Karomona pointed at some fawn-coloured candy floss, also called cotton candy, lying in the grass. I looked at it and then at him. He picked it up and tore it in half, giving a handful to Gwynn and the remainder to me.

"Lion droppings," he said in voice brimming with pride. "About two weeks."

The shapeless, odourless mass took on a new dimension as I realised I was holding animal fur that had passed undigested through a lion. Lion crap definitely was cool.

"This lion, he eat impala," Karomona explained, jabbing at the fur in my hand. "This time I show you the impala, next time we see the lion!"

Abruptly, Karomona stood, and, with a spring in his step, led us to the *mokoro*.

"I guess he considers our outing a success," Gwynn said with a question mark in her voice.

I nodded. "It's a good lesson, I suppose. Not every walk will bring sightings of the Big Five."

"No. But it's being here that makes it so special." Gwynn frowned. "And do you really want to meet a lion, on foot, with no weapon?"

Having once been forced to stare-down a pride of lions feeding on a kill without the benefit of a weapon in my hand, I could see her point. It was not an activity I would recommend, especially not if all our guests were like Bonnie and Chuck. Not much in the developed world prepared one for raw Africa.

CHAPTER 7

By the time we reached the camp, I was more than ready for the breakfast Barbara offered us. Sweaty as I was from our hike, I grabbed Andrew's hand and dragged him to the dining room without even bothering to freshen up. Bonnie and Chuck were already seated. They looked as weather-beaten and famished as I felt. I collapsed, exhausted, into my usual chair, with Andrew, smelling slightly salty, next to me. Barbara and Rodney took their places at the head.

"Gorgeous day, isn't it," I said to Bonnie, between gulps of orange juice. Trudging through the bush in the sun was thirsty work, even though I had scooped up a couple of mouthfuls of water as Karomona poled us back down the river to camp.

Bonnie wiped her brow with her napkin. "Got a bit hot at the end of our walk."

"Summer in the Kalahari," Barbara said, nodding her head. "The temperature is nasty."

"Not as bad as spring," Andrew added. "That heat is just murderous."

"It was worth it, though." Chuck helped himself to fruit salad and yoghurt. "We saw giraffe, two buffalo, and, of course, loads of birds."

Bonnie fanned herself with her hand. "It must be ninety degrees, and it's only ten in the morning. Spring is worse than this?"

"Enough with the weather," Rodney said. He turned to Andrew—I didn't think Rodney had actually registered my existence yet. "How did you enjoy your session with the Doctor?"

"The Doctor?" Andrew looked up from his pile of scrambled eggs and toast.

"You noticed Karomona's fingers, I presume?" Barbara said.

"Hard not to." Andrew rested his knife and fork on his plate. "What happened?"

Barbara plunked her elbows on the table and leaned forward conspiratorially. "Before I can tell you what happened to Karomona's hands, I need to go back to his early childhood. As you know, all parents think their children are the most gifted brats ever born, and Karomona's were no exception."

Barbara clearly had an issue with kids. It eased some of my tension about Sandy's brood. They couldn't be nearly as awful as Barbara painted them. "But it wasn't long before Karomona justified his family's confidence," Barbara continued, "because he began to experience strange, life-like dreams. They showed him people's illnesses and the herbs to cure them."

Rodney cleared his throat noisily. "More toast. Anyone? Anyone?"

Everyone ignored him, including Barbara. "His parents sent him to a *sangoma*—"

"A what?" Bonnie interrupted, breakfast forgotten, face intent on Barbara.

"An herbal healer."

"Tosh!" Rodney interjected. "Back in the good old days, we used to call them witchdoctors, which, if you ask me, is what they are. Charlatans and blackguards, all."

Barbara threw a scowl Rodney's way. "Witchdoctors dabble in black magic. *Sangoma* use white magic to heal people or help them solve their problems."

"Black magic! White magic! Someone must surely want more toast?" Rodney swooped a breadbasket around the table.

Barbara pushed it aside. "No, they don't. They're more interested in Karomona." She smiled at the rest of us. "Anyway, the *sangoma* he went to live with taught him to interpret his dreams. Once the cause of the sickness was diagnosed—usually an enemy had asked an ancestor to curse the sufferer—the *sangoma* showed Karomona where to find the herbs to drive out the evil spirits and to placate the dead. Only then would the patient recover."

"The damn fool boy and his even more stupid parents allowed that charlatan quack to break Karomona's fingers," Rodney cut in. "Since then, he's been unable to bend his knuckles." A gasp rose from around the table. "There, done. Now, Andrew, how's your breakfast?"

Commenting on the bacon must have seemed somewhat facile after Rodney's revelation, because Andrew slumped in his chair, saying nothing.

Chuck filled the silence. "That's positively barbaric. And his parents allowed it to happen? I can't believe it."

"You won't believe half the things these so-called civilised people do," Rodney snapped, clearly disappointed he hadn't scotched the topic. Still, he added, "As part of his training that quack even told Karomona to swim every day in crocodile-infested waters."

"And *did* he get eaten by a crocodile?" Bonnie asked, barely veiled sarcasm in her voice.

"No," Rodney said, equally acerbically. "The crocodiles decided there was more intelligent life in the river to eat."

"Oh, Rodney!" Barbara pumped her fist on the table. "That *sangoma* made Karomona into a very powerful man. Everyone is terrified of him, because a man who can drive out evil spirits can just as easily drive them in. And he happens to be the best tracker in the delta."

Rodney snorted. "Until a few weeks ago, when he got lost for two days. Top that. The great tracker managed to lose himself and a bunch of guests in a thunderstorm. Took three days and half the planes in Maun to find them."

Barbara gasped, and her eyes widened. Rodney sucked in a breath, looking around guiltily. Clearly, no one was supposed to know about that embarrassing incident.

"Time to feed the fish eagles," Rodney said, clambering to his feet.

"Good idea," Barbara agreed with forced enthusiasm. "Go, fetch your cameras everyone."

Barbara and Rodney dashed out of the dining room, leaving me, and everyone else, speechless. There really didn't seem to be anything to do other than to leave our eggs to congeal while we got our cameras.

Once we had reassembled at the bay, Rodney appeared, holding a chunk of raw steak. Two fish eagles, perched on a dead tree on the opposite side of the river, screeched frantically. Rodney moved to the water's edge, cut a section of papyrus stem, and tied the meat and the stem together with two strands of long grass. "Steak doesn't float, but papyrus does," he said to Andrew, as if he had decided Andrew would be the one performing this task. "Important point, because fish eagles feed off the surface."

With the avian audience going wild with anticipation, Rodney turned to the rest of us human spectators. "Cameras at the ready." He gave a piecing whistle, waved his arm above his head, and threw the meat high into the air. It didn't go far, landing with a plop a few feet away in the water.

One of the eagles leaped from its perch and winged towards us. It turned a broad arc as it reached the bay, and I gasped at the rush of air blasting my face as it powered past. With perfect control, it swooped low, dropped its talons, and scooped up its breakfast. Steak safely grasped, it flew back to the dead tree, calling a "thank you" before tearing the meat apart.

Everyone, including me, broke into spontaneous clapping.

"Feeding the fish eagles is a winner," Rodney said. "The interesting thing is, though, only the male responds. The female just shouts comments in the background. Sounds familiar doesn't it, Andrew?"

Andrew was too smart—or scared—to rise to that one.

Barbara turned to us. "So, camp managers, do you want the job?"

I didn't even have to look at Andrew to know the answer to that question.

CHAPTER 8

December through March: that's how long it took for Andrew and me to negotiate our way through house sales and estate agents, car salesmen, and pro film equipment dealers. Finally, we found ourselves at a small provincial airport outside Johannesburg, waiting for our flight to Maun. We were surrounded by two suitcases of clothing, a camera in its case, a tripod, an Apple Mac with a twelve volt converter, a steel box full of tools, and a basket containing a very disgruntled Siamese cat. These and our Land Rover were all that remained of our diminutive empire.

The road we had travelled to get us from the fish eagle to this terminal building had been nothing short of miraculous.

Once back in Maun, in the balmy afterglow of our camp visit, Sean had seemed pleased with our decision to manage his lodge. We didn't know it then, but his smile of delight was a rare treat.

We had filled our two-day drive home from Maun with talk about our future life, coloured with frightened anticipation. Going to the Okavango remained a huge gamble, in which the stakes were everything we owned in exchange for the great unknown.

It seemed worth the risk.

The day after we returned to our small thatched cottage, we put our world up for sale. Our two houses, two of our cars, the aeroplane, the top-end film editing equipment, and numerous computers had to go.

"Nothing worth doing is easy." I used that phrase daily to whip my flagging spirit when, after a few weeks, nothing had sold.

Soon, I had to use it on Andrew, too, as the anchors tying us to Johannesburg tightened their grip.

Before leaving Maun, Sean told us he would apply for our work permits. He seemed positively sanguine about the process. "A piece of cake. I'll have them in three weeks. Work starts at the end of January. Be ready."

January came and went, and the promised work permits did not materialise.

Sean was cagy when, after days of trying, we finally reached him on the phone. He mumbled, "This is Africa. Can't rush things."

Continuing with our sales efforts required an act of pure faith. Our faith was obviously lacking because, by the end of February, we had sold nothing of importance.

Then, in just four days, everything, and I do mean everything, changed hands. After ditching a load of debt, we paid off the Land Rover and put a small sum into savings.

Now we were committed.

Still, there was no sign of the work permits. Desperation peaking, we moved into the spare room at Andrew's parents' house and settled down to wait.

And wait.

Woodie was not impressed. Neither were Andrew and I.

Borderline panic set in. With nothing to do and all day to do it, we spent our time struggling to get Sean on the phone. An almost impossible task, it seemed, until one day Sandy picked up. She gave us our first command as our new boss.

Through the snaps and crackles on the telephone line, I heard her say, "I want you to meet Morag. She's been managing the camp in your absence. She's on her ten days' leave and is down in Joburg, visiting family. Call on her. Introduce yourselves. She'll be training you when you get to camp."

If we get to camp, I thought morosely. Still, I scribbled down Morag's phone number and gave her a call.

It turned out that instead of visiting family, Morag was moonlighting at a small gift shop not far from where we were staying.

We agreed to meet.

On the appointed day, Andrew and I sauntered into the gift shop, looking for someone who looked like a Morag. Only one person occupied the tiny space—a stout woman in her early forties with long red hair. She occupied herself by rearranging lavender cushions on a shelf crowded with teddy bears.

"Morag?" I asked.

"That's me." Her mother must have been able to see into the future when she named her, because Morag definitely resembled a Morag.

"I'm Gwynn. This is Andrew. We're the new Tau Camp managers."

Morag looked at me. Then she looked at Andrew. Then back at me. Her eyes hardened, if that was possible, given they already looked like quartz. "I'm too busy to talk about the camp now. We'll handle all that when you arrive." With a swat of her hand, she puffed up a stuffed-to-bursting cushion, sending the display of teddy bears tumbling to the floor.

My mouth opened and closed, but no sound came out.

Andrew broke the silence. "Sandy said to call on you."

"And you have. Now you can go, because I'm busy."

I looked pointedly around the shop, verifying that we were the only customers.

Inexplicably, Morag ignored the gesture. A flash of ire hit me.

Andrew must have noticed, because he grabbed my hand. "See you when we see you." He dragged me out of the shop.

Morag and her extraordinary behaviour dominated our conversation over the next few weeks. With nothing more concrete to suggest, we decided frosty welcomes had to be a Tau Camp thing—something we both vowed to change.

If we ever got our work permits.

When Sean finally contacted us at the end of March, we said nothing about Morag because his news was too good to spoil. "I'm sending you some air tickets. You're coming, work permits or not."

It seemed insane, but what choice did we have? Tau Camp just had to work out for us.

Back on the tarmac at the airport, I glanced at my watch again. I had been looking at it every five minutes for the last four hours. Our plane to Maun was delayed, and no one could tell us why. We had cleared customs ages ago and—in the absence of a functioning departure lounge—waited on the apron next to a twin-engine Piper Seneca we had been told would take us to Maun.

Despite being March—autumn in southern Africa—the sun beating down on us was cruel. Worse, Woodie hadn't stopped yowling since we left home at first light, and nothing I did pacified her. I was as bad-tempered as she was.

Another hour passed.

Then, a uniformed pilot sauntered towards us, clutching a handful of papers. "This is hello and goodbye," he said. "Screw up with the arrangements. Some genius double-booked me." He bent down and smiled at Woodie. "A cat, huh? Siamese. Pretty. Got three at home. Anyway, gotta fly. Someone will be along shortly to get you guys to Maun." He disappeared into *our* plane, started the engines, and taxied away.

Andrew pulled me out of the prop wash, and we both slumped down next to Woodie.

"He can't be serious," I moaned. "Even if we make it to Maun today, we'll miss our connection to Tau Camp."

"Great. Homeless in Maun, with an angry Siamese cat."

"Excuse me," another pilot said, looming over me. This one curled his lip at the cat box. "What is that?"

"A cat," I replied, in no mood for humour.

"I see that. But I'm allergic to the buggers. That *thing* is not getting on my plane."

I leapt to my feet and thrust my jaw out at him. "That *thing*, as you call it, is getting on your plane. And she's flying to Maun. With us."

"No way, lady. Not unless you want us crashed somewhere in the desert."

Back pulled straight, I locked eyes with him. It didn't help; he still towered over me. But I wasn't letting a little height difference deter me. "That cat has a ticket to fly to Maun. Today. With us."

"It's not getting on my plane."

"Then find another pilot. And plane."

"There aren't any."

This was *High Noon* all over again.

I knew I was being unreasonable—the man did have an allergy, after all—but it wasn't Woodie's fault the company screwed up. And what was I supposed to do? Abandon her at lost luggage until they organised another flight for her? Not a chance.

Andrew nudged me, and I spun to face him, hoping he had a solution to the impasse. "Maybe if she goes at the back?" he ventured.

"Not happening. Dump it." The pilot started towards a plane on the other side of the apron. "There are lots of wild cats around here. It'll soon settle in."

"I'll cover the box with a wet towel," I hissed, barely resisting the urge to hit him.

He must have got the message that he courted a black eye, because he hissed back, "Drench the towel."

Within fifteen minutes, we were in the air. We sat in stony silence, listening to the drone of the engines and a faint meowing coming from the back.

This was not how I'd imagined I'd enter paradise.

CHAPTER 9

Night was closing in over Maun when Gwynn and I landed—safely, despite the pilot's predictions to the contrary. Once through customs, we heaved Woodie and our luggage into the arrivals hall, hoping someone would be there to meet us. We weren't left standing long before a smiling woman walked up to us with her hand out in greeting.

"Hello. My name is Sepei. Welcome to Tau Camp." I recognised her from our LSD trip. She'd been the one trying to persuade Mick to squeeze a few more tins of peas onto the plane. She grabbed one side of my toolbox before leading us to a pickup truck parked outside. Still beaming, she helped ferry the rest of our junk to the vehicle and then dropped us off at the familiar offices of Okavango Safaris on the main street.

Sean and Sandy were waiting for us.

The first question off my lips was about our work permits.

Sean shrugged. "Not yet. But they'll come."

"And now?" Gwynn asked, looking drained after the harrowing day.

"Work waivers," Sean said breezily, flapping a piece of paper at us. "One of you will have to come to Maun each month to renew them. Don't forget, or they'll kick you out of the country." He looked down at the cat box.

Disgusted beyond measure, Woodie had finally stopped howling on touch down at Maun airport.

"So this is it. The cat. Doesn't look like much. Watch out for genets. They'll have her for a snack before you can blink."

Gwynn glared at Sean, but said nothing. About the size of small, low-slung terrier, except with a long, bushy tail, genets hunt mice, small birds, and insects. Woodie might have been a featherweight, but this was insulting. Still, I sympathised with Gwynn's reticence to answer back. Like her, all I wanted was a room, a shower, and a meal.

As if sensing our moods, Sean said, "Too late to get to camp tonight. You can sleep in our guest cottage."

Tiredness robbed me of the will to complain.

Our bosses' house was located on the banks of the Thalamakane River, Maun's main water source. The failing light limited appreciation of the view as we stumbled through swarms of mosquitoes behind Sean. He led us to a small thatched room at the river's edge.

Strangely, it had no bathroom.

"Shower and toilet are outside." Sean indicated a reed screen a few yards away. "We're now entering hurricane hour." Gwynn and I exchanged puzzled looks but Sean didn't elucidate. "Don't let it put you off. Come up to the house for supper when you're done here." Shoulders sagging despite his own advice, he ambled back to his home.

After a day in hell, we were alone at last. It was time to let Woodie out of the cat box.

Woodie usually showed her disapproval of changes in her routine by going on hunger strike. Not tonight. She downed a bowl of water and polished off two helpings of tinned fish without coming up for air. One look at the spartan cottage, with its double bed and mosquito net, she decided she didn't like the view, and climbed back into the cat box.

"I can't leave her." Gwynn's body writhed and her hands wrung. I could see she was battling back tears.

"But you can't stay here, either. Sean will think you'll dump his guests for the cat."

Gwynn sighed. "I know." She tried to cuddle Woodie through the cat box door, but was rewarded with a scratch and a snarl. The Siamese wasn't making this easy.

I went to clean up, leaving Gwynn to sort through her emotions. Naked in the open air shower under a trickle of lukewarm water, I wished the autumn night wasn't so cool.

Gwynn arrived. "The show goes on," she said, stripping off. "I'll make it up to her when we get back from dinner."

After a tussle for the best spot under the nozzle, I decided to let her win. I leaned against the reed wall to wait for her to finish and dislodged a squadron of mosquitoes. Towel in hand, I flicked left and right, trying to knock the buggers from the sky. A monster landed on Gwynn's leg, and I lashed out. Gwynn squealed with pain as the corner of the wet towel struck. But at least I squished the little bugger. It left a splatter of blood on her thigh.

"Lovely," Gwynn moaned as the blood washed away in the shower. "Next time warn me, so I can hit you back."

"Be thankful. I saved you from a chowing."

"Too late. That one already had me." She cocked her wet head at me. "You know what the one mosquito said to the other?"

"Nah."

"'Should we take Gwynn outside, or should we eat her in here?' The other replied, 'Take her outside? Are you crazy? The big boys will have her for sure.'"

I snorted a laugh. "Very funny." It was good to hear her joking, no matter how lame the joke.

When the tepid water ran out, we dressed and headed off to schmooze with our new bosses.

A scream rent the night air not fifty paces from their house. It wouldn't have sounded out of place in *The Shining*. That was followed by more yells, this time a mature voice. Then more childish shrieks.

We approached with caution.

On the veranda, we found the source of some of the noise.

A servant bathed a little boy in a large zinc tub. Given his punches and wild kicks, he wasn't enjoying it.

Neither was the maid. She yelled back at him, telling him to sit and be quiet. The boy's fist shot out, landing a punch on her nose. She retaliated by shoving soap into his eyes. The kid screamed even harder. It struck me then that he looked like a miniature version of Sean.

It had to be one of Sean's "monsters."

"Oh, boy," Gwynn muttered. "Is it possible Barbara was right?"

"It could just be a once-off occasion," I said, wishing that were true.

Gwynn gave me a please-let-it-be-so look, followed by a don't-let-him-do-this-at-the-camp look.

Then we heard another set of wails, this time coming from the house.

Leaving the little boy and the maid to their fisticuffs, we wandered through the rambling mansion. The din led us to the kitchen, where a boy, only a little older than his brother, howled on the table in the centre of the room. He was also a carbon copy of Sean.

The insults Sandy was shouting at Sean over the racket soon brought us up to speed with the action.

This was their eldest son. He had been practicing a karate chop on a creeper in the garden when the resident snake had taken exception. It had spat at him.

"And you, you bastard, you're not even taking it seriously," Sandy yelled above the kid's screaming.

Sean shrugged. "This is Africa. Kids get bitten and stung and spat at every day." Turning to us, he asked, "You guys want a drink?"

"Spat at by a snake?" Gwynn replied, looking anxiously at the child.

Sandy seized upon that weakness. "Yes, Gwynn, a bloody great spitting cobra! Enough venom to blind an adult, forget about a six-year-old boy. And what does he care?" She shoved Sean in the chest. "Nothing."

Sean rolled his eyes and led us back to the veranda, where his other son shrieked in the bathtub. He poured the drinks, handed them around, and slumped into a wicker chair. "Like I said, hurricane hour. It'll be over soon. Sit."

It was like I'd stepped into another world.

CHAPTER 10

Maun may have been a backwater, but getting high-paying tourists around the delta was big business. Sean's chunk of that industry ran like a well-oiled machine, thanks to three women who bustled about the office when we arrived at work the next morning.

The only one I recognised was Sepei. All hopes of Sean introducing us to the other two were dashed when he disappeared into his cave and shut the door.

A blond woman in her mid-thirties stepped forward. "I'm Joan, the travel agent here. It's my job to send guests to both Tau and Scops Camps."

"Nice to meet you." Andrew smiled at her.

Joan didn't smile back. "I'm also your link to the outside world, so the most important thing you need to know is how to answer when I call you on the radio." She pointed to two communication radios behind her desk and rattled off, "VHF. It works most of the time. As long as the weather's good. And HF is for when it's lousy." She glared at us, eyes flashing.

Andrew and I exchanged now-what-have-we-done-to-offend looks, but no answer seemed forthcoming.

Instead, Joan continued, "Never, ever leave the radios on overnight. The batteries are solar powered, so they'll be dead by morning, and then I can't get hold of you. And that makes me as mad as a hippo in labour with twins."

"Roger that." Andrew puffed his chest out with aviation efficiency. "What call signs do we use to reach you?"

"Calling 110 will get you Scops Camp," Joan barked. "Maun office—me—is 637. You're 638. When you hear some call 638, jump. It's me, and I get seriously pissed off if I'm kept waiting." Joan's glower deepened. "That means one of you stays close to the reception where the radio is kept. Always. Not like Barbara and Rodney, who spent most of the day in their hut with their feet up."

"Yes, ma'am," was all I could think of to say. I wondered if a salute would be too much. I regarded it a privilege to work here but, apparently, Joan didn't share my views.

Then, as if she'd read my thoughts, Joan's worn face cracked a tiny smile. "Okay, okay, I'm not as bad as all that. In fact, I make your life possible. Me and Verity." She pointed to a slight woman beaming at us from across the office. "That's Verity. She pays you, so I suggest you be very nice to her."

I shot Verity my most ingratiating simper.

Her grin broadened, showing a mouth full of brilliant teeth.

"And you've met Sepei," Joan continued. "She makes sure you eat. It's her job to shop for both camps."

"Everything from fillet steak to concrete bricks," Sepei said. "Come, I show you." She grabbed us each by an arm and led us out into the bright sunshine.

We spent the next few hours scouring Maun's two cash-and-carry warehouses for the items Morag, who was back at the helm at Tau Camp, had requested Sepei purchase for the camp.

To say that Maun's merchandise was limited was being kind.

"Never be in a hurry," Sepei advised us for the tenth time. "Sometimes it takes weeks and weeks for stock to come." She looked at a sheet of paper clasped in her hand and shook her head. "*Eish!* Morag, she ask for gum poles and chicken mesh. Impossible. Maybe next of next week, when the truck comes from Gabs."

Next of next week? I understood enough Setswanan pidgin-English to realise that two weeks would pass before the next supply of building materials arrived from Gaborone, Botswana's capital, over five hundred miles away to the south.

That was a real problem. Over breakfast, Sean had made it clear that he expected his camp fixed up as a priority after Rodney's neglect.

"Building supplies. Not easy to get?" Andrew asked, tugging his beard.

Face forlorn, Sepei shook her head again. "It's a big *matata*."

This was long before Timon and Pumbaa of *Lion King* fame rocked us all with *Hankuna Matata*, so I had no idea what *matata* meant. Sepei soldiered on before I could enquire.

"The other *matata* is that the stock can only fly when there's space on the planes. People, they come first, and the guides and staff are always jumping on board, snatching the seats." She said this as if it were the bane of her life.

I was beginning to glean what the word *matata* meant.

"And gas bottles! They are an even bigger *matata*. They can only fly on empty planes, so it can take months and months to get gas bottles to the camps."

Both camps used gas for cooking, fridges, and some lighting. Gas bottles were as important as bread and milk.

"And then Scops Camp also needs its other stock for their shop." Sepei must have seen our growing concern because she leaned in close, and repeated, "Never be in a hurry."

"And fruit and vegetables?" I croaked. "I don't see any in the wareouses."

"Other than cabbage and butternut." Andrew pulled a face. He hated cabbage and butternut squash equally.

"Fresh comes from Gabs on Tuesday and Thursday. If it can catch a ride on the plane."

"And if it can't?" I asked in an even weaker voice.

"Then it's a *matata*. That's why I send you tinned peas, cabbage, butternut, and gem squash."

"This is beginning to sound like the Berlin Airlift," Andrew said. At the rate he was tugging on his beard, he wouldn't have a hair left by the time we got to camp.

"Perhaps the most challenging part of the job," I added.

Rookie mistake. But what did I know then about the *matatas* awaiting us at Tau Camp?

* * *

At three in the afternoon, Sepei announced it was time to meet our plane. Sean was at the airport. He pointed to a blue and white Cessna 206 and said, without a trace of pride, "The first in my new fleet. Okavango-Air is taking to the skies."

He was nothing if not entrepreneurial. I had to admire that.

Sepei loaded some of the morning's shopping into the Cessna's belly pod and looked at our pile of luggage with a pained expression. "*Eish*. It's a *matata*. No space."

I understood her problem. And, as camp manager, it was now my problem. "Just the cat and one of the suitcases, Sepei," I said, opening our two bags.

Andrew helped me shuffle our clothes around until we had one case filled with enough stuff to tide each of us over for a few days. The laundry department had better be efficient. Done, I zipped the suitcases and Andrew heaved one of them back into Sepei's truck. He gazed at his camera gear, toolbox, and computer, then, with a sigh, strong-armed them into the truck. Getting to work on fixing the camp would have to wait.

While the guests bound for Scops Camp climbed on board, Sean introduced us to the pilot. "Andrew. Gwynn. New Tau Camp managers. Andrew can fix things." He looked at me as if wondering just what it was I could do.

Heartwarming.

"Wes," the straw-blond Australian pilot said, sticking his hand out in greeting. "So you fix things, then, Andrew? Bloody marvellous. If you want to endear yourself to us pilots, then do something about the bloody awful runway."

"What?" Andrew asked, leaning in.

"Make it longer, mate."

I thought back to the cricket pitch we had landed on, hemmed in on both ends by open lagoons and palm trees, and realised that some *matatas* at Tau Camp might be impossible to solve.

CHAPTER 11

A troop of baboons playing on the runway welcomed us when we landed at Tau Camp. They scattered as the plane trundled past, stopping on the side of the strip to watch us disembark. For wild animals, they were fearless. Meeting planes must have been a regular item in their day.

But, interesting though they were, I was expecting a human welcoming party. Gwynn and I might have been flippant about wanting to run a hotel, but I was very conscious that I had zero experience. I was rather counting on Morag's help to get started. With a bit of luck, she'd left her bad mood at the Johannesburg gift shop.

As if she knew I'd been thinking about her, Morag stepped out of the grove of trees hiding the camp.

A leggy dun-coloured dog trailed her. It had a pointed nose, a large bulge in the middle, and a whip-like tail, narrowing to another point at the tip. It looked like every other Botswanan dog I had ever seen. Due to generations of interbreeding, local dogs had earned a breed title of their own—Ngamiland Pointer. Smiling broadly as only dogs can, it lolled its tongue at us in greeting.

I wish I could say the same about Morag.

All we got by way of welcome was a curt, "So you've arrived." Without waiting for a reply to the obvious, she turned to the staff streaming onto the runway. "Stock. Get it sorted before the baboons rip it apart. Luggage and cat goes to number nine. Then go. Come, follow me." She patted the dog and they both started towards the camp.

It took me a moment to realise she'd aimed the last instruction at Gwynn and me. As human relations went, this wasn't looking good.

What was it with these people? Every person associated with camp management had a massive chip on their shoulder. There had to be a common denominator. I'd always been taught that a fish rots from its head. As mild as he appeared, perhaps Sean wasn't the easiest boss to work for. Unless it was Sandy who got everyone worked up. Time would tell. As for me, I'm a friendly guy, and Gwynn. . .well, Gwynn is Gwynn—what you see is what you get. Right now, my wife wore a stunned expression, rather like a bludgeoned fish. I shrugged, took her hand, and we fell into step behind Morag.

She stalked to a cottage built from the same reeds as the rest of the camp. Situated to one side of the runway, it had a private garden of prickly grass and palm trees, screened by a reed wall. The cottage itself looked cool and inviting. It would make an ideal home for Woodie, which would make Gwynn happy. That would make me happy, so I hoped it was our new home.

Morag's voice broke into my musings. "You live in a *letaka* hut. Same as everyone else around here." She turned to leave.

"*Letaka*?" Gwynn said, clearly grasping at anything to strike up a conversation.

Morag's eyes narrowed and her voice sounded incredulous. "You don't know what *letaka* is?"

"No. Should I?"

"And you want to run a camp in the Okavango? Amazing." Morag's voice could've cracked ice.

"I didn't know the study of African architecture was a requirement for running a lodge," Gwynn snapped back.

This wasn't going to end well. For anyone.

I took a deep breath and stepped between them. "I'm guessing *letaka* is the local name for the reed walls, right? And I'm also guessing this is our house. Gwynn, maybe you should get Woodie settled in. She's been in the box all day."

I hoped Gwynn would clutch this face-saving exit with both hands. With a scowl at Morag, she bent down to pet Woodie through the bars. I let out a breath. Trapped for the second day, Woodie was too ticked off to even yowl. Gwynn picked up the box and flounced passed Morag into our doorless hut.

Morag turned to leave. "We have no guests, so I've given the staff the night off. We'll be eating at Scops Camp. I'm leaving in half an hour. Don't be late, because I'm not waiting."

"We'll be ready."

She whistled for her dog, which was sniffing up a tree. When it ignored her, she called a sharp, "Hazel! Come here. Now." Vaguely brow-beaten, Hazel ambled off after her.

I joined Gwynn in our new lounge.

"There's a psycho if you're looking for one," Gwynn said, still holding the cat box.

She was right, but I wasn't adding fuel to this fire. "Help me check the place out for cat safety before you let Woodie out."

That sent Gwynn scurrying.

It took less than a minute to explore our new home. It was all one room, divided into three sections with *letaka* walls. On one side, stood a king-sized bed draped in a mosquito net, and on the other, a sitting area with two wicker chairs and small table. Behind these, a long, narrow walk-in cupboard, and a shower, basin, and toilet. The front wall, opening onto our garden, was about a meter high. Airy. That's how best to describe it.

And that was a problem for Woodie.

"I see a *matata*," Gwynn said.

Not wanting to deal with this, I grabbed my binoculars—they had at least made it onto the plane. "There's a bird on that bush I don't recognise."

"Woodie," Gwynn said, ignoring me, ignoring her. "How are we supposed to lock her up for a few days and put butter on her feet?"

Butter on her feet? Gwynn really thought that old wives tale about buttering a cat's paws would work to stop Woodie running away? Laughter bubbled up before I could stop it.

Then saw I her face.

I cleared my throat, coughed once, and spluttered, before saying, "Just let her explore. She won't go far from us."

Gwynn's hands found her hips. "And when we go to Scops Camp?"

I didn't have an answer. Neither did she.

Woodie gave a plaintive whine. I opened the cage and she slunk out, not talking to us. With trepidation, I watched as she smelt every corner of the cottage and every blade of grass in the garden. Her hair rose with each new, unfamiliar scent. By the time Morag arrived to fetch us, she looked like a Siamese toilet brush. She took one gawp at Morag and dashed to her new hiding place amongst our clothes. Gwynn had stashed them on the top shelf of our doorless wardrobe as a refuge for her. It didn't look like Woodie intended coming out any time soon.

I doubted I'd get my wife moving, either.

CHAPTER 12

I left my cottage with a prayer in my heart that Woodie would be waiting for us when we got home. If I could have skipped this dinner, I would have. But something suggested that Morag would see that as weakness, which she'd exploit until I bled. As inexplicable as her behaviour was, I couldn't risk that. Not with my present and future riding on our success at here. Andrew squeezed my hand. I smiled grimly. No one was going to derail this for us.

Morag set a brisk pace down the runway. At the end of the strip, the path disappeared into a small grove of trees, then onto a shallow floodplain. The ground was dry and firm, given the low water level in autumn.

The walk melted my anger away. I nudged Andrew and grinned, feeling a kind of ownership of the real estate. The fact that we could run into an elephant or a lion at any moment added to the thrill.

We had been walking for half an hour when I figured I had calmed down enough to make peace with Morag—striding a few yards ahead of us. "Does this happen often?" I asked. "Empty camp and dinner at Scops?"

She didn't reply.

How mature of her. I rolled my eyes.

Andrew repeated the question.

This time, she turned to look at him—and simpered. "No. So we take full advantage of it when it does." Still addressing Andrew, she added, "It's Kyle's birthday. He and Milly manage Scops. So a celebration seemed in order."

"Cool," I said, hoping for a cut of the conversation. "We love celebrations."

Morag turned her back on me.

What *had* I done to so offend her? I twirled a dark curl around my finger, walking in silence until we reached Scops Camp.

Morag led us to the bar—the heart of the camp. Andrew and I plunked down onto stools made from palm-trunks and rested our elbows on the counter—an upturned *mokoro*, holed and scarred from years of sailing on the delta, and now singed by a thousand cigarette butts.

I was busy identifying the dozens of animal skulls and snake skins mounted on the *letaka* wall when a man spoke in a cheerful voice.

"Morag! You're here." He slapped us on the shoulders. "And you must be Andrew and Gwynn. Great." The speaker was younger than me. In his early twenties, he looked like the kind of guy who drifted on the tide of wanderlust, each night ending up at a different backpacker's hole somewhere in the world. For now, he had washed up onto the shores of Noga Island to manage Scops Camp. Who knew where he would be tomorrow? I liked him. "I'm Kyle," he said, pointing to a wiry blonde girl wearing a tie-died T-shirt and khaki shorts. "And this is Milly. Welcome to Scops."

Milly looked us over, and then burst into a grin. "Well, well. Tau Camp managers propping up the bar at Scops Camp. Now there's a first."

"Huh?" Andrew answered in surprise.

"Oh yes. We folks at Scops have always been lower than baboon crap in the eyes of the Tau Camp managers. It looks like the tradition may die at last."

"But Morag's here too. And she's been managing the camp in our absence," I said, trying to grasp the politics.

"She's not a manager, just a teacher. That doesn't count," Kyle said.

Morag frowned and I wondered about that.

"I think if the two camps work together we'll have more fun." Andrew grinned at Kyle—and then said something that had me slumping back on my stool. "I bet you guys have never won a volleyball match. We should have an inter-camp challenge"

"Andrew, what's got into you?" I said in a loud whisper, hoping Kyle heard. "You're hopeless at ball sports." I wasn't much better, but this was so out of character for Andrew it was frightening. It had to be all the fresh air. Or something.

"Beaten at volleyball? No way." Kyle decided to ignore my comment. He shoved two beer cans at us. "Scops Camp are the Noga world champions. Undisputed for years."

"Why? Haven't you had anybody to play against you before this?"

"Andrew, shut up!" I said, laughing. "Neither of us can hit a ball straight, and who knows if the staff at Tau have even heard the word 'volleyball'?"

A swarthy man hopped over to the business side of the bar, propped his elbows on the *mokoro*, and beamed at us. He had a staggeringly white row of front teeth. "*Rra* Andrew. We at Scops, we know what to do with a volleyball. You Tau guys had better watch out because we are cunning and clever! And I'm the new captain of the Scops team," he clicked his fingers suggestively, "and I take bribes easily."

Laughing, Milly punched him on the arm. "Englishman is the world's worst ball player. That's why we shove him behind the bar anytime someone mentions the words 'ball' and 'game' in the same sentence."

"Englishman. Is that your name?" I asked.

"Yes. I don't even have a Setswana one." He loped off to help a guest to a drink.

"It's like the story of the Bushman," Andrew said. "A couple of years ago, a group of explorers in the southern Kalahari had a problem with their Land Rover."

"Like most people with their Land Rovers," Kyle interrupted.

Andrew smiled wryly. "True. Anyway, their gearbox broke and they had to dismantle it. Lucky for them, they had a workshop manual. But when they left, they forgot it. A Bushman family found it. As it happened, they lived in a village that had begun English lessons. One thing led to another, now there's a kid there called LT Seventy Five Gearbox."

We all laughed; then Kyle said, "Masterful defensive tactics, Andrew. Confuse us with stories so we forget to take you up on the volleyball challenge. You running scared?"

"Scared? Not us," Andrew declared with confidence that astounded me.

"Done!" Kyle slapped the bar. "One month from today. Here at Scops. The Okavango Delta Volleyball World Challenge. And after the game, we'll stuff ourselves on Milly's cooking." He leaned over and kissed Milly's neck.

She swatted him away with a laugh.

A cold voice spoke from the sidelines. "And how do you intend to fulfil that engagement?" Morag looked directly at me, as if I, not Andrew, had staked out Tau Camp honour. "You can hardly bring Tau guests to Scops Camp, can you?"

I hadn't thought of that. But neither had Andrew. Or Kyle. Or Milly.

"I might *only* be a teacher, but *clearly*, I know more about running a lodge than you do." Morag stood up and stalked off to join a group of

Scops Camp guests.

"The hell with her," I muttered under my breath. "From this moment on, I'm praying for an empty camp on volleyball night. And that she's gone by then."

It was late when Morag led us back to Tau. A billion stars blazed down at us as only the Kalahari can display them. It was then that I realised what Andrew and I had achieved. We were here, in the Okavango. I felt like running through our old suburb in Johannesburg, into the houses and shopping malls, shouting it out for everyone to hear.

The stars hummed, listening attentively. I knew they understood.

CHAPTER 13

I awoke to the joyful cackle of a francolin and the manic call of a Heuglin's robin—not familiar bird calls in a Johannesburg garden. The cool morning breeze rustled our mosquito net. I could feel Woodie lying under the covers between us, like she always did. I reached down to stroke her. Gwynn's hand was already there.

"I hope she'll be okay while we're working," was Gwynn's morning greeting.

"Regretting bringing her?" I knew asking that was about as bad as saying I thought Gwynn had put on weight, but I had to know.

"No regrets," came the prompt answer.

I didn't really expect anything else.

We lay together, savouring the moment before we met our new lives. My stomach churned with excitement and nervousness.

Gwynn finally broke the silence. "I wonder what our first guests will be like?"

"I bet it's a crotchety old German destined to lose his underpants in our laundry."

Gwynn had just started chuckling when a crashing of branches overhead, followed by hysterical barking, jolted us out of bed.

"That's Hazel, Morag's dog," Gwynn said. "It sounds like she's being attacked."

"Baboons!" I shouted, dragging my clothing together. "C'mon, let's move."

Within seconds, we were both dressed. Woodie watched with slit-eyed disapproval as we abandoned her again and raced out of our garden.

Hazel's barking led us through the camp to the kitchen. We skidded to a halt at the door, stopped by six baboons. Some were perched on the counters, while others squabbled over the contents of the dustbin. None were shorter than five feet tall, and all weighed in at about ninety pounds. So they weren't small, especially when adding fearless aggression to the mix.

Still, filled with zealous determination to defend my new home, I left Gwynn at the front door, grabbed a stick, and dashed around the back, through the scullery, into the kitchen.

The air was heavy with the smell of baboon poop and the contents of the dustbins strewn over the floor. With Gwynn stationed at the front door, for a brief, heady moment I thought we'd trapped them. Now we could thump them for daring to raid our kitchen. But in a blur of brown they vanished—straight through the scullery roof.

Now I knew why Morag had ordered the gum poles and chicken-mesh.

The scullery roof had collapsed. I had a perfect view of the baboons' bright red backsides as they perched in a sycamore fig tree, barking abuse at us. Refusing to be defeated, I waved my stick menacingly, while Gwynn shouted.

They ignored us.

It was positively humiliating.

Then the pitch of Hazel's barking changed. She sounded quite frantic, so I shot through the kitchen door and out onto the path to join her. A huge male—the alpha, I guess—strode towards me. With every hair standing erect, Hazel lunged at him, stopping short before the final assault.

Until that moment, I'd never fully comprehended just how giant five feet could feel, how colossal ninety pounds could seem, or how large a baboon's incisors could be. The stick I brandished suddenly felt like a matchstick.

My bravery evaporated.

The baboon moved towards me, arrogance in every rollicking step.

I threw a handful of figs at him.

That surprised him.

He stopped, watching me with cunning black eyes.

Hazel growled low in her throat, waiting for a command. I licked the sweat beading in my moustache. From being in control, I was now out of my depth, wishing I had something more substantial than a stick with which to defend myself.

Then, like me, the baboon seemed to decide that a frontal confrontation would be a very bad start to the day. He barked imperiously at his henchmen. They obeyed, scampering across the leafy canopy. I heaved a sigh of relief. They dashed out of the camp, over the runway, and into the bush on the other side. The alpha followed, sauntering up the path.

We both knew who'd won that round.

"Welcome to Tau Camp." Morag actually laughed as she joined me. "Chasing baboons is a bit of a pointless exercise. They raid the camp as soon as it's quiet. There's nothing you can do about it."

Surprised by her warm greeting, I replied, "Thanks for the insight. I suppose we should clean up the mayhem in the kitchen."

"Don't bother. The kitchen staff will do that. They'll be here in about an hour. Got to get the camp ready for the guests."

I was about to reply when Gwynn joined us. "So who's coming today?" she asked, her voice bubbling with enthusiasm.

The light died in Morag's eyes.

Without saying a word, she pointed us in the direction of the reception desk, whistled for Hazel, and headed into the lounge.

I shook my head in puzzlement, unable to understand why she had taken such an intense dislike to Gwynn. "You didn't know her before?" I asked. "Maybe someone you ticked off at primary school?"

Gwynn looked indignant. "Primary school? I bet I was still wearing nappies when that old bag was in primary school!"

Knowing I was on the brink of saying all the wrong things, I headed for the reception desk to find the magical documents that would tell us what guests we could expect today. A clipboard with a bunch of diary schedules—flight sheets, they were called—caught my eye. As I paged through them looking for today's date, my eye fell onto a familiar name.

My heart stuttered.

Michaelino X2. They had spent three days at the camp, departing the day before we arrived. I had to know if they were the same couple I had thrown out of my editing room. I put on a friendly face and went to Morag. "Michaelino times two. Do you remember them?"

Morag patted the sofa next to her for me to sit. Too strung out to resist, I obeyed.

"Remember them! How could I ever forget? They were the guests from hell. Joan, in the office, told me they had a fight on the tarmac at Maun Airport, so he arrived without her. She only got here the next day, all sorry, like a cuddle-bear. But it only took about ten minutes, and they were at it again, going at each other like banshees."

"What were their names?" I asked, already guessing the answer. There couldn't be two terrible Michaelino couples around. The world just wasn't big enough for that.

"Jack and Jane," Morag said. "Do you know them?"

"They're the reason I'm here."

CHAPTER 14

By seven o'clock, the other staff began to trickle into work. I watched them set about their chores, knowing they were scrutinising me as closely as I was eyeing them. In all this activity, Morag seemed riveted to her chair in the lounge, reclining there with the abandon of a fully paid-up guest. Worse, Andrew, chatting with her, seemed to have caught the same sitting-around-doing-nothing bug. I joined them. "Stuff's happening out there. Morag, I take it you're going to show us around?"

Morag heaved herself to her feet. Andrew and I fell into step behind her.

Her first stop was the kitchen. It had been cleaned, ready for the day, and now five unnamed staff stood stern-faced and motionless before me. You could have cut the atmosphere with a meat cleaver, like the one hanging from the pot-rack above the dull stainless steel prep table. Only one person—a handsome guy in his mid-twenties—looked directly at us. The rest looked at their feet or averted their eyes. But instead of introducing us, Morag walked to the other side of the room, leaned against a fridge and watched us.

It was unsettling.

The handsome guy stepped forward and gave a half-bow. "*Dumelang, Rra en Mma*," he said in the vernacular, meaning "hello sir and madam." "My name is Matanta, and I'm pleased to meet our new managers."

I smiled and held out my hand. Matanta grabbed it, giving me a full-on traditional Tswana handshake involving much gripping of hands and wrists. He pointed to a round-faced man with a drooping moustache and, with perfect seriousness, added, "This lump of lard is Robert. You must be careful of him because he isn't a *Motswanan* like all of us. He comes from Angola."

Beaming as if he'd just been paid the greatest compliment, Robert clasped my hand. "Maybe I'm from Angola, but that shouldn't scare you. I'm not a terrorist, like Savimbi's boys." He referred to the controversial Angolan rebel leader. The civil war in Angola raged at this time.

"Our other chef, Seatla, is on maternity leave," Matanta volunteered. "Robert and I will be glad when she's back because the overtime has been *very* bad."

It dawned on me why Matanta was so eager to help. Sean had mentioned that, not only was Matanta head chef, but he was also the deputy camp manager. It was all window-dressing, though. In Sandy's words, "European guests didn't want to be entertained by black people barely out the bush." I shook my head as I recalled her words. Apparently, European guests preferred moody redheads who said too little and glared too much.

While these thoughts ran through my head, the remaining three staff stood restlessly in line, waiting their turn to be introduced.

With a disparaging wave of his hand, Matanta said, "And these others. You'll soon learn who they are. But *this* is our kitchen!" I followed his gaze around the reed-and-chicken-mesh room. *Sans* Barbara and the baboons, I saw it clearly for the first time.

The words "clean" and "sanitary" didn't spring to mind.

The stained concrete floor was shot with cracks, the gas range blackened with age, and the once white melamine working surfaces chipped and grey. Two upright fridges—one of which looked as if it had been built in the fifties by Chevrolet—stood next to an equally ancient chest deep-freeze. I couldn't see the third fridge clearly because Morag's squat bulk leaned against it. But I didn't miss the rusty steel storage cabinet—complete with buckled doors—sagging in the opposite corner. It brimmed with everything necessary to prepare a good meal: broken bags of flour and sugar, packets of yeast, opened tins of tomato paste, half-filled bottles of mayonnaise, and spices and herbs.

I silently took it all in.

And then I fell in love.

This kitchen, as old and worn as it was, felt like home.

A smile spread across my face. Matanta smiled back. Bounding across the room, he eased Morag out the way so I had an uninterrupted view of the upright fridge she'd been hiding.

It was a brilliant white, brand new piece of kitchen equipment.

"Meet our Fresh Fridge," Matanta said as if he were introducing a living-breathing entity. "We keep our fruit and veg in here." He turned back to the '50s model and stroked it reverently. "This *medala*—that means 'very old' in our language—is our Everything Fridge." He smacked the top of the deep-freeze. "And this last one, we call The Cupboard."

"I'm sorry, the what?" I asked.

"The Cupboard. What did you think I said? Freezer?"

"Well, I was rather hoping you did, after all it looks a bit like one."

"Open it, and you'll see why we call it The Cupboard."

I opened the heavy lid, and I put my hand inside. The over-ripe meat said hello. The contents were about half a degree colder than room temperature. I recoiled. "Is that meat okay?"

"If we eat it today. Rodney didn't like fixing anything. He liked his slippers too much." Ignoring Morag's hiss of disapproval, Matanta added, "So, almost everything is broken, or is about to break, or I have already fixed it a hundred times." He looked at Andrew. "You can fix things?"

"I know my way around a toolbox," Andrew replied. "Show us more."

Matanta propelled us into the scullery.

He allowed the inadequate drainage and collapsing roof timbers to speak for themselves. The floor was awash with oily dishwater, while sycamore figs from the tree above lay trodden and rotting underfoot. The scullery stank like a dirty distillery. Matanta made a show of sniffing the air, then turned to us. "The baboons like this place."

I prodded the Swiss Army knife attached to Andrew's belt. "I think you're going to need a little more than this, MacGyver."

Andrew looked vaguely panicked.

Next, we found ourselves in a well-stocked larder the size of the average person's lounge. Rusted shelving strained under the weight of tins and bottles, bags of sugar and flour—and a few broken jam jars. The baboons couldn't be blamed for those because the pantry door had been locked during their raid. Neither could Barbara and Rodney. Those breakages fell right into Morag's turf.

Morag sucked in a breath as if she recognised that, too. She peeled a piece of broken jam-jar off the shelf and, with a flick of her red tresses, tossed it into the dustbin on the other side of the kitchen. She would be a good addition to our volleyball team, if she would just finish scratching the bite from whatever it was that had bitten her.

That wasn't happening anytime soon, I realised when she said, "The kitchen may not look wonderful, but every guest who comes here congratulates me on the standard of the food." She prodded one of the watching staff. "Get in there. Clean it." Turning to Matanta, she added, "The menu for today is: Lunch: spaghetti Bolognese, tomato and mozzarella salad, and a green salad. For dinner, we will have butternut soup, fillet steak with roast potatoes, cauliflower cheese, and beans with almonds. For pudding, please do a chocolate mousse." She walked out the kitchen calling over her shoulder, "Gwynn, tomorrow you do the menu."

How was I supposed to know what the chefs could prepare? Talk about being thrown into the deep end. My mouth dropped as I wondered, yet again, what Morag was doing here, because helping us learn the ropes was not high on her list of priorities.

Matanta must have seen my shock, because he gave me a sympathetic smile as he reached for a couple of tatty, grease-stained files. "Our recipes, *Mma*."

"Thank you, *Rra*." He grinned at the compliment of being called "sir." "Hopefully, I'll get a chance to look at these this afternoon." I put them back on the shelves. "Andrew, we'd better keep up."

We raced out of the kitchen just as Morag disappeared into the large reed-fenced enclosure in the centre of the camp. It turned out to be a laundry, with lots of hanging space for washing lines slung between palm trees.

Morag pointed to a small room, little more than a reed overhang. Three women waited next to concrete sinks, filled with wet washing. "Impeleng, Tokololo, and Mankana," Morag said. "The laundry ladies. They're good workers, but temperamental. And you must keep a special eye on Impeleng, the head of this department." She gestured to the youngest of the three, a girl of about seventeen, sporting a rebellious face. "Impeleng is very hardworking. But she's young and difficult to handle." Impeleng scowled. Morag ignored it. "To compound matters, Impeleng, along with half the other girls on this island, had an affair with Matanta. She recently had his baby. Of course, since Mesho, one of the waitresses, has been living with Matanta for years, no one other than Impeleng admits it ever happened."

Impeleng stamped her right foot and shouted, "*Lekgoa!*"

I had no idea what that meant, but it sounded as if she was swearing. Morag ignored her, but Mankana, the eldest of the three, put a steadying hand on Impeleng's shoulder. Impeleng folded her arms, giving Morag a voodoo-stare.

Morag didn't seem to notice. "Anyway, Impeleng's kid's a spitting image of Matanta. And Mesho, I might add, is still on maternity leave. She's just had another one of Matanta's children. I've lost count on how many he's bred now."

I swallowed hard. Like the kitchen, managing the housekeepers was my department. Other than dishing up top class meals, my second concern centred on dealing with the staff. Here a soap opera unfolded before my very eyes.

Morag now faced Impeleng. "Number two. Get it ready. The guests will be here at noon. That's in less than an hour".

CHAPTER 15

Morag's tour of the camp continued. In our ramblings, I'd noticed three red-uniformed men sweeping up nature's attempts to untidy the grounds around the cottages. Morag now led us to meet them. They were watering and digging over the sorriest vegetable garden I'd ever seen. The sterile, grey Kalahari sand had been coaxed into producing a few rows of stunted marigolds, some struggling herbs I didn't recognise, and a huge red chilli bush.

Morag looked at the garden in despair. "It's bloody hopeless really, but we have to try because vegetables are so expensive, and the supply so erratic." She put her hands on her broad hips. "The baboons don't give us a chance, though. Every time something green appears, they're in here like locusts. Chilli is the only things they don't eat, hence the big bush."

While Morag rambled, the three gardeners watched me closely.

Morag now waved an arm at them. "Sean insisted on red uniforms so the pilots can see them when they're working on the runway. But they're much more useful for spotting this lazy lot when they skive off to sleep in the bush during the day."

It was comforting in some weird way to know that Morag was horrible to everyone, not just to Gwynn.

"Andrew, meet your team. This is Olututswe, head of maintenance." Olututswe, a tall, slight man nearing retirement age, stood erect, with his feet together, displaying yellow teeth in a broad, confident smile. "He's the only person on the island who knows how the sewer system works, because he built it."

Next to Olututswe waited an old, semi-upright man leaning on a home-made rake.

Morag gestured to him. "Alfred is the *medala*." Although I was probably more than half Alfred's age, I read in his eyes and in his humble bow that I was the boss, and had been from before we met.

"He's also the only one around here who eats barbel," Morag continued. Also known as catfish because of their whiskers, these almost prehistoric bottom-dwelling fish looked and tasted like mud. Not something most people relished.

Finally, Morag introduced the last of the maintenance trio. "Thekiso."

He was young enough to be in high school.

Thekiso stepped forward. "I like to speak English. It is good to meet our new managers."

"Hello, Thekiso," I said.

"Thekiso," he corrected.

"Yes. Thekiso," I repeated.

"Thekiso! Thekiso!" Olututswe interrupted; clearly distressed by the way my Western tongue mangled the Tswana name.

The distant rumble of an approaching aircraft suspended my lesson in Tswana phonetics.

"You haven't checked the room!" Morag gasped.

"*I* haven't checked the room, is what I think you mean," Gwynn corrected so only I would hear.

Still, Gwynn and I dashed back to the cottage where the laundry ladies were putting the finishing touches to their cleaning. Those girls sure worked fast. Just as well, given that the Cessna was touching down at that very moment.

Breathing hard, Gwynn and I bolted back up to the runway to meet it and our first guests. We arrived at the edge of the strip just as the pilot turned the plane hard and opened the throttle. The prop wash cloaked us in great clouds of white dust and leaves. I can't imagine why I didn't see it coming.

The doors burst open and we had a look at our first guests.

Not what I expected.

A long-haired man, sporting multiple ear piercings, climbed awkwardly from the plane. A small brunette dressed in grubby denim shorts and a faded India-print blouse followed him. They looked like dollar-a-day travellers—definitely not the type of guests we'd met when we visited the camp in January. Still, I stepped forward, determined to give my rehearsed greeting a try. Then, I noticed a middle-aged lady and gentleman huddled on the backseat of the plane.

Kyle, who seemed to have materialised out of nowhere, slapped me on the back. "Nice change at Tau Camp! The new managers even acknowledge that Scops Camp clients exist." He gestured to the scruffy pair, and smiled at me.

"Oh, they almost had a free cottage," I said blithely, moving in to help Mrs—Crikey, with everything going on, I hadn't found out their names. Anyway, whoever she was, I rushed forward to help extricate her from her seat. "Welcome to Tau Camp," I said, flashing my friendliest smile. "I'm Andrew."

"I'm Herb Van Hoeven, and this is my wife Mary," Herb said in a broad Dutch accent. He grabbed my hand and shook it firmly, while I considered how nice it was when people tell you their full names.

"We saw elephants as we flew over the swamps," Mary enthused. "This is our first visit to Africa, and I have always wanted to see real elephants."

"Then you've come to the right place." I looked around for Morag, hoping she'd take the lead in getting Herb and Mary settled into their cottage. She was sorting through the supplies Sepei had squeezed on board. With a curt nod to me, she organised the staff swarming around the plane into a sherpa-style ferry to carry the stock, and then disappeared with them into the camp.

Gwynn and I were alone on the runway with our new guests. Cursing under my breath, I was about to pick up their luggage when a wizened man stepped up—he looked half-Motswanan and half-Bushman—but he was wearing the khaki uniform worn by the guides.

I sighed with relief as he held out his hand to Herb, saying, "*Dumelang, Rra en Mma.* I am Lecir, your guide to show you the Okavango. I must also carry your bags." He scooped up the cases and nodded at me, probably a hint to tell me to start moving my butt towards reception to check this lot in.

Feeling like the rank amateur I was, I led the way in silence. I couldn't help but wonder how Lecir knew we were the new managers. I would love to have known what rumours had been flying around the staff village since our arrival yesterday.

Confronted by the paperwork at reception, I again looked around for Morag, but she was conspicuous by her absence. Gwynn gave me an encouraging smile and engaged Mary in conversation, leaving only Herb for me to look stupid in front of. He was smiling, confident I had it all under control.

And then it struck me: Herb hadn't a clue of what should happen now. I could've offered him a beer and chat, and he'd be none the wiser. I decided to do it my way. Travel agents handed out lots of bits of paper when booking guests into—or onto—things. I asked Herb for his bits and soon had a small pile of vouchers on the desk in front of me.

Then I remembered the indemnity.

It was nowhere to be found on the desk. I delved under the counter. Somehow, the pad of forms had managed to get hidden inside a water-marked ledger, coated with so much dust I swear no one had used it in years.

Strange that.

As I placed the indemnity in front of Herb, I remembered Rodney's comments when we'd signed that form all those months ago. He wasn't someone I wanted as my mentor, so I said nothing about being eaten by crocodiles. Formalities complete, we took them to their cottage.

"This is just how I imagined it would be," Mary crooned. Then, with a tinge of nervousness aimed at the waist-high wall and door, she asked, "There's no chance of animals getting in during the night, is there?"

"This is probably the safest place on Earth," Gwynn assured her, exuding confidence as if she'd welcomed a hundred guests. "The only room we lock here is the pantry. And that's only to keep out the baboons." Seeing Mary's panicked expression, she quickly added. "They only raid the camp in the mornings. We don't even lock up the bar. The animals don't drink."

Mary put on a brave smile and laughed at Gwynn's little joke. "You've used that line before. Probably countless times on nervous fools like me."

Gwynn and I exchanged a small victory smile. Then I saw Gwynn's brow crinkle with worry. Muttering about a meeting with Morag, she left me outside the Van Hoevens cottage and headed for the kitchen.

I braced myself for the fall out.

CHAPTER 16

Morag wasn't in the kitchen as I suspected, but Matanta was there. He handed me a pink sheet of paper that looked rather like a grocery shopping list.

I looked at him blankly. "What am I supposed to do with this?"

He shrugged. "Maybe ask Morag, *Mma*, because she gave them to me to give to you."

My core temperature rose. It was definitely time that woman and I had a little chat. I turned to find her, but Matanta grabbed my arm. "Maybe later you can solve that *matata*, *Mma*." He leaned in close so none of the other kitchen staff could hear him. "But now we should have lunch, yes?"

I looked at my watch. It was nearly one o'clock. "Lunch is served now?"

"Always, *Mma*," Matanta whispered. Then he shouted across to a young waiter, "*Ari, Ari*. The *lekgoa* are waiting for their food."

Struck by the youthfulness of the lad, I didn't bother asking Matanta what *lekgoa* meant. Ari couldn't have been older than fourteen or fifteen. Ari jumped to attention, scooped up a tray with the lunch, and headed for the door before I could even check the food.

"Ari," I called, hoping to stop him before he vanished.

Instead of pausing, he sped up, dashing out the room.

Matanta must have seen my surprise, because he laughed. "You just told him to move his rump, *Mma*. *Ari* means hurry. And his name is Kekgebele. He wants to be a chef when he grows up. Like me."

"Then let's ari-up and help him learn," I said, feeling like a complete idiot.

Matanta was diplomatic enough to smile at my awful joke. Then he shrugged. "He can't read, *Mma*. His father is… difficult. He doesn't believe in school. Very hard to be a chef if you can't read recipes."

Matanta had a point, but still I wanted to help. "Maybe when he's working with you, you can show him things. Help him."

Matanta must have approved because he beamed at me with his infectious smile. "*Em, Mma*. I'll do it. I like Kekgebele. He's a good kid."

In that moment, Matanta and I clicked. I can't describe exactly what happened, but I just knew he was going to become very important to me, and I sensed he felt a bond, too.

As if building on that, Matanta pointed to the dining room. "I think your food is getting cold."

I grinned at him. "Yes, *Rra*. I'm on my way."

Andrew had mustered the Van Hoeven's into the dining room. There was no sign of Morag—ever ready to ease us into our new job—so it seemed we were doing our first official meal at Tau, solo. But, I asked myself, how hard could it be, inviting people to eat and then talking to them while they did so?

I let out the breath I'd been holding.

Right on cue, as if to help us along our way, Mary commented on the weight of the chair as she struggled to drag it away from the table. I let Andrew answer while I checked out the food.

As much as it burned me to admit it, the food under Morag's watch looked and smelled delicious. I instantly gave Matanta the credit, thrilled I wouldn't be hanging my head in shame this mealtime. So, basking in his reflected glory, I waved a hand at the display and invited Herb and Mary to dive in.

With plates loaded and wine glasses filled, we settled down to get to know each other. The conversation flowed easily—after all, Mary and Herb wanted to be here. They had a deep interest in everything about Botswana, the Okavango, and the camp. And I was just as interested in their lives, left back in England. Herb, it turned out, was obsessed with lighthouses. So obsessed in fact, he and Mary actually lived in one, which he was painstakingly restoring.

Enjoying the food and the company, I allowed myself to relax so much that it came as a bit of a shock when Mary said, "How long have you been here?"

Andrew and I exchanged embarrassed glances. Clearly, he also wasn't that keen to admit this was our first day on the job.

But we needn't have worried about framing a reply, because Morag answered for us.

"Today's their first day on the job, and I guess it shows." Morag and Hazel eased into the dining room as if they'd been waiting in the wings for just this moment. Smiling smugly, Morag settled at the table and grabbed a plate of cheese.

I'm not a violent person, but right then I could have gladly stabbed her with a bread knife.

"Well, who would have believed it?" Herb replied. I looked at him, trying to detect veiled sarcasm in his words, but I didn't know him well enough to judge.

Mary was more effusive. "But you do it so well. I thought you'd been here for ages."

I couldn't resist a sideways glance at Morag. Her face was deadpan, her ice-shard eyes staring at her gorgonzola.

"So Andrew, when do the flood waters reach here?" Herb asked, changing subject. He'd have to be blind, deaf, and dumb not to have noticed the tension between us.

Andrew's eyes widened and his mouth dropped as he scrambled for an answer.

Morag answered for him. "The flooding of the Okavango Delta is caused by summer rainfall in the Angolan highlands. The bush telegraph says the waters have already reached both Shakawe and Seronga—small villages to the north of us. The people in Shakawe say the flood is excellent. The folks in Seronga, further south where the panhandle splits into the actual delta, say the waters are already subsiding. So who knows? I guess we won't find out until mid-June or July when the waters finally reach us."

"So, if Gwynn and Andrew are the managers, what do you do here?" Mary asked Morag in a sweet, tinkling voice.

Mary wasn't the only one who wanted the answer to that question, so I leaned forward to listen.

"I'm a teacher, of sorts. Sean, the camp owner, has employed me to train the guides. Birds are my specialty and that's where the guides are weakest. I also happen to be best friends with Sean's wife, Sandy. Altogether, I'm invaluable to them."

Best friends with Sandy? That explained a lot of some things, but very little of other things. Like why she wanted to sabotage her friend's business by not teaching the new managers the ropes. There had to be a reason, I just had to figure it out—before I killed her and sent her gift-wrapped remains back to Sandy on the next flight out of here.

Wearing that friendship like a bulletproof vest, Morag fixed her horrible eyes on me and added with obvious glee, "I'll be living here on the island, at a place called Otter Lodge." For someone as cold as Morag, she sure knew how to look smug.

Still smirking, she turned to Andrew. "Otter hasn't been lived in for a while and it needs some maintenance work to make it habitable. I'm hoping you'll make it a priority." Without waiting for a reply, she addressed our guests. "Why don't you have a nap? Come back at four, and Lecir will take you on your first outing."

Dismissed, Herb and Mary shuffled their chairs back and began a slow walk to their cottage.

Morag stood up to leave, too, but I grabbed her arm. "Not so fast. Matanta gave me a pink shopping list. What am I supposed to do with it?"

"And while we're talking about paper work," Andrew added. "What do I do with the vouchers and things the Van Hoevens gave me?"

Morag gave me a condescending look as if I were the only one who had spoken. "We do admin in the mornings when the guests go out. Now it's time to attend to the staff, and to look after the guests."

"But you've just sent the guests to bed," I said, unable to believe how annoying this five-foot of nothingness could be. "And we *are* staff."

Morag turned to leave. It was clear the only way I'd stop her would be to rugby tackle her. As my rugby playing was as bad as Andrew's volleyball, that would be counter-productive. And who knows how Hazel, glued to her ankles, would feel about that.

Always unpredictable, Morag stopped to simper at Andrew. "Sean asked me to prepare a bird walk for Tau guests to follow when strolling on the island. The chief guide, KD, is going to help me. I'm meeting him at the runway now." She flicked her hair over her shoulder and set off down the path.

I scowled after her retreating form.

"Calm down," Andrew ordered. "She's obviously pissed off you got the job as manager."

"Me? What about you? I'm not doing this alone, you know?"

"I know. I don't get it, either. But she is friends with Sandy, so—"

"Don't even go there," I snapped. "I *am* not letting that influence me." I bit my lip, and then added, "If Sean and Sandy wanted her as camp manager, they would have given her the job. They didn't, so she must just suck it up."

"Good. That's the spirit. Just no fighting with her. It won't get us anywhere."

Typical Andrew. He was always the peacemaker. Tedious, if you asked me.

He smiled, as if reading my thoughts. "Anyway, running the camp can't be that difficult. We'll figure it out as we go." A placating kiss landed on my cheek. "Now, I've things to do with my new maintenance team."

"I'll walk with you to the kitchen," I grumbled. But what I really meant was I'm going to find Matanta because if it's war with Morag, then I need an ally.

CHAPTER 17

Sadly, the kitchen shift had changed and Matanta and his team had gone. Nervous about claiming my new domain, I stood in the shadow of the door as Andrew hurried away to play MacGyver. After a few moments, my quiet skulking was rewarded by the sounds of sweet singing coming from the scullery.

I stole in to look.

A chubby young girl stood on a red beer crate, singing while washing the lunch dishes. It was then that I noticed how high the sinks were. Without the crate, her feet would be sloshing in the oily dishwater leaking from the sink onto the floor.

She turned to face me. "*Dumela, Mma.* I'm Betty."

Her somewhat plain face was lifted to real beauty by huge brown eyes. I recalled seeing her earlier in the day when Matanta showed us around the kitchen. That meant she should have gone home when the morning shift left. It rang alarm bells. "Are you the only scullery lady?"

"*Em, Mma.* We are short staffed in the scullery."

Great. So I was missing a chef, a waitress, and now a scullery lady, too. I guessed hiring staff was a little more complicated here than just slapping an advert in the local rag. I was nibbling on the inside of my cheek when a voice behind me said:

"And me, I'm Lesego." I turned to see a lanky teenager with a cocky smile. "Did Morag tell you I'm not happy with my pay? The waiters in Maun get much more money than me, and I have to live and work in the bush."

I had no idea how much he earned, but his tone said that living in the bush was the greatest inconvenience possible. The last thing I needed now was a wage dispute to go along with my recruitment drive, so I answered evasively, "There's a time for everything, and the time to discuss your wages will come."

"Lesego!" an outraged voice called from the door.

It was Robert. He grabbed Lesego by the arm and jerked him across the kitchen, berating him in Setswana. With a sulky look in my direction, Lesego snatched up his tray and headed for the dining room. Without saying a word, Robert continued with his kitchen chores.

I walked through the camp to see what was happening in the laundry. A relaxed, peaceful atmosphere greeted me. The three women sat chatting, while Impeleng, the only one whose name I remembered, worked her way through a pile of table linen with a gas iron. Some of the other off-duty staff lay sleeping in the sun. The only way I could tell they were staff was by their uniforms. Learning the names and faces of our twenty fellow team members was going to be more of a challenge than I had anticipated.

Feeling weighed down by yet another thing to cope with—without the help of a mentor—I made my way to our cottage to find my sorely neglected cat. Woodie hunched into a small ball, hidden amongst my clothing in our wardrobe. My heart ached as I scooped her out of her hiding place. Secretly, I wondered if bringing her here was the right thing. My guilt soared as she nestled into my neck. She and I were headed for a cuddle on my bed when I remembered Joan and her confounded radio. As much as I wanted to curl up with Woodie, I could hardly skive off on my first day here, could I? So, adding 'disgruntled' to my list of miseries, I took Woodie and headed back to the reception area.

Woodie was having none of it.

Yowling in terror, she leapt out of my arms—her claws leaving great gouge marks behind them—and raced back to the safety of our cottage. I stood in the path, torn between going back to her and my new responsibilities. Duty finally won out over love, and I slouched off to reception, and flung myself down into a chair to wait for the radio. To make matters worse, Tom, the resident camp cat, sprawled out on the sofa opposite me. He snored softly, obviously without a care in the world. I had the sudden urge to throw a scatter cushion at him, but resisted it. It wasn't his fault Woodie was scared, Morag horrible, and I was stuck at reception.

The more rational part of my brain knew I was being silly. After all, I'd wanted to be here so badly, I'd given up just about everything I owned for the privilege of listening for radio calls that may or may not come. But now the reality of camp life didn't seem to measure up to the dream.

There weren't supposed to be evil witches like Morag in paradise.

People like her were reserved for fairy tales or women's prisons. And this wasn't a fairy tale. If it were, huge grin plastered on her face, my cat would be at my side, taking on this world with me. Instead, she cowered in my cottage and I was in the lounge, alone, while Andrew had fun fixing up the island with his team.

It all seemed so unfair.

I'm ashamed to admit it, but I was so deep into my pity-party that it took the sound of a broom thumping against furniture to bring me back to the present. Lesego was sweeping away the dust I had tracked onto the highly polished ochre floor.

"So," he said, leaning on his broom. "Do you know my name?"

"I'm still learning all your names. And this is time to sweep, not talk." I know I was in a bad mood, but his cockiness wasn't winning him any friends here.

Clearly too thick-skinned to notice, he continued, "Well, *Mma*, you are very slow. My name is easy. Lesego. It means lucky."

I stood to face him. "Lesego, it might surprise you to know that *yours* is indeed one of the names I have remembered—and not for the best reasons, either. You are full of cheek, and I don't like cheek."

Lesego grinned provocatively, then sauntered off back to the kitchen, leaving me to my poisonous thoughts.

CHAPTER 18

It was late afternoon when I made it back to Gwynn and our cottage. Brimming with excitement about my first day in paradise, I couldn't wait to share my news. Gwynn wasn't there, even though Woodie waited in the wardrobe. Deflated, I trotted down to reception.

Gwynn sat in the lounge, staring morosely out at the bay.

I did a mental reverse on my enthusiasm. "Hey, how come you're not up with Woodie?"

"She didn't want to come down here," Gwynn replied, not even looking at me.

I shifted Tom off the sofa and sat down right in her line of sight. She looked away. Oops. *Matata*. I proceeded with caution. "So why aren't you with her?"

"Joan said someone was supposed to man the radio at all times. Remember?"

I'd forgotten about Joan and the radio. Feeling a twang of guilt, I asked, "Did she call?"

"No."

That explained Gwynn's bad mood. I shelved my excitement, and asked tentatively, "So, what else have you done other than sit here?"

"I've taken a deep dislike to Lesego. He's a cheeky little swine."

I had no idea who Lesego was, but still I joked, hoping she'd crack a smile, "Not another person you don't get along with?"

Without moving a facial muscle, Gwynn replied, "He's moaning about his pay."

Hmm. Bad joke. I tried again. "Everyone moans about their pay."

"Not to their brand new boss, they don't. Apparently, every other waiter in Botswana earns more than he does. And he told me I'm very slow, and that his name is Lesego. It means lucky."

I really wasn't in the mood for this, but I played along. "And then?"

"I told him I don't like cheeky waiters. I think he also hates me now. But he can get in line behind Morag." Gwynn must have finally heard the self-pity in her voice, because she winced, and then forced a smile. "Tell me about your afternoon. I know you're dying to."

Okay, I'm a callous swine, but she didn't have to ask me twice.

"You won't believe the junk on the other side of the runway. No wonder the baboons live near the camp. There's probably enough garbage there to feed them for a year. I can't believe Sean knows about this. Rodney just dug huge holes in which they dump the rubbish. Olututswe says they burn the paper and make compost with the green stuff, but I don't believe it. The place is a disgrace and one of the first things I'm going to do around here is clean it up. And would you believe, there's even an abandoned International 4x4 and Land Rover over there."

Gwynn smiled as my words tumbled out. "You look happier than I've seen you in months."

"I've also looked at the runway sprinkler system. Sean told me to spray it every day before the planes land, to settle the dust and to stop the strip from blowing away. Olututswe says the pump hasn't worked for months and half the sprinkler nozzles are broken." I grinned. "Some look as if they've been chewed. Olututswe says hippos graze on the grass next to the strip at night. We should see them from our cottage."

"That'll be fun." Gwynn brightened visibly.

"I saw two old water pumps in the shed, so maybe I can cannibalise one and get the other working. I think I'll make that my first job." With that, I stepped into the CIM room, a little storeroom next to reception where camping equipment, tools, and other odds and ends were stored. It was the first time in years that I'd felt challenged and content at the same time.

"Don't worry," Gwynn called to me from the lounge, rather pointedly, I thought. "I'll wait here for the Van Hoevens. Someone should welcome them back from their outing,"

I decided to ignore her tone. "You're a brick. See you back at the cottage later."

A quick glance at her face and I knew I wouldn't get away with abandoning her at reception for much longer. Clearly some kind of shift system was needed. But for now, I was too excited about my new job.

* * *

The sun was going down when I finally closed the work shed door on my water pump project and headed for our cottage.

Gwynn stood in the middle of the lawn, tears streaming down her face.

"And now?" I asked.

"Woodie. She's gone."

"Gone? Gone where?"

"If I knew that I wouldn't be standing here. I'd be finding her!" Gwynn snapped at me.

This wasn't the time to argue, so I bolted to our wardrobe to see if Woodie was there.

"I've already searched it. I've searched everywhere," Gwynn said, following me.

"Let's just check again," I replied, heart sinking way beyond my boots, settling deep down in the Kalahari dust.

We pulled all the clothes out of our wardrobe. Next, we stripped the bed. Then we shifted the two chairs and coffee table, the only other furniture in the house.

There was no cat.

That left the garden.

Or I hoped it left the garden because the thought of her wandering off into the bush was not one I wanted to pursue.

We stomped across the spiny grass, hoping to flush her.

Nothing.

We peered under every shrub, calling and calling.

Still nothing.

"What more can go wrong here today?" Gwynn cried. "This is a very high price to pay to be in paradise."

I didn't know what to do or say, other than to keep searching.

At last, a small, plaintive cry caught our attention.

She was *somewhere* in the garden. Where I couldn't imagine, because we'd searched every inch of it.

Again, the cry.

"She's hurt," Gwynn wailed. "I can't believe it. Something must have attacked her. Maybe she was bitten by a snake, or perhaps a raptor tried to carry her off."

Gwynn was being irrational, but I wasn't about to tell her that. "She's alive and here. That's what matters. Let's just keep looking."

Another mew, a little clearer this time.

"She's in the cottage," Gwynn said, running inside to look again.

Still no cat.

"I don't get it," Gwynn sobbed. "Where is she?"

"Woodie," I called again, with some exasperation.

As if sensing this game was getting old, Woodie gave a positive meow. It was coming from the rolled-up reed blinds hanging from the roof rafter where our front wall should have been. I hadn't noticed them before.

Gwynn ran over to the blind, calling.

My heart skittered when I saw Gwynn's eyes widened in shock. She gently pulled Woodie out from the rolled-up blind.

Our confident city-slicker cat trembled pathetically, her little body covered with scratches, blood, and matted fur.

Gwynn kissed her and then asked in a tear-muffled voice, "What do you think did it? A wild cat?"

"They're nocturnal," I reminded, and then hesitated, not wanting to share my thoughts. But the truth had to be faced if we were ever to live in peace here. "I wouldn't be surprised if it were Tom. He looked mighty ticked off when I tossed him off the sofa. Maybe he came up here to vent his fury."

Gwynn looked up in surprise. "Tom? But—but he seemed so content this afternoon."

To prove Gwynn wrong, Tom stepped around the reed fence into our garden, hissing as if he owned the place, which, admittedly, he had until we'd arrived.

Woodie sank her claws into Gwynn's arm, trembling even harder.

From then on I didn't like Tom one bit.

My logic told me it wasn't his fault. He'd had the entire island to himself before this little upstart appeared. But then so had Morag, and her behaviour was little better than Tom's. Although I couldn't openly fight Morag, I could sort out the cat. So I did, chasing him out of our yard.

"I must stay with her," Gwynn said, sitting down to examine Woodie's injuries.

Just beginning to realise the impracticality of having a city cat in the African wilds, I replied hesitantly, "Okay, I'll go and check on the staff. And tonight I suggest we lock her up in the CIM room while we have supper. Just until we can sort Tom out." I left Gwynn disinfecting Woodie's wounds with Betadine cream from our first aid kit.

They were still busy when I returned ten minutes later.

Gwynn looked up from her ministrations. "Anything to report?"

"No sign of Morag. Alfred lit the fires in the donkey boilers (a small wood-burning furnace plumbed to the showers for heating barrels of water) so we'll have hot water. Matanta is in the kitchen preparing snacks and dinner. Kekgebele is setting the table. Lecir asked me which guides to call for the guests tomorrow. Like I had the answer to that."

"Did you ask Matanta for help?"

"Didn't have to. He was right there. He suggested I call Kamanaga. You know, Morag is a great help. Don't know what we'd do without her." I headed for the shower. "Oh, and by the way, Lecir and Herb said they saw a lion on their walk. Apparently Mary almost wet herself."

* * *

Half an hour later, with Woodie safely ensconced in the CIM room, Gwynn and I joined Herb and Mary around the campfire. The four of us enjoyed a drink while admiring the distant palm trees, black sentinels against a vivid red, orange, and pink sky. The moment the sun dipped below the horizon, a sticky humidity settled over my skin as sweet lily-scented air drifted in from the river. It could not have been more tranquil.

The peace was short-lived.

A fierce scream tore through the dusk, followed by a hysterical yowl.

We all jumped with fright.

Then it struck me that the sound was coming from the CIM room.

Gwynn and I, joined by Morag and Hazel who had just arrived, rushed over to investigate. I flung open the door, expecting to see Tom and Woodie battling it out, but the room was empty. The sound of fighting receded through the camp. It was then I noticed that the reed walls didn't reach the roof—like that was news at Tau Camp. I could have kicked myself.

With no time to lose, Gwynn, Morag, and I ran after the cats, with Matanta bringing up the rear. Not to be out done, Hazel raced up and down the pathway, barking manically.

Morag grabbed Tom, and Gwynn and I finally caught Woodie at the entrance to our cottage. After spending a few minutes comforting her, Gwynn hid her in the rolled-up blind where she seemed happiest.

Steps heavy, we returned to our guests.

Morag, with Tom on her lap, sat with Herb and Mary at the fire. His eyes were closed as he blissfully leaned into her cuddle.

"Tom's being a real bully," Gwynn said, looking at them both with open loathing.

"What do you expect?" Morag replied. "You knew there was a cat here when you decided to come. Your cat must take her chances because Tom was here first."

I could see Gwynn wasn't going to let this pass unchallenged. I shook my head, wondering if there was a special Tau poison—something in the air, maybe?—that turned every discussion between senior camp management into a free-for-all to 'entertain' the guests. Before I could stop her, Gwynn shot an apologetic look at the wide-eyed Herb and Mary, and said to Morag, "Let's talk. Right now."

Morag put Tom down and followed Gwynn the few yards to the dining room. In true Tau fashion, Gwynn attacked before I'd even entered the room.

"Yes, Morag," Gwynn snarled, sounding remarkably like the fighting cats. "I thought you'd say that about Tom. And I suppose I must take my chances, too, because you were here first? Well, understand something—Woodie might not win the fight against Tom, but I will win against you. And the reason for that is simple. You are *just* a teacher of sorts and I am *just* the manager. It's the manager who decides what animals live where, not the teacher. As manager, I have decided: one more stunt like that, and Tom will be on the next *mokoro*, headed for Scops Camp."

I sucked in a breath. Although I spoke glibly about running the camp on our own, we still needed Morag's help. I hurried over to douse the flames.

Then I stopped.

Gwynn might like playing with fire—she does, literally—but this was no arson attack. Morag had made it abundantly clear she had no intention of teaching Gwynn anything to help her run the camp. My wife had taken the only face-saving option available to her—to go it alone. Pity she'd done it so publicly.

Morag stared at Gwynn. Then, she said, "But I am friends with Sandy. You can't—"

"That does not make you bulletproof," Gwynn snapped. "So don't bother throwing it in my face again. I'm impervious." She folded her arms across her chest, tilted her jaw up, and grilled Morag with flashing green eyes.

I held my breath, waiting for Morag's reaction.

It was as unexpected as Tom's attack on Woodie had been predictable. Morag walked out the room and disappeared into the night.

Still, something told me this wasn't the end. Morag didn't strike me as the kind who'd roll over and play dead just because someone snapped at her. The next few weeks were going to be interesting as these two struggled for ownership of this patch of jungle.

With a huge sigh, I took Gwynn's hand and dragged her back to face her guests.

They looked embarrassed.

"I apologise," I said in my most apologetic voice. "But Morag is making life somewhat difficult."

Surprisingly, Herb came to Gwynn's defence. "I sensed something like this might happen, but I didn't think we would still be here to see it. Whatever happens, Gwynn, I wish you well in this lovely place. And, for what it's worth, I think you and Andrew are already good managers."

"Thank you, Herb, but I'm still sorry," Gwynn said, quickly recovering from her anger, like she always did.

"I'm not," I said, now that I knew the guests weren't about to fire us. Yes, brave, I know. "Like Herb said, a showdown with you and Morag was inevitable. Now I can stop worrying about who's going to throw the first bomb. Oh, and a direct hit, I think."

Gwynn struggled to restrain her smile as she led Herb and Mary to dinner.

Our first night as managers of Tau Camp wasn't a late one. After dinner, Gwynn and I locked up the pantry, and walked slowly through the shadows to our house.

The camp was full of sound. A tiny Scops owl purred its insect-like call, while crickets chirped merrily all around us. Ahead of us on the path, a fiery-necked nightjar called its mournful cry, "Good Lord Deliver Us." Appropriate I thought. Far in the distance, we caught the sound of hyena yapping and laughing.

Then a new, unfamiliar noise.

We stopped to listen. It was a high-pitched, monotonous squeaking, rather like a rusty sign swinging in the wind. I was about to suggest we go and find it, when Gwynn whispered, "Woodie will be waiting for us."

Sighing, I left the mystery unsolved, and we went to greet our cat. She was still where we'd left her after the fight. Tom, too engrossed in snitching tidbits from the table, had not troubled her again.

I was just drifting off to sleep when Gwynn poked me in the back. "You awake?"

"I am now," I mumbled.

"Just to let you know, I've shed all the tears I ever intend crying over Tau Camp. Starting tomorrow, I own this world."

I smiled. This was the girl I'd married.

CHAPTER 19

The buzz of the alarm clock jerked me awake. I looked at the time in disbelief. Five thirty. It felt as if I'd only just gone to bed. Worse, my entire body ached from yesterday's unaccustomed walking. Sadly, that was a testament to how unfit I was, given that I'd spent most of yesterday afternoon moping in the lounge.

I wasn't the only one in pain, because Andrew groused, "I guess we've got to move, but I don't think I can."

"Are you aching too?"

"Muscles I didn't even know I had."

"The guests will be up soon," I replied, wishing I wasn't so painfully diligent.

"And the baboons."

That decided it.

After dressing, we bade Woodie farewell and headed for the kitchen.

Halfway down the path we met Lesego. I called out a greeting, hoping to make up for my rudeness yesterday. He seemed please I'd remembered his name and fell into step with us. A few paces on, Andrew stopped, pointing to something in the bush not far from the kitchen door. I stepped off the path to pick it up—a large black saucepan.

"Damn," Andrew muttered. "Did we miss the baboons?"

"No, *Rra*. They're still on the other side of the runway, sitting in the sun," Lesego replied.

"Well, something or someone got into the kitchen and swiped that pot," Andrew said, walking purposefully to the door. There he stopped and his hand flew to his mouth.

I quickened my pace and then also stopped. The wood-and-mesh kitchen door lay on the floor in six tangled pieces, one corner still attached by a loose hinge.

"*Eish!*" Lesego gasped. "What could make such damage?"

"You live here, and you don't know?" Andrew asked, stepping into the kitchen.

I followed, immediately stumbling over the oven warming-draw and two heavy steel pots. My mouth gaped as I found my feet. My kitchen looked as if a giant had picked it up and shaken it.

A large black dustbin, which had held the accumulation of yesterday's rubbish, had been tipped over and the contents strewn over the floor. Next to it, a smaller plastic dustbin, used for collecting greens for the compost heap, had also been emptied, and then shredded. Tupperware boxes and bowls lay scattered everywhere, some of them sporting teeth marks. The plastic coating on the oven door handle had been gnawed away. All five knobs from the stove were gone. And, most frightening of all, the heavy gas range had been dragged at least three feet across the floor. The rubber gas pipe, stretched to breaking point, had stopped its progress.

"The burner on the fridges . . .they're open flames," I croaked, almost scared speaking out loud would ignite the gas. Our archaic fridges used a small flame as a heat-exchanger to turn bottled gas into. . .well, to be honest, I'm not sure because it certainly wasn't cold air or ice.

"If that oven had moved an inch further," I continued, "the pipe would have snapped and the gas would have exploded. We'd have lost the whole kitchen."

"Imagine the radio call to Maun," Andrew said. "Hello, Sean. Our first day was great. Today not so good. We blew up your camp."

We both giggled—then stopped simultaneously when we spotted the *piece de resistance* of the carnage.

The door of our shiny, brand-new Fresh fridge hung open, the shelves neatly positioned on their racks with the greens untouched. Below, the floor was coated white with millions of tiny polystyrene balls. Our plastic junkie visitor had munched its way into the door lining, releasing the insulation. If that was not bad enough, it had also chewed the rubber door seal, which lay in three pieces in a sea of synthetic snow.

"What on Earth happened here?" I turned to see Herb and Mary standing behind us, ready for their morning walk.

"We were doing waiter training. But it's not going very well," Andrew said.

Lesego gave him a this-man-is-mad look while everyone else laughed.

"I thought for a moment it was the cats fighting," Herb volunteered.

"Good one, Herb! Fortunately not, though. They'd really have wrecked the place," Andrew replied.

"Then what do you think it was?" Mary asked. From her fearful tone, she didn't see the funny side of all this.

"I'd say we were visited by a hyena," Andrew said. "Amazing that we heard nothing last night. Did you?"

"Not a sound. We both slept like the dead," Herb replied.

Now looking decidedly nervous, Mary asked, "But aren't hyenas dangerous? I mean would they attack a person? Would they come near the cottages?"

"Spotted hyena, and this was probably a spotty, can be quite vicious," I said.

"Especially if they're in a pack," Andrew added for spice.

"Do you think a pack did this?" Herb asked. His face glowed with excitement.

"Maybe," Andrew said with a mischievous grin.

Mouth trembling, Mary started wringing her sunhat.

I took pity on her. "I think we'd definitely have heard something if a pack of hyenas had torn through the camp. I would say this was a solitary animal."

"But aren't they dangerous?" Mary repeated.

"Yes, of course they are," Herb yelled at her. "You heard what Gwynn said." Having shut his wife up, he continued with unbridled enthusiasm, "Do you think he'll come back tonight? I'd love to see him. I've read that their jaws have the strongest bite out of all the African mammals. And they can be very nasty. Perhaps we can wait up for him? Hide behind a bush."

I looked at Herb in delight. In one breath he'd admitted hyenas have a nasty bite and a bad temper, in the next, he was begging to be allowed to stay up and, from the scant protection of a bush, eavesdrop on this one's dustbin raid. It was classic; you couldn't make this up.

"Herb," I asked innocently, "did you know hyenas often drive lions off their kills?"

Before he could reply, Andrew butted in. "Yes, they also attack campers during the night, biting their faces or feet if they sleep in the open. I remember one camping trip to the Savuti in southern Chobe when we ran into hyena."

Herb leaned forward, mouth open, hanging onto Andrew's every word. I bet he was looking forward to hearing that one of the party had been dragged off into the night.

"We'd made a stew in a heavy cast iron pot," Andrew continued. "After supper, we filled it with water and left it to soak. During the night, we were visited by a spotty, and in the morning the pot was gone. We saw the tracks where he'd dragged it about hundred yards into the bush."

As I expected, Herb's face registered mild disappointment with that outcome. Mary just looked terrified—a bug just seconds before the chameleon's tongue lashed out.

"*Eish! Matata.*" This was followed by a rapid series of tongue clicks.

We turned to see Lecir, Herb's and Mary's guide, standing at the door, shaking his head.

"A hyena come to cause trouble in the kitchen." Lecir waved his arms to make his point. "It will come back now, many, many times." He poked Andrew in the chest with knobbly finger. "You must shoot him. Hyena in camp is no good." Having declared his verdict, he clasped Herb and Mary firmly by the arm and walked them out of the kitchen. "Today, we go for long walk. Find hyena. Then I bring you back for breakfast."

They had just left when Morag took their spot. She shook her head, also clicking her tongue. Was that a Tau Camp thing?

"You're the teacher," I said to her. "Any ideas for warding off hyenas?"

She must have still been ticked off with me after our fight because she turned her back and made a point of looking at Andrew. I snorted; she'd have to try harder than that to get me down today. It was obvious by her silence that she had no bright ideas to offer.

Sounding somewhat overwhelmed, Andrew said, "He better not come back or else I'll have to schedule the construction of a hyena-proof door into my maintenance programme." He shot a disgruntled look at the Fresh fridge as if it was at fault for being mauled. "As it is, I must see if I can fix the fridge this morning."

"Fix the fridge? Not possible," Morag said.

She didn't know Andrew like I did. Once on a fix-it mission, a few pieces of chewed plastic would not defeat him.

Andrew shrugged. "I'm sure I'll figure something out."

"Don't forget you have to come to Otter Lodge with me today, too." Morag's voice brooked no argument.

"Okay," Andrew said, annoyingly. What was his game? He knew I couldn't stand her, so why was he sucking up to her?

Once we were alone, I asked. "Why are you helping Morag? We have more important things to sort out."

"I'm going to make a deal with her. I'll fix up Otter in exchange for her help with the admin. And when her house is fixed, she won't be living here anymore."

Ah. . .why hadn't I thought of that? "Brilliant. Good boy. Off you go." I waved him on with a grin. "I think today is going to turn out very well indeed."

I stayed in the kitchen while Andrew tackled Morag. I couldn't hear their conversation, but soon they were sitting together in reception, shuffling papers and ledgers. Andrew and I'd agreed, because he's more methodical than I am, that he'd handle the bulk of the camp admin. The kitchen paperwork was my baby. I would have to find someone else to help me with my pink shopping lists.

Right now, that was the furthest thing from my mind. My kitchen had been trashed, and I had guests coming into camp in a few hours.

CHAPTER 20

Concentrating on bookkeeping was impossible. All I could hear were laughter and jokes coming from the kitchen. The morning staff were cleaning up the chaos from the hyena attack. I'd expected them to be annoyed at having to start the day by scrubbing, but no, they sounded as if they were having a party. Jealous, I took a break from Morag and headed over to join them. It was then I noticed Gwynn standing in the shadows, grinning. She quickly put her finger to her lips to silence me and beckoned me over to watch.

Thekiso, my young maintenance lad with the unpronounceable name, was on his hands and knees on the floor. Growling fiercely, he lunged at the oven door. Then he turned and charged the fridge. Robert grabbed a wooden spoon and chased him around the kitchen. Thekiso then pounced at Betty. She squealed in terror and ran across the room towards the scullery, slipping on a ripe fig that brought her down on her bum, much to everyone's raucous delight.

Then Robert spotted us.

He coughed loudly to attract attention. Thekiso obviously didn't hear because he dashed towards Robert, waving a torn dishcloth above his head. Robert pulled himself erect and barked Thekiso's name, making our ferocious 'hyena' look up in surprise. Robert gestured with his head towards us. Thekiso's dark face paled as he froze, crouching on the floor with the dishcloth between his outstretched hands. Slowly, he panned around. The moment he saw us, his eyes clamped shut in embarrassment.

A sudden hush settled on the kitchen and I knew Gwynn and I had just arrived at a crucial crossroads in our lives at Tau Camp. What we did now would determine whether the staff respected us as people, or merely tolerated us as managers.

I could see Gwynn was thinking exactly the same thing. Without hesitation, she stepped over to Thekiso and patted him on the shoulder. "You're a brilliant hyena. Even I was scared."

Only Robert gave a quivering, nervous laugh.

"But you see, Thekiso, this hyena likes plastic, not cloth," I added, surreptitiously watching their faces. It took a moment for them to register that I wasn't angry.

Then, like magic, the tension evaporated. Everyone, including Thekiso, cracked up laughing.

I learnt a valuable lesson that morning. This was Africa where patriarchal societies dominated. Gwynn might be the manager, but I was the chief, and it was only after I'd spoken that the law was set and the final judgment given.

Robert suddenly became serious. "This hyena is bad luck. They bring very bad magic."

"Why?" I asked, my curiosity piqued.

But Robert became all business-like. "When Matanta comes we'll tell you all about hyenas. But now I must make breakfast. Lesego must set the table and you, *Mma*, must give me the menu for today."

I could see from the wide-eyed panic rippling across Gwynn's face that she had been too busy being depressed yesterday to give the menu a second thought. She quickly flipped through the grimy recipe files. "Let's have quiche and salads for lunch," she began hesitantly. Then she yanked open the Everything fridge. "And for dinner. . . we'll start with—" she licked her lips and smiled, "my personal favourite: deep-fried camembert cheese with marula jelly. And then," she opened The Cupboard—our freezer—gasped at the smell, and slammed it shut. "The chicken rotting in there, perhaps you'll turn it into a mushrooms and sour cream casserole. But do it soon."

Robert smiled. "*Em Mma*. And pudding?"

"Um. . .apple pie and custard." Satisfied with her decision, Gwynn pinned up the menu on the notice board.

We left the kitchen—only to be confronted by Impeleng and her cleaning team.

"How many *lekgoa* today?" Impeleng asked.

Lekgoa. That word again.

Gwynn and I stared at her blankly.

Impeleng repeated the question with a hint of impatience. I called Robert over to translate. He laughed when Impeleng, now tapping her broomstick on the ground, repeated herself for a third time. "She has a *matata, Rra.* A problem. She doesn't know how many guests are coming today, and what rooms to make up, so she said, 'how many *lekgoa*?' *Lekgoa* is Setswana for white people, so we call the guests *lekgoa.*"

"Don't you get any black guests?" I asked.

"Yes," Robert replied. "Or as we say in Setswana: *em* or *er.*"

"And what are black guests called?" Gwynn asked.

"We make them honorary white people for their stay and call them *lekgoa* also."

Clarity restored and yet another lesson in Setswana complete, Gwynn thanked Robert and instructed Impeleng to prepare number three. We had one party of two *lekgoa* coming in today.

The excitement over, I looked over at Morag and the bookkeeping. There was no avoiding it.

Gwynn grinned at me. "Enjoy. I'm going to check on Woodie."

I watched her go with a brooding sense of resentment that she was free and I wasn't. Now I knew exactly how she'd felt yesterday afternoon.

About nine thirty, Gwynn came back down to reception. The desk was still spread with voluminous sheets of ledger paper, each covered with a tangle of figures. I know I must have looked perplexed. Morag, also looking confused, was chewing thoughtfully on a pencil.

"How's the admin going?" Gwynn asked, looking disgustingly relaxed and cheerful.

"I've managed to confuse myself while teaching Andrew," Morag admitted.

"Let's begin again," I suggested for the third time.

"Herb and Mary are on the way back," Gwynn announced.

Morag threw down her pencil and leapt to her feet. "I've done my part, Andrew. Now you have to come to Otter with me today."

Done her part! "Not even close," I said to her departing back. "We carry on after breakfast until we get it right."

"Then I suggest you learn faster."

I opened my mouth to say something cutting, but Gwynn grabbed my arm. "Fighting with Morag is what *I* do. Now come, breakfast is ready—including a nice big bowl of yoghurt."

I made a vomiting sound, rather like Woodie throwing up a hairball. "You know my views on yoghurt. Didn't you make anything worth eating?"

"Yoghurt. And fruit salad and juice, cold cereals, oats porridge, eggs to order, crunchy bacon, fried tomatoes with mushrooms, and toast and jam, of course."

My mouth watered. "Are you sure that's enough?" I asked as we headed for the dining room.

Gwynn skidded to a halt. "You don't think so?" Why do women always doubt themselves? "Just as well I got Robert to make some sweetcorn fritters, too."

It struck me that we must be among the most privileged people on Earth. Here we had free access to delicious food and drinks, prepared by someone else, served by someone else three times a day, every day, on an elaborate baronial table in an environment that would be the envy of most people on the planet. And we were being paid to eat it. What more could you ask out of life?

Other than a bit more sleep, it was perfect.

CHAPTER 21

Perfection, Andrew called it. Hmm, perhaps up until breakfast was finishing and Mary turned to me with a wistful look in her eye. "Lecir suggested we take a picnic lunch today to a place called Baobab Island. Apparently, we'll sit under the trees like hedonists while he serves us. We would love to do it, if possible."

Was it possible? How did I know? I didn't even know if Baobab Island existed. And why did I always get the potentially embarrassing problems? Mentally kicking Lecir for his over-eagerness, I plastered on a fake smile. "I'll go and brief the kitchen."

Matanta had joined Robert at the stove. I addressed my remarks to him. "What's Baobab Island?"

"Ah!" he said. "The *lekgoa* want to go on a picnic." He shouted across to Betty, "Run to the laundry and get the cooler boxes."

As she complied, I asked, "So Baobab Island is the usual picnic spot?"

"One of them, *Mma*." Matanta smiled at me. "You'd like it. Small island with just two trees. A little baobab—" Fingers angled skyward in the usual African gesture used to indicate height, he pointed to the low ceiling. I assumed the baobab was indeed a young tree. "And an umbrella acacia. Very nice place. Maybe one day when we have an empty camp, you and the Chief can go picnic there."

"Sounds great. And when was Andrew promoted to chief?"

Matanta gave me an arch smile, and, instead of answering, started to sing, "So, what do the *lekgoa* eat today, *Mma*? Must I make a special quiche to go on picnic, and one to stay at camp?"

It was my turn to say ah! "So we need another menu." I grinned at him. "Something tells me Tau Camp picnics are not like the last picnic Andrew and I had. We ate soggy egg mayonnaise sandwiches straight out of the tin foil, and drank Coke from a can."

"No, *Mma*." He continued his tuneless song as he walked to the Everything fridge and extracted a large Tupperware basin. "Maybe I do cold meat, potato salad, mixed salad, cheese, biscuits, and fruit?" With a smile, he placed a generous helping of meat into a second Tupperware— it had a few chew marks from the hyena, but that couldn't be helped. He snapped the lid closed before dropping it into the cool-box.

"Perfect," I replied. "I couldn't have done it better."

Matanta held his hand up for a high five, and then said, "I hear you like our new hyena."

"Thekiso, I like very much. The other one I'm not so sure about," I replied, slapping his palm.

"I think we'll have fun together, *Mma*."

I had been conscious of Robert during our exchange. He said nothing, but his eyes hadn't left me either. I turned to face him, and was surprised to see a deep scowl marring his jovial features. Before I could delve into what it meant, Morag poked her head around the door.

"I take it you intend to feed the fish eagle?" Her voice was as cold and condescending as usual. "He's been screaming for the last five minutes."

I hadn't heard him.

Matanta couldn't have heard him, either, but he burst into a chant, "Time to feed the *audi*, time to feed the *audi.*"

Robert made a croaky impersonation of a fish eagle calling.

"*Audi*? Does that mean fish eagle?" I asked, ignoring Morag.

Matanta nodded as he handed me a small piece of fillet steak pulled from The Cupboard. "*Audis* do not always eat fish. They also eat dead animals." He glanced pointedly at Morag. "Unlike some, they're not fussy. Rump, fillet, they don't complain."

Morag scowled at him and marched out the kitchen.

Hmm. . .Matanta didn't like Morag. This was information a girl like me could use.

CHAPTER 22

The fish eagle didn't disappoint. There was a clatter of camera shutters like a celebrity press conference as it swooped down onto the bait. The only trouble was the timing—every photographer was about a second off.

"Fantastic," Herb shouted. "I promise I'll send you one of my photographs for your pinboard in reception."

I didn't have the heart to tell him he'd just taken a picture of a small splash in a lily pond. Sadly, the fish eagle excitement was short lived and I now had to face more bookkeeping with Morag. She saw me coming to reception to join her, picked up her pencil, and sighed. An hour later, she was no closer to helping me unravel the mysteries of Sean's accounting system.

Then I heard a welcomed distraction.

Gwynn, Matanta, and Lecir were down at the bay, helping Mary and Herb and their picnic onto the *mokoro*. I joined them. Lecir loaded in a fold-up table and camp chairs, a roll of toilet paper shoved on the end of a spade handle, a cooler box of drinks, and another cooler box of food. Once his passengers were safely aboard, he took his spot at the back of the boat. He shoved his pole into the water. Gwynn gave the prow a firm push. They were off—and I was instantly jealous.

Gwynn must have been too, because as Lecir manoeuvred the *mokoro* out into the main channel, she said, "Makes one want to come back as a *lekgoa*."

"Maybe next time we have an empty camp we can duck off and

have a picnic under a tree."

"That's what Matanta suggested. Sounds great." Gwynn gave me a sideways glance. "But you'll have to learn to pole first."

I rubbed my hands together in anticipation. "I need one of those poles the guides use to punt with."

"*Ngashi.*"

I waited for a translation of a new Setswana word.

"The poles are called *ngashi.* And the best ones are made from the Silver Terminalia tree. Matanta told me. So when do your lessons start? I'm sure he'd teach you."

My sigh bested the call of the mourning dove. "Not until I've knocked off a few things on my ever-expanding fix-it list."

Morag's bark, reminiscent of the alpha baboon, pulled me back to the books. As I plonked my butt down onto the stool next to hers, she announced, "I've been meaning to tell you that the staff salary reviews are overdue. It should have been done last month, but Sean was waiting for you to join."

That would explain Lesego's wage gripe.

I wanted Gwynn here for this discussion, but as I called her over, Morag said loudly, "I hardly think we need all three of us." She fixed Gwynn with an imperious eye and added, "I'm sure you have rooms to check."

Gwynn plunked her elbows on the desk and smiled sweetly at Morag. "Miss this? You must be kidding. I love talking about money. Almost as much as I like spending it."

Morag opened her mouth to object, but I got in first. "Gwynn and I are a team. We do this together."

"Anything you like, Andrew," Morag said in an even more saccharin voice than Gwynn's. She handed me the staff salaries book.

I shook my head as I paged through it; whatever Sean's faults, he couldn't be accused of being generous. Even Matanta earned a pittance.

"It isn't quite as bad as it looks," Morag justified. "Each staff member also gets a hundred Pula credit to spend at Scops Camp's shop. It's the only shop on the island, so everyone has to buy from there."

"And it's owned by Sean. Talk about giving with one hand while taking with the other," Gwynn pointed out with unassailable logic.

Even Morag pulled a face at that injustice. "Sean is happy to look at an eight percent increase for the staff, but I think we should push for more for Robert and Lesego."

"Lesego? Why him?" Gwynn demanded.

Morag gave a tired sigh. "When you've had as much experience running this camp as I have, you'll know that he's an excellent waiter."

"Then I suggest he works on his first impressions," Gwynn said with a mulish cast to her jaw.

"This is not about 'first impressions'," Morag replied, as if Gwynn were a dumb kid. "It's about doing what's fair for a good and loyal staff member. And remember, I've been here long enough to see past 'first impressions'."

Gwynn was revving up to reply, so I intervened. "Okay, Morag. Based on your recommendation, we'll include Lesego in our salaries crusade. But what about Matanta? Obviously, if anyone is going to get a raise around here, he should. Apart from anything else, he's the deputy manager."

"As you wish." Morag's disdainful tone told me she didn't care much for Matanta.

Childish, I know, but that knowledge sent Matanta soaring in my estimation—and from Gwynn's eager nodding, she agreed.

Morag shoved a piece of paper and a pen at me. "As manager, you must write the motivation letter to Sean."

I knocked together a credible begging letter, asking Sean to hand over some more cash for his staff. The letter would go off on today's plane.

Gwynn scowled her disapproval as she read my missive. "You do realise that if Sean agrees to this, Lesego will earn almost as much as Robert? That will probably make him the most expensive waiter in all the Okavango. . .forget that, the whole of Botswana, maybe even southern Africa . . . I could go on."

Morag's eyes narrowed. "There's a waiter at Fish Eagle Camp who earns more. And that's just down the river from here. So much for what you know about things."

Thankfully, the radio crackled into life. I lunged for the mic. "638. Go ahead Joan."

"Nice 'n prompt!" came Joan's crackly reply.

"As you said, you make our lives possible," I said, sounding smug. "What can I do for you?"

"Sorry for the short notice, but I'm sending you another two guests on the 12:30 flight. Weson X 2. And I've changed the Cessna to an Islander."

My heart did a high jump. A Britten-Norman Islander was a twin-engine, ten-seat, high-winged flying delivery van. Maybe Sepei would have managed to pack my toolbox into it. I really hoped so.

I saw Gwynn's eyebrows rise and registered that Joan also said she was sending us some new guests. I glanced at my watch. It was just after eleven. Plenty of time to get a room ready, but what about a guide?

Morag said, "Andrew, you'd better send Thekiso to the staff village to call another guide. And I think we've done enough admin for the morning. Let's hit Otter Lodge."

I wanted to ask Gwynn if she'd manage on her own, but knew she wouldn't thank me for it. At this point, she'd rather have chewed off her own arm to feed to the hyena than admit defeat in front of Morag.

She must have read the concern in my eyes, because she leaned over to kiss me. "Go. Have fun." Then in a more serious tone she added, "Getting Otter habitable is certainly the number one priority round here."

* * *

Otter Lodge perched at the edge of a tranquil lagoon on the other side of the island, about ten minutes from the camp. Like everything else, it was a large reed structure built between the trees, except this time, it rose two levels. The missing sections of walls and roof suggested it had survived a small tornado.

"Baboons," Morag said, following my gaze. "I employed some kids to chase them away, but it's pretty hopeless. The blasted animals still wrecked the place. That will have to be fixed before I move in."

I tugged on my beard. "Um...who makes the reeds?" I knew nothing about building reed houses.

"Mother nature, I suppose," Morag said with an irritating laugh.

"No. I mean the walls."

An air of melancholy settled on Morag's face, probably at the failure of her joke. "Old women from the staff village. They bind the *letaka* together to make what the locals call *mabinda*. That's then turned into walls and roofs. If you want, I can arrange for three women to start working on it." My face must have registered my surprise—where did this helpful Morag come from?—because she simpered, "In the interests of teamwork, and all that."

"I'll ask Olututswe to bring them to the camp so I can brief them." I hopped up the stairs into the house and made a point of scanning the kitchen-cum-lounge.

Baboons had defecated all over the wicker furniture, and dead centipedes and spiders littered the sink. Nothing that couldn't be cleaned. The only possible delay to Morag moving in seemed to be the *mabinda*.

"How long do you think it'll take the women?"

"First, you'll have to order the *mabinda* twine from Sepei. While you wait for it to arrive, the women will go into the delta to collect the *letaka*. Budget two weeks for that. Then another two weeks to peel the reeds and to stitch them together. Then the actual repairs have to be done. I suppose about six weeks."

Six weeks.

I sighed. I'd rather hoped we'd be shot of Morag by the end of the day.

Wishful thinking. Without replying, I climbed the narrow wooden staircase to the bedroom, a large square room overlooking Otter Lagoon. Like all Tau bedrooms, the centrepiece was a bed and mosquito net. It looked so peaceful I could have lain down and slept all afternoon.

"The water boiler has never worked properly," Morag said, interrupting my daydream. "We flew in a gas expert, but he couldn't get it going. I'd have coped with cold water, but the solar panel is broken, too, so no electricity." She raised her eyebrows. "Do you know anything about gas and solar panels?"

"Solar panels are a breeze, so I'll have your electricity running in no time. But gas? Well, I'm no expert, but I'll give it a try." When Morag's face fell, I added, "I'm sure the problem will succumb to logic."

I certainly hoped so because I was relying on logic to fix most of the *matatas* on Noga Island. And logic said the release of gas to the boiler was triggered by water pressure. So no water pressure, no gas. No gas, no fire. No fire, no hot water. Simple.

The trickle of water coming from the tap confirmed my suspicion, sending me off looking for leaks in the system. But after scrambling through the undergrowth, following the water pipes, I came up blank. They were as tight as Sean's wallet. I was about to start scratching my head when another thought struck.

The water was pumped straight from the lagoon and, as clear as it was, there had to be floating debris in it. That implied some kind of filter system. A quick scout around revealed the in-line filter. I whipped it open and triumphantly removed a few leaves. Brimming with confidence, I now turned on the closest tap.

A mere trickle mocked me.

It was back to the filter. This time I studied it more carefully. A wisp of grass on the wrong side of the filter inlet caught my eye. I prized it out it with tweezers, replaced the filter and retested the system.

Scalding hot water.

"Your gas is working," I called out to Morag.

"What?" She tripped over her feet in her haste to reach me.

"The gas. It's working." *Keep it casual, low key like I do this every day.*

"No way! What did you do?"

"Magic touch." Like her, I wasn't about to give away too many of my secrets. "Now for the solar panel."

I waded chest deep into the lagoon to a single pole on which a filthy panel had been mounted. A quick splash of water cleaned it. Then logic, again. One of the cables had been pulled out, probably by a passing hippo. So, with one eye watching for crocs and hippos, and the other on the job, I reattached it.

This may sounds crazy, but standing in crocodile-infested water, fixing the panel was one of the most thrilling things I'd ever done. This was the grit you never got to experience as a tourist. It made every moment of every challenge we'd faced to get here worth it.

Back at the house, I checked the battery. Dead. But the voltage from the panel was healthy.

"Order a new battery and you're in business," I said to Morag.

"I'm stunned." She sidled up to me, purring like a cat. "Thank you. You truly are a marvel."

I grunted and collected my tools. She skipped along next to me as I headed back to camp in time for the arrival of the Islander.

CHAPTER 23

The arrival of the Islander was a big event, drawing not only the usual crowd of maintenance and kitchen staff but everyone else who worked at the camp. The only MIA was Morag. She disappeared into the bush the moment Gwynn came into view.

Gwynn grinned at me as the plane door flew open. "This is so exciting! I wonder what Sepei sent us?"

That was indeed an indictment on camp life. Sorry, Sean, but it isn't the guests who really stir the soul. It was the promise of supplies needed to keep them happy that created the real thrill.

"You want to sort the stock while I get the admin done with the guests?" I asked with a tinge of envy, craning to catch a glimpse of my toolbox. It was being elusive. I did spot my camera case and tripod, though. That was good.

"Perfect," Gwynn said, "I'll just say a quick hello to the guests, then join you as soon as Matanta and I are done."

* * *

I was finishing up the paperwork that welcomed the Schultz and Weson parties into the camp when Gwynn bounded in, giving me a thumbs-up. "Toolbox accounted for."

Keen to get it open, I motioned to her to take the very talkative Hans Schultz and his very quiet wife, Gretchen, to their cottage while I dashed the Wesons to theirs.

Morag stopped us in our tracks.

She greeted the guests and said, "Let me introduce you to your guides."

I shot her an are-you-crazy look. Surely after all her many months of running Tau Camp, she knew the guides were introduced to their guests at the strip? Apparently not, because she stepped forward, telling Dylos, a stocky man with a lopsided smile, to carry the Schultz's bags. Then she introduced Kamanga to the Wesons.

Everyone looked confused.

"Morag, I've already assigned the guides," I whispered. "Dylos is going with the Wesons."

"Oh! Well, in that case, I need you all to sign an indemnity before you go out onto the water. In case you get eaten by crocodiles."

"Andrew has already made us sign our rights away," George Weson drawled in a deep southern American accent. "You can now safely feed us to your crocodiles." He looked first at Morag, then at me, his raised eyebrows suggesting he'd just stepped into a loony bin.

"Well then, let's go to the cottages." Morag swept out of the reception and headed towards number two, where Herb and Mary were staying. Unsure of what to do, all four guests started after her.

This was insane. I raised my voice. "I think we'll do it this way. Gwynn, you and Kamanga take Hans and Gretchen to number six. And Dylos and I'll take George and Linda to number three."

The last thing I saw before striding out of reception was Morag blushing. Scarlet. It was strangely satisfying in a perverse way, although it did nothing to cool my fury. Or my own embarrassment. It also drove all thoughts of my toolbox from my mind.

After settling George and Linda into their cottage, I returned to reception to confront her. Gwynn was the only person there. She was sorting through the mail that had come in with the Islander. She turned to speak to me, probably to comment on Morag, when we heard a harsh, cutting voice behind us.

"How dare you two behave like that!" A white-faced, thin-lipped Morag stalked into reception. "You two think you know everything. Well, you don't. Let me remind you that I've run this camp single-handily for two months. You two started yesterday and now you think you know everything."

I was officially pissed off.

Sucking in a quick breath, I thrust my face up to hers. "Are you schizophrenic, or do you just do this to annoy me?"

Morag blinked, and, for a moment, I saw panic on her face and heard it in her voice. "Andrew, I – I don't mean you—"

"Where were you yesterday when the Van Hoevens arrived?" I demanded. "You had no problem dumping us then. But now you think you can embarrass us by barging in and taking over. Badly, too." Gwynn touched my arm, trying to calm me down, but I wasn't about to be placated. "There are single-celled organisms rotting in the bush who could do a better job of teaching than you can. So how about taking a hike down the runway to go and make your bird walks—or whatever it is you're supposed to be doing around here."

I stopped my tirade and looked around.

Gwynn was biting her lip with an unreadable expression on her face.

Worse, Morag looked at if she were about to cry, whether from rage or misery, I couldn't tell. But there was no backing down now, or she'd walk over us forever. I stared back at her with a stony expression.

For a full minute, nobody said anything.

Then Morag's hands found her hips. "If that's how you feel, you can run the camp on your own. I'll be moving out tomorrow and I expect Otter to be ready."

We both knew how pointless that demand was.

It didn't stop Gwynn murmuring, "Nothing would give us greater pleasure."

With the coming of the Islander, I hadn't had a chance to tell her about the state Otter Lodge was in. I broke the news now. "Morag's with us for another month, at least."

My words were greeted with absolute silence. It wasn't my greatest moment, I admit. But the woman had to be psychotic with her erratic behaviour.

Finally, Gwynn spoke. "Great. That should do a lot for the atmosphere around here." She gnawed the inside of her mouth before adding, "Morag, maybe we can at least try and be civil to each other. For the guests' sake, if nothing else."

Again no one spoke. It was on the tip of my tongue to ask her what her problem was with us when she walked off. She had not gone more than ten paces when she called back, "Andrew, I don't want to fight with you. The two of us could make a good team."

I shook my head in wonder.

Gwynn slumped against the desk. "Oh, joy! I see she fancies you enough to leave you in peace, but what about me?"

I chose to ignore the ridiculous comment about Morag fancying me.

When I said nothing, Gwynn added, "A strange thing happened while you were at Otter. Robert called me over to speak to him. In private. Just as well, because he tore my ear off." She saw my wide eyes and added, "Yes. I know. Weird. Anyway, he was very unhappy with my menu. Apparently, quiches and apple pies and picnics all on one day are a bit of a stretch. Not now, when the camp is empty, but when it's full. He told me Morag would never have given them a menu like that and I've no right to call myself a manager. And, what's worse, if I carry on giving rubbish menus, I won't survive with Matanta. He says Matanta has trained every manager who ever worked here, and if I don't buck up my ideas, Matanta will chew me over and spit me out. What do you think of that?"

She could have told me Robert had grown wings and flown and I'd have been less surprised. "That hardly seems likely. Matanta has been really helpful."

"I know. But that's not the point. Why do you think Robert even said it?"

"Morag doesn't like Matanta," I said. "That's obvious."

"Morag doesn't like anyone. Except you, Lesego, and—"

"And Robert," I said. Where had Gwynn got this crazy idea that Morag liked me? I knew she could be insecure, but that was just nuts.

"Precisely," Gwynn said. "I rest my case. Her two favourites on the salary increase list. I think she's trying to buy them off so they'll side with her."

"This all sounds a bit too cloak-and-dagger for me," I said.

"Huh! You think? Give me a few days and I'll slap the evidence on your desk—right on top of all those lovely ledger sheets you and Morag like playing with."

Before I could frame a suitably scathing reply, I heard someone striding to reception.

Gwynn, looking over my shoulder down the path, rolled her eyes. "I don't believe it. He's actually going to do it. I told him lunch was about to be served, but he wouldn't listen. And I warned him it was too hot, so they'd see nothing if they go walking now."

It was burning at about ninety degrees of dry, sweaty heat—and that was under the trees where it was cool. It would be hell walking on the islands now.

"What are you talking about?" I peered over her head at Hans and Gretchen, marching down the sandy path towards us.

"Ready for lunch I see," Gwynn said, pointedly as the couple stepped up to the reception desk.

They looked nothing like two people headed for a blow-out meal at Tau Camp. Hans, with his ramrod-straight back, wore a military pith helmet, giving him a decidedly Prussian general air. Gretchen, short and dumpling-like, followed a few paces behind. She wore an enormous straw hat. Lunch was clearly the furthest thing from their minds.

"*Ja, Ja*. So ve are here at last," Hans said, striding passed us into the lounge.

I followed.

The bay of water looked peaceful, made even more so by the pair of spotted-necked otters diving amongst the reeds. A jacana strutted over the lilies.

Hans surveyed the view. "Ze swamps. They are very beautiful. Very beautiful indeed." He nodded at me. "Vell done!"

"Oh thank you. But really, it was nothing," I said.

Gwynn walked away, her hands covering her mouth.

I looked at Hans. Nothing happening inside. My razor-sharp wit was completely wasted on him.

"Ve are ready to go on ze boat."

"Lunch is served," Gwynn called, louder than necessary. Then she took Gretchen's arm, hoping I think, to lead her away from her husband's insane idea of going game-watching at midday when all the animals—smarter than humans—would have taken cover in the deepest bush.

"Did someone mention lunch? We're starving." Linda and George had arrived.

"Step this way," Gwynn said, still holding Gretchen's arm.

Like a lamb, Gretchen followed Gwynn, but her eyes darted nervously back at Hans. He stood resolutely at the bank, waiting for his *mokoro* trip.

Then Hans's nose twitched, and I guessed he'd caught the smell of the quiche.

To say he elbowed his way to the table isn't exactly polite, so instead I'll settle for: after gently shoving the other guests aside, he eased himself to the head of the buffet queue, where Kekgebele served him first.

Linda, standing behind him, suddenly exclaimed, "Oh, George!" She pointed at the cheese board. "Isn't it pretty?"

Kekgebele had excelled himself; the board was a work of art. He'd poled out into the bay and had picked a perfect lily pad and two lily flowers, one pink and one blue, and laid them on the board. The bottle-green leaf highlighted the yellow cheddar, cream-coloured Brie, and blue-veined Roquefort to beautiful effect.

"I'll just have to try some," Linda said, helping herself. "Sorry to ruin the picture." She turned to the table. "And the table napkins! They're lilies too! The waiter must have spent hours folding the linen."

He probably had, but the effort was wasted on some of our guests.

Hans pinned George with his agate-coloured eyes. "Your accents tell me you are both from za USA." Before George could reply, he continued. "*Ja*. My wife and I, we have been to America. In fact, we took our two daughters to America for six weeks holiday. We had a wonderful time. We vent everywhere from New York, to Orlando to see Mickey Mouse."

I looked at Gretchen. She stared out over the bay, her mind obviously far from America.

As Hans' detailed itinerary droned on, the Weson's began to fidget, edging to the table with their plates of food.

Gwynn took Linda's arm. "Have a seat. Andrew will pour some wine. Now, George, what do you do for a living?"

Looking relieved, George sat and answered quickly, "I am a sociology lecturer at—"

"Zat is interesting, *ja*," Hans interrupted. "Now me, I am retired. I was working all my life for Siemens. Except, of course, during ze var. Then I was a tank driver in ze Afrika Korps. With Field Marshall Rommel. Ze Desert Fox." He chuckled proudly.

Gretchen continued to stare at the bay.

"Zis food. . .it's very excellent," Hans droned, taking a seat next to Linda. "I must congratulate you. Not like ze food we ate in America."

I could see Linda and George groaning inwardly. "Every day in America it was just dufnuts, dufnuts, and more dufnuts."

Gwynn raised her eyebrows at Linda and mouthed, "Dufnuts?"

Linda mouthed back, "I haven't a clue."

"*Ja*. Even my daughters got so tired of ze dufnuts. They serve every kind of dufnut you can think of. Dufnuts with chocolate. Dufnuts with jam. Dufnuts with cream—"

"Oh! You mean *doughnuts*." George sniggered.

Linda looked away, her face red with suppressed laughter. I buried mine in my napkin. Gwynn quickly offered everyone some more wine, but when that didn't stop her peals of laughter, she escaped to the kitchen. By now, George's shoulders were shaking so much, he slopped his wine over the tablecloth.

"And you know what else?" Hans demanded, oblivious of his audience's mirth. "In America you do not see ze clothes on ze table like you do in Europe." Clothes? I was about to risk correcting him, when he jabbed his lily-shaped napkin with a fork. "Or even here in darkest Africa. *Nein*. It's all just plastic. Everything in America is plastic. Except the Spruce Goose."

George grabbed Linda's long, flowing skirt, swept it up and spread it over the corner of the table. "Clothes on the table, like that?" He and Linda were both laughing openly now.

Hans nodded. "*Ja*. Just like zat."

Unable to contain my laughter any longer, I cast about for a change of topic.

Meanwhile, Gretchen stared out over the bay.

A glossy starling came to my rescue. Dark blue with iridescent feathers like beaten brass, they are curious, fearless, and raucous. This one was also hungry.

"Why, George!" Linda cried through her tears. "Would you look at that little bird over there? He's helping himself to the cheese. Isn't that just the cutest thing you ever saw?"

The starling dug his beak into the cheddar, then stopped, cocked his head to one side and turned his beady bright eyes onto us.

I glanced over at Gretchen. She was looking animated for the first time since arriving at the camp. Cooing in delight, she clasped her hands together, and leaned towards the bird.

Hans curled his lip, looking at me with disapproval. When I did nothing to chase it away, he flicked his napkin at it.

The starling cackled in surprise, and fluttered off to join his friends in the trees, where they waited their turn to attack the cheese.

The light died in Gretchen's eyes. Without a murmur, she turned again to stare out over the bay.

Hans stood abruptly, yanked Gretchen's chair out from under her, and declared emphatically, "Now we go out on ze boat."

Realising there wasn't a moment to lose, I dashed up to the laundry to call their guide. Following the example of just about every other intelligent creature in the delta, Kamanga was peacefully asleep under a tree.

Bad luck for him. Hans had given his orders.

"Kamanga," I called. "The Desert Fox is ready to go out to chart the islands."

Kamanga woke, sat up, and rubbed the side of his head. It was clear from his mutters, he thought the new Tau Camp manager insane.

I laughed. Maybe mental illness was catching.

Kamanga pulled himself slowly to his feet and asked in a bemused voice, "The *lekgoa* want to go out now? In the heat? They'll see no animals. And these *lekgoa* speaks very strange. I cannot understand him."

"Nor can anyone else," I said, patting him on the shoulder. "Just do your best."

With that, Kamanga picked up his pole and headed down to the bay.

CHAPTER 24

The Wesons rested before their afternoon outing. Woodie slept peacefully in the sun in our garden. Morag and Tom weren't anywhere near me—or Andrew. He busied himself unblocking the French drain outside Herb and Mary's cottage, leaving the rest of his maintenance projects—as critical as they also were—to wait. That left me minding the radio. Again.

Instead of sitting in the lounge moping, I headed to the kitchen. And Matanta. I was determined to find evidence of the Robert/Morag collusion. Then I would enlighten my painfully dim husband to the fact that the Ice Queen was after his body.

"So, *Mma*," Matanta began as I joined him at the prep counter where he rolled pastry for the apple pie. "I heard the laughing at lunch. It seems the German is funny. That's strange for Germans."

"He is," I plonked my elbows down on the counter opposite him and rested my chin on my hands. "But he doesn't mean to be funny."

"They're usually the funniest."

Pleased he'd opened the discussion, I said, "I'm learning to speak Setswana. I've added at least twenty words this morning."

"That's good. Barbara and Rodney weren't interested in learning. Sandy can't be bothered. Sean tries, a bit, but not much." He gave me an almost shy look. "Gwynn. That's a strange name. I've never heard it before."

"It's Welsh. Short for Gwynneth. But never call me that, because I won't answer you." He raised one eyebrow. "My mother only ever called me Gwynneth when she was cross with me."

"Mothers!" Matanta waggled both his eyebrows at me. "You know what mine did to me?" When I shrugged, he said, smiling, "She named me Torn Trousers. Now how's that for a name?"

"Matanta means Torn Trousers?"

"I had thirteen brothers and sisters, but I never met one of them. They died, all of them, before I was born. When I came, my mother said, 'No, this boy is just torn trousers, like all the rest. So, I'm not going to love him enough to give him a proper name.'" He paused, waving his rolling pin at me. "You understand that no one keeps torn trousers?"

"She was smart, your mother. By naming you that, she ensured you lived."

Matanta chuckled, nodding. "People have told me many times to change my name, but I never will. I'm Torn Trousers. The survivor."

The survivor.

I liked that.

As I was quickly coming to realise, part of my survival at Tau Camp depended on befriending Matanta. I leaned in closer to him. "Robert said a hyena is bad luck. Is that true? Apart from the obvious things like chewed fridges and blown up kitchens, of course."

Matanta's dark eyes studied me. "A hyena is a very, very bad animal." He continued working with his pastry with a zeal that surely could not be good for it. I was wondering if I would get anything more out him, when he added, "But you know, a hyena is not always an animal. Sometimes it's a person who comes as a hyena because he wants to make trouble for you."

My thoughts immediately sprung to Morag. Morag the Hyena, coming back in the dead of night to cause even more problems . . . Morag the Hyena, gnawing the knobs on the stove . . . Morag the Hyena, chewing on the dustbin . . . Morag the Hyena, not knowing how to do the paperwork—

Laughter welled up inside me, but I contained it because Matanta was searching my face for traces of scepticism. At that moment, Kekgebele and Betty joined us, standing unobtrusively to one side.

"Yes," Matanta continued, perhaps fooled by my poker face. "The people who have the power to become hyenas are the Bushmen. The Tswana people like me, they don't like the Bushmen because they are very strong. They have magic that is much stronger than the best of our *sangomas*."

Betty and Kekgebele nodded their heads in agreement.

"One night, Robert and I were in Maun," Matanta continued, wrapping a dented pie tin in pastry. "We were at a party at a friend's house and there was a Bushman there, and he'd drunk too much beer. One of the other guys got cross with him and told him to go, but the Bushman started to fight with him. Now, the Bushmen are small, and they can't fight one of us with their fists and win. But this one wanted to fight, so the Motswanan started to beat him. First, he grabbed the Bushman with both arms and threw him on the ground. Then, he fell with his knees on the Bushman's chest. We heard the air coming out of his lungs and I knew he didn't stand a chance." Matanta fell quiet. Nothing moved in the silent kitchen until he said, "Just when we thought the Bushman would be killed, we saw his body change. The Motswanan couldn't hold him because he was too strong. Then the Bushman threw the guy off and stood up. But, he was no longer a man—he'd turned himself into a hyena. Then, seeing the fire, the hyena got a fright and ran away."

"And you saw this?" I asked, searching his face for signs of mirth. There were none.

"You ask Robert. He was there, too. On my life, that Bushman turned into a hyena." There was no hint of laughter in his voice, either.

I turned to Betty and Kekgebele. Their serious mien said they believed every word.

"And you and Robert hadn't been drinking beer?" I asked in my best investigative voice.

"I started drinking plenty of beer after that," Matanta said. Then he smiled. "And I haven't stopped."

I don't know what happened that night in Maun, but I know firelight can play tricks on superstitious minds. Matanta and Robert probably saw fear combined with the threat of death give the Bushman the strength to throw off his tormentor.

Or maybe he had done exactly what Matanta had said: turned into a hyena.

I wanted to believe it was true.

Leaving Matanta to his baking, I wandered back to my post at the radio. Andrew was there, writing furiously on a tatty piece of paper.

Without looking up, he said, "Have you any idea just how much stuff I have to fix? And the list is growing—probably as we speak."

I tilted my head, cupping my ear dramatically. "Hey, listen, I think I just heard the toilet in number four break."

"Not funny," Andrew groused. "Especially considering I've spent the last hour up to my armpits in crap."

I made a poor attempt at suppressing a laugh. "So, is the soak-away soaking again?"

(For those with more advanced plumbing—the running water kind supplied by your local city council—a soak-away is a kind of French drain. A deep hole, dug in the ground, is filled with rocks or beverage cans and bottles, which allows water from showers, basins, and toilets to seep away quickly and discreetly. The hole is covered with soil and grass to hide the evidence. And the smell.)

"Give me a hug and I'll tell you," Andrew said, grinning.

I grimaced. The malodorous scent of sewage hung around him like a limp cloak.

Andrew laughed. "I think the cans have rusted away so Thekiso is busy digging it up to find the problem." He gestured at his crumpled paper. "But I have to get in an urgent order for maintenance stuff. Maybe we'll get another Islander soon, and I want to be prepared." He started reading off his list. "A new battery for Otter. Six more gum poles. A couple bags of nails. Twenty two-by-fours. Some lavatory cistern spares. A roll of twin-flex. Three rolls of *mabinda* twine. Chicken-wire—"

"Enough already!" I pulled a wad of paper off a clipboard sitting on the desk and plastered it to his chest. "Use these, or you'll just have to write the list over. And I don't think I could stand hearing it again."

"Ah," Andrew grunted. "Stock requisition forms? That makes sense. Did Matanta tell you about these?"

"No. I radioed Maun this morning, while you and Morag were at Otter. Sepei and Verity explained my pink shopping lists to me. Apparently, we're supposed to do orders on Sunday, so Sepei has the week to find the stuff."

Andrew looked up from his scribbles. "Weren't they surprised Morag hadn't taught us all this?"

"If they were, they're too tactful to say anything."

Not caring that it wasn't Sunday, Andrew shoved his order form into the mailbag to go out on the next plane. Then he leaned against the desk in chatting mode. "What else have you done, while I've been working my butt off?"

"I spent a productive hour with Matanta in the kitchen."

"Getting chummy with him, are you? This doesn't perhaps have anything to do with Robert's comments, does it?"

"I admit that sucking up to Matanta was part of a nefarious plan for securing allies in the war against the Ice Queen, but then I started talking to him. He's really nice."

Andrew grinned. "So now you don't want to use him anymore?"

At least I had the decency to laugh. "I know you don't believe my whole conspiracy theory, but Matanta has no time for Morag, either. A snake could bite her and he'd step right over her. And he's not stupid, he knows Morag is going to be around here long term, so I figure he's also looking to strengthen his defences."

"I think you're being paranoid. Matanta is just professional."

"Really? Any idea what the word *matanta* means?" When Andrew shook his head, I added with relish, "Torn trousers. His mom named him that because he was the only one of thirteen kids to survive."

"He told you that? It sounds kind of personal."

"Not as personal as his avid belief in Bushmen who turn into were-hyenas." I smiled at Andrew's bemused expression. "Ask him to tell you about it. Or, better still, ask Robert. He was there, too, the night a Bushman turned into a hyena. It would be interesting to hear his take on it—if he's even willing to share."

I had the pleasure of seeing Andrew tug at his beard. I guessed he was thinking back to Robert's reticence to speak when we asked him why hyenas were bad luck. Knowing Andrew, I left that thought to brew with him and changed the subject. "Now, how about a shift system? One day, I do the early morning and you do the afternoon. Then we swap. That way we can both get some time off in the day."

This time he didn't even stop to think. "Deal."

"Good. Enjoy your afternoon fixing the toilets—while listening for the radio. I'm going to sleep with Woodie. Wake me when the sun goes down."

CHAPTER 25

I looked down at my sleeping wife and cat. They looked so peaceful. Too bad, since I was about to wake them. I bounced down onto the bed. "The Van Hoevens are back from their picnic. They had a grand time."

Gwynn groaned. Woodie opened one eye and glared at me.

"The other guests have also come back from their outings. And, ta-ra-ta-ra . . .I've fixed the Fresh fridge door."

Gwynn sat up, rubbing her face. "I thought you were fixing toilets?"

"Enough about the stupid toilets. Listen to my fridge story." She leaned forward dutifully. "I used a candle to heat the plastic lining, which I then remoulded back into shape. Then, I mixed up some fibreglass and resin, and patched the holes."

"Does the door actually close?"

"Huh!" How dare she doubt me? "I was on a roll today. Silicone rubber is wondrous stuff. I used it to fix the seal." I paused, still seeing doubt. "Okay. The fridge will never be perfect again, but now it blends ever so nicely into the rest of our kitchen. Robert and I are calling it The Hyena fridge."

"Robert was there?"

"Yes, and he and I got along just fine."

"Did you ask him about the hyena?"

"No, I was too busy—"

"Being a fix-it hero," Gwynn interrupted.

She smiled her approval and my chest puffed a little. I covered it up by saying, "Now, Woodie and I think it's time you got up and had a walk with us along the runway."

"*Walk?* Are you insane? My whole body is aching from walking."

"Tell someone who cares." I jumped to my feet. "C'mon, it's beautiful out there."

Muttering something about slave-drivers, Gwynn dragged herself off the bed. I scooped Woodie up, and the three of us strolled out onto the runway.

Tentatively at first, and then with obvious delight at being out of the house, Woodie rolled on the sand. Nicely coated in powdery white dust, she darted in and out of the long grass, sniffing out every hole—probably made by snakes. Without a care, she disappeared down one of them, leaving only the tip of her tail visible. Pity she wasn't this brave where Tom was concerned.

A little way down the strip, a group of lechwe looked up at us with cautious dark eyes. Golden-brown antelope with white bellies, they used the waters of the delta to hide from predators. They were having dinner on the coarse grass skirting the runway. It reminded me that night was approaching and our guests would be looking for their meal soon, too. We started for home.

"Would you still have come if you had known how exhausting running a lodge would be?" I asked as Gwynn stooped to drag Woodie out of yet another hole.

"Of course. I wouldn't have missed it for the world," came her quick reply as Woodie wriggled in her arms. Gwynn dropped her, allowing her to continue exploring.

"Even though we're on call virtually twenty-four hours a day?"

"To be honest," Gwynn admitted, "I hadn't really thought it through properly when I suggested we come here. But regrets? No."

Just as well, since we had only been here for three days. It felt like weeks had passed.

Back in our cottage, I flopped down on one of the chairs—the first time I'd actually sat in this room. I was about to point out that disturbing fact when a black beetle, easily the size of a chestnut, droned by the front of the house. It veered sharply into the lounge, did a low level pass above our heads, and then buzzed off outside again.

I smiled. Just being in a place that made a visitation like that possible was worth any amount of time spent fixing toilets.

As I was undressing for my shower, a movement next to the toilet caught my eye. I peered closer, straining to see in the gloom around the toilet bowl.

"Hey, Gwynn," I called softly. "Did you know we have a pair of bats living next to the toilet?"

"Bats!" Gwynn bounded into the bathroom, eyes blazing with excitement.

The bats, about two inches long, were hanging upside down from a copper pipe running to the toilet cistern. Almost reverently, we watched them. Rhythmically, they swung their furry little bodies, shrouded in beautiful, paper-thin wings, from side to side. Their black eyes sparkled in their rat-like faces.

"I think I'm going to call this one Moriarty," I said, pointing at the one on the right.

"Moriarty? From the *Goon Show*?" Gwynn turned up her nose.

"Yes," I said, somewhat defensively. Since my earliest childhood I had been a *Goon Show* addict, something Gwynn never quite understood. "And I'm going to call the other one Moriarty, too."

"Both of them?" Gwynn objected. "You can't do that."

"Why not? Can you tell them apart?"

As if fully in agreement with me about their names, the Moriarty twins spread their wings and flittered off into the dusk.

CHAPTER 26

Herb and Mary were describing the delights of their picnic to the Wesons when we arrived at the pre-dinner campfire.

With a mischievous grin, George nudged me with his wine glass. "How did Hans and Gretchen's game viewing go?"

Right on cue, Hans and Gretchen joined us.

Without a word, Gretchen sank down onto a chair and stared out at the bay.

Hans remained standing, looking a little deflated. "We had a long ride in the boat. Then the boy took us for a walk. But we did not see very many animals. Kamanga said it was too hot. He said we should have waited for the late afternoon when the animals come out."

"I'm surprised Gwynn didn't tell you that, too, before you left," Morag said, pushing a shocked tone into her voice.

I was saved from answering by a loud grunting coming from the river.

"Ah ha! And what makes that grunting sound?" Hans looked excitedly towards the water and I could almost see him thinking: So. . .there are animals here, after all.

"It's a hippo," I replied.

Morag darted a disgruntled look at me as if she resented me answering. "He's spent the day lying in the shallow water, and now he's making his way into the main channel. From there, he'll pass onto the island. It's suppertime."

The hippo honked a few more times and we all peered into the channel just upstream from the camp, hoping to get a glimpse of him.

We were disappointed.

"So hippos feed on land?" George asked. "I thought they ate fish and stuff in the water."

Again Morag answered first. "They come out to feed on grass, often walking for miles during the night."

"They're pretty house-bound during the day," Andrew added. "They can't come out of the water for long because they get sunburned."

"You're joking, right?" Mary asked.

"No." Morag now glared openly at Andrew. "They can't take the sun. That's why they only come out at night."

Clearly, Morag didn't like other people knowing too much about animals. That irritated me, so I kicked back in my chair and said in my best story-telling voice, "When God created the animals, the hippo lived on land. But they hated it. Every day spent in the baking sun was torture, especially when they'd come down to the river to drink. Finally, one brave little guy plucked up the courage to knock on God's front door. He asked if he could be allowed to spend the day in the water."

I pointed skyward to the heavens. "I wasn't there, but from what I've been told, God didn't like the idea at all. He said something like: 'No, because if I let you in the water, you'll eat my fishes.'

"As you can imagine, the hippo was bitterly disappointed. But he refused to give up. A real little fighter, this guy. So, over the next few days, he thought about his problem. Then an idea came to him."

I leaned forward, conscious of everyone watching me—including Morag. "He rushed back to God and said, 'If you let me lie in the water, I promise I won't touch your fishes, and, as proof, I'll eat nothing at all during the day.' Apparently, God raised one perfect eyebrow, so the hippo added, 'Instead, I'll come out of the water at night and eat grass.'

"God looked at the hippo for a long time before asking, 'How can I trust you?' The hippo had a ready answer: 'That's the best part of the plan, Lord. I'll only ever do my droppings at night. And when I go, I'll spray my poop over the ground so you can inspect it. And you'll see, there'll be no fishes.' God agreed. And from that time forth, hippos have spent their days in the water, coming out at night to feed. And when they poop, they spray their droppings wide, and they honk, which means, 'Look, God, no fishes!'"

Everyone laughed.

It even raised a smile from Morag, but she quickly suppressed it. "Gwynn's story belies the fact that hippos are extremely dangerous animals. They kill more people each year in Africa than any other mammal. It's for that reason, the local people like to be off the water come dusk."

Morag's words fell into a void of silence.

Finally, Herb stirred himself. "Talking about dangerous animals. Andrew, have you told everyone else about the hyena?"

"*Nein.* We have not heard about this animal." Hans turned to Andrew accusingly. "What have you been hiding from us?"

"Name, rank, and number is all I'm giving," Andrew said, eliciting a few laughs from everyone except Hans and Gretchen.

She still stared out at the bay.

"Last night a hyena came into camp," I said. "He raided the kitchen, and ate some of our best appliances. It's possible he'll come back."

"*Ja,* now that would be *wunderbar!*"

"I'll send the kitchen staff out to give him a telegram, if you like," Andrew replied. "Something like this: Have deputation of people to meet you. Stop. Be at the dustbins behind the kitchen at 21h00. Stop. Dress: informal. Stop. Bring own wine glass and cutlery. Stop."

I heard a soft scuffle and looked up to see Kekgebele standing next to me. "Dinner is served, *Mma.*"

The timing seemed appropriate.

Everyone moved to the dining room. Andrew poured the wine, while Kekgebele dished out the deep-fried Camembert and marula jelly starters.

Crisp and golden on the outside, once cut, the sharp-smelling cheese oozed out onto my plate, melting into the insanely sweet marula jelly. Combined, it lured me into a taste explosion like nothing else on Earth.

The chefs had again excelled. It made me wonder who had been on duty the night we'd eaten drunken chicken with Barbara and Rodney. Then I remembered Matanta speaking about a third chef, Seatla, who was on maternity leave. It had to have been her.

Once my plate was scraped clean, I sat back, listening to our guests chatting and laughing like they'd known each other for years. Even Gretchen was engrossed in a conversation with Mary.

"Poor Hans," Andrew whispered in my ear.

I smiled. All the chatter had drowned out his voice, and he looked quite glum as he stared out across the bay.

Someone touched my shoulder.

I jumped, spinning to see Matanta grinning at me.

He leaned in close. "*Mma en Rra.* There's a genet in the scullery. If you come now, you'll see him."

Andrew turned to the table. "Sorry to interrupt, but there is a nocturnal visitor in the scullery. If we go quietly we will see it."

"Ah! The hyena!" a whispered cry went up around the table, followed by the scraping of chairs.

"I hope they're not disappointed," I said to Andrew as we crept towards the kitchen.

I could have spared my worry. No one could be disappointed at the beautiful sight that greeted us.

The size of a large domestic cat, the grey and black spotted genet sniffed around the reed walls in the scullery. He tilted his pointed snout up, fixing his bright eyes on us. Flicking his banded tail, he scampered out into the night.

"Strong little guy, considering how he ripped into your fridge," Herb said, smiling at his own joke.

"This animal is smaller than a hyena, *ja*?"

"Are they dangerous?"

"Only to insects, mice, and small birds," Morag whispered, in reply to Mary's predictable question.

Something akin to love in Morag's voice made me look at her. Her face had softened, as if she were a mother cooing over a beloved child. In that instance, I saw a different side to Morag, a side I could relate to, even like. A flicker of hope ignited in my chest. Maybe, if she left my husband alone, we could build on this common ground of our love for African wildlife.

I now regretted my silly story about the hippo. It had done nothing to build relationships. I promised myself to try harder to make things work between us.

Herb looked intently at the spot where the genet had been. "Do you think it is worth waiting for that hyena?"

Andrew, Morag, and I shrugged. Who could possibly tell if a wild animal, free to roam anywhere he wanted over the many thousands of square miles of the Okavango, would choose to come back to our kitchen?

A murmur of disappointment spilled through the group. Perhaps realising the lateness of the hour, and the early morning that awaited them, our guests drifted off to bed.

Then, Morag surprised me even more.

Without saying a word, she joined Andrew and me at the bar, helping us re-stock the fridge. She even joined our debate on whether to disconnect the gas to the stoves and fridges in case the hyena did come back.

"I think we should disconnect," Andrew said.

"But, what about the meat in the freezer," Morag objected. "It may be autumn and the nights are cool, but still not cold enough to stop things rotting."

I was about to ask if she had ever opened The Cupboard, but changed my mind. "I agree with Andrew. The last thing we need is a gas fire in the kitchen."

Morag gnawed on her lip. "Hmm, and a fire would rip through the camp . . . okay, I'm with you. Fridges off."

Maybe genets should visit the camp every day.

CHAPTER 27

The new shift system meant it was my morning to sleep in, but I chose to do something else. Binoculars in hand, I set off on a walk down the runway to check the irrigation sprinkler nozzles.

What a way to spend a workday morning!

Up at five-thirty, I hit the morning rush hour of baboons, letchwe, and impala as I headed for the strip, while listening to the early morning broadcast of bird song, and news from the arrow-marked babblers.

It was like I'd died and gone to heaven.

By seven o'clock, when the day shift arrived, I'd checked every nozzle, replacing some, putting others in my pocket for later repair. I joined the staff, and we entered the camp together.

All was quiet.

I made my way to reception to meet Gwynn.

"It seems Herb got his wish," she said, by way of greeting. "Hyena came last night."

One look at her face and the positive effects of my morning therapy were blown away. "Damage?"

"We can just about write off the Hyena fridge. All your work on the seal is in bits, and the lining has been mauled again. He also had another go at the stove. Just as well we turned off the gas." She took my hand and led me to the kitchen. "And, while the guests think it's all wonderfully entertaining, Lesego's a bit ticked off this morning. Major clean-ups for three days in a row just aren't cricket. Or so he's telling me."

"Cricket?" I said, suddenly seeing opportunities. "He knows about cricket? What about volleyball?"

I never got an answer because Morag stepped out in front of me. She glanced down at our clasped hands, and then said stiffly, "Andrew, I know you're short-staffed in the scullery, and I think I've got the perfect girl for the job."

"Thanks." I pointed at Gwynn. "But employing staff to work in the kitchen is her domain. You two should discuss it."

"Her name is Petso," Morag said to me, openly ignoring my comment—and Gwynn. "I met her today on my walk down to Otter. She was under a tree, stark naked, bathing in a large zinc tub. I heard her singing long before I saw her." Morag gave a throaty laugh. "When she saw me she became shy. But when I asked if she'd be interested in working at Tau Camp, she leapt out of the bath and jumped up and down with excitement. I told her to come to the camp today to meet you. She's behind the kitchen with Betty."

"Like I said, employing kitchen staff is definitely Gwynn's baby." I pushed Gwynn in front of Morag and headed to the kitchen.

Gwynn stopped, digging her heels into the sand. Then she stunned me by bestowing a smile on Morag. "Thank you. I appreciate your help."

Morag snorted. "I didn't do it for you."

Shaking her head, Gwynn now pulled me around the back of the kitchen.

Clad in a short, hand-me-down-kind of skirt and a thin T-shirt, Petso was a slight girl in her early teens. Her only defect, as far as I could see, was one leg, which was slightly thinner than the other. I later learned it was from a brush with polio. Although pretty and scantily dressed, she radiated pure innocence. She stood before Gwynn, not daring to raise her eyes from the ground.

"Petso!" Robert, who had joined us, suddenly shouted. "Look at the manager when she speaks to you." But there was no condemnation, only mirth-filled approval in his voice.

Petso looked up at him, and then at Gwynn, and smiled the biggest, broadest smile I've ever seen.

Gwynn smiled right back and led her into the scullery. "So, Petso, would you like to work here?"

Petso stood in wide-eyed wonder, looking first into the kitchen, trashed by the hyena, and then at the pile of dirty dishes and pots from last night's dinner stacked on a rickety little camping table in the corner of the scullery. Her face beamed.

"Have you had a job before?" Gwynn asked. When Petso shook her head, Gwynn explained, "As dishwasher, you must make sure there are always clean plates and glasses for the *lekgoa*. Then, you'll have to prepare lunch for the guides. And you must also help the chefs with whatever they ask."

"Yes," Robert interrupted. "If Matanta or I tell you to run to the laundry, or to make food for us to eat, or to mix the bread dough, then you must do it without being cheeky."

Petso looked first at Robert and then at Betty. Betty, who was clearly keen to see another scullery lady employed, said something in Setswana. Petso turned back to Gwynn and beamed even brighter.

"If you work the early morning shift, you'll have to be at work at seven o'clock sharp—not a minute later," Gwynn said.

"Yes," Robert butted in again. "Because if you're late then The Chief," he pointed at me standing to one side, "will be very cross with you." Petso's eyes widened once more. "And he is very fierce. See those red bushes growing out of his face. Chiefs with red bushes growing out their faces eat naughty girls for breakfast."

Pesto's face fell and she took a quick step back.

I was about to object that my beard in no way turned me into an ogre when Gwynn said, "Thank you, Robert, but it's been a long time since The Chief ate anyone, so I'm sure Petso will be quite safe." She placed a reassuring hand on Petso's shoulder and the girl relaxed. "Now let me finish explaining the shifts. We don't just work during the day at Tau Camp, we work at night too."

"With no break, either." Robert's smile betrayed his discouraging words. It was obvious he wanted Petso in the kitchen.

"The night shift ends at nine o'clock," Gwynn said, trying to keep the interview on track. "Do you still want the job if you have to work so late?"

With her hands clasped in front of her, Petso swung her body into a little skip, and then constructed her first complete sentence. "*Em Mma*, I want to work here."

A cheer went up and all the kitchen staff clapped.

Robert immediately shouted, "Pets! Run to Scops Camp and buy me twenty Texan Plain. *Ari.*"

Petso, looking uncertain, turned to comply.

Gwynn grabbed her arm, while shaking a finger at Robert. "First, we must get you a uniform. Because you work night shift, you'll have to move from the village to stay closer to the camp."

"She can stay with me at Romance Island," Robert offered leeringly.

"Thank you, Robert," Gwynn said. "But I say she lives at Honey Camp, with Betty. She's way too young and sweet for you, so keep your hands off her."

"Matanta lives at Honey Camp," Robert wailed. "And if she stays there with Betty, he'll have her for sure."

"No, he won't," Gwynn said even more firmly "He has more than enough problems with all his current girlfriends. Now, you all just leave sweet little Pets alone." She turned to me. "Let's go settle her salary."

Within a few minutes, Petso, now re-christened Pets, was laughing gaily, her arms in suds up to her elbows.

I stood back and looked at Gwynn. "So how do you know so much about where the staff live?"

"Matanta. He's the font of all knowledge, willingly shared."

CHAPTER 28

Breakfast: my favourite meal of the day. Our guests seemed to be enjoying it, too, judging by their satisfied silence. Finally, Linda wiped the egg off her mouth and spoke. She and George had just completed their first morning walk.

"Dylos is a total scream. You'll never guess what he said before he took us out." Everyone looked at her expectantly. "The moment we climbed out of the *mokoro*, he lined us up like a pair of naughty school children and gave us a lecture. It went like this—"

"The Okavango is a very, very dangerous place," George interrupted.

"George! It's my story." Linda slapped him on the arm. "He said, and I quote: 'The Okavango is a very, very dangerous place. So, if you see a buffalo, you must climb a tree. If you see a lion, you must stand still. If you see a leopard, you must not look him in the eyes. If you see an elephant, you must climb under a bush.' Then he made us repeat it back to him. Only when we were word perfect, would he take us for our walk. But, by then, we were giggling so much, I think we chased all the animals away. Dylos isn't very happy with us."

"Lecir said something very similar to us on our first morning," Mary added. "It gave me quite a turn. I wondered why the guides don't carry guns."

"Because they're more likely to shoot themselves—or worse, you—if we let them loose with firearms." Morag sat down to join us. Late, as usual.

"But I still don't get it," Linda said. "Why the speech? I would never climb a tree if I saw a buffalo. And I doubt George could either—even if he tried." She gestured to George's rather large paunch.

"Oh yes you would, if you saw the right kind of buffalo." I smiled at George's girth, "Not even that would stop him."

"That sounds like the introduction to a story," George grinned, clearly unperturbed by the reference to his girth.

"It is. One of my best friends scaled a tree with an arm in plaster from his hand to his shoulder—all because he saw the right kind of buffalo." I bit into my toast, happy to leave it there.

Herb was having none of it. "Andrew, you cannot possibly leave us in suspense after that opening."

What could I do but comply? "Before I met Gwynn, a bunch of friends and I came up to the delta. Jonty had his arm in plaster. Anyway, our guides took us for a long walk and we bumped into about a hundred buffalo. In numbers like that, they're as innocuous as cows. It's the stragglers or lone animals that are the ones to watch. Our guides let us get quite close, figuring it would be safe. But what they didn't see was a bad-tempered bull standing to one side—until he charged. Only, they didn't tell us he was coming. So, the first we knew was when the guides bolted up the nearest tree."

"Talk about a healthy sense of self-preservation," George said.

"No kidding. Matched only by us three guys. We also took off, leaving the three girls shouting and waving behind us."

"Now that's what I call being a gentleman," Linda said with a twinkle in her eye.

I laughed self-deprecatingly. "Can't be beat! Anyway, plaster and all, Jonty was the first to climb to the top of our tree. I only dared look back once I was safely on a branch. The girls were still screaming their heads off, running full throttle towards us. Then I saw the buffalo had stopped. Without words, my mates and I agreed to say nothing. If there'd been enough time, we'd have placed bets on which girl made it to the tree first."

"I have no doubt your girlfriend immediately severed all ties with you," Mary said primly.

"Do you think he'd have risked that with a girlfriend?" Gwynn now chimed in. "My husband's not that dumb. They were all just good buddies, so no harm done."

Everyone laughed. Everyone that is, except Morag. She glared at Gwynn, shoved her chair back noisily, flung her napkin down onto the table, and stalked out of the dining room. Lucky for her, Sean lived in Maun and didn't see any of her antics. Surely, not even her friendship with Sandy could have protected her from this kind of behaviour?

An uncomfortable silence settled. These were definitely becoming tedious.

Gwynn sighed, and then leaned into me, whispering, "Time to feed the fish eagle, maybe? Break the tension. Just like Barbara and Rodney did."

I never thought I would copy their example, but clearly it was a tried and tested remedy for getting camp managers out of sticky spots. "I suggest you get your cameras because we're going to feed the fish eagle."

Amid the clattering of chairs, Gwynn headed to the kitchen to get the meat. I walked to the bay and started preparing the float.

A twittering voice stopped me in my tracks. "Andrew, let me help you with that." Morag's hand slithered onto my arm, clasping me tight.

I ignored the loony and carried on tying my float. It was then I felt eyes boring into my back.

Surprised, I turned to face my challenger.

Gwynn stared at me. She scowled, and then vanished into the kitchen.

The moment the feeding was over, I joined her.

She leaned on the counter, watching Matanta gather the ingredients for lunch, her face still dark and brooding.

Although I had no idea what I'd done to earn her fury, I laid down a peace offering. "Hey, I suggested to everyone we go for a post-breakfast, pre-lunch swim. I thought you might like getting away from camp for a bit."

"Everyone?" Gwynn asked, not bothering to look at me.

"Well, almost everyone. Not. . .you know who."

"Her name is Morag. Say it," Gwynn snapped. "And here I was planning to be nice to her today. Shows what an idiot I am." In a brief flurry of animation, she slapped herself on the forehead, and then her elbows sank back down onto the counter with her hands supporting her head. "What I don't get is why you encourage her."

It struck me that talking about Morag in front of the staff really wasn't very bright. It smacked of Sean and Sandy—and Barbara and Rodney. "C'mon, let's go to reception."

Gwynn slouched even deeper over the counter. She was going nowhere in a hurry.

Matanta turned to the only other staff member in the room, Petso, sloshing her way through her first pile of breakfast dishes. "Hey, Pets. I need a smoke. Run to the laundry and ask Dylos to give me a cigarette." Without hesitation, Petso leapt off her beer crate and bolted out of the kitchen. "And some matches," Matanta called after her. He waved his hand at me, as if indicating that I had the floor.

So, with the coast almost clear, I replied to Gwynn, "Morag's just sucking up to me so I'll fix her house, her solar panel, her plumbing—"

"Her plumbing!" Gwynn's head shot up, eyes flashing. "How can you be so naïve? The only plumbing she's interested in is yours!"

My mouth dropped. "You can't be serious."

"Oh, yes I am. And I've been trying to tell you this for days, but you're too dense to listen."

That ticked me off. "You don't think you're taking this whole thing a bit far?"

Wrong choice of words.

Gwynn's face blanched and she hissed, "Am I? Then tell, why do you let her hang onto you like she owns you?"

Oh jeez. . .and the day had been going so well.

I scrambled for an answer that wouldn't have me sleeping on the couch for a week, when Matanta laughed.

"Women! *Lekgoa*. Motswanan, they're all the same. Nice. But trouble." He shot a glance over his shoulder, probably to check we were really alone, and then confided, "Like the gorgeous little Impeleng in the laundry. She's made so much trouble for me, but what man could resist her?" He cleared his throat as if he couldn't believe what he was about to say. "Even a woman like Morag can be trouble."

I rounded on him. "So you think Morag has the hots for me, too? She has the sex appeal of a box of matches!"

"Of course," he replied in a matter-of-fact voice. I wasn't sure which statement he was agreeing to.

Still I protested, "Never! She's too—" I scratched my head, thinking, "too *mental* to be interested in me. One minute, she's biting my head off, the next she's..." My voice faltered.

I was going to say all over me, but I didn't think that would improve my relationship with Gwynn. Also, it made me see Morag in a new light, and what I saw was terrifying. My eyes widened and I looked at Gwynn with pure panic. Not that I got any support there—she was still glaring at me.

"*Rra*, Morag's an interesting one," Matanta said. "I've been here at Tau Camp a long time. Eight years I've worked for Sean. I started doing maintenance, but I didn't like it because there's no proper maintenance here, just reed huts to fix, and toilets to unblock. I like building with bricks, so six years ago I moved to the kitchen. For the past five years, I've been Sean's deputy manager. So trust me, I've seen many managers come and go in this camp. But the biggest *matatas* always happen when a new manageress arrives before the old one has left."

I glanced over at my angry wife and released a breath. Her face had relaxed and she was listening intently to Matanta. I could have hugged him—except that real men don't hug. And Matanta probably didn't hug either.

"Sean also made that mistake when Barbara and Rodney came," Matanta continued. "Now, me and the other staff, we didn't like Barbara or Rodney. They treated us like children and they didn't like black people. You just have to look at Rodney's stupid signs all over the camp to know that." Rodney had plastered the kitchen, laundry, and reception area with belittling notices aimed at the staff. "But I felt sorry for Barbara because of the previous manager who stayed here on the island. She was terrible, just like Morag is to you, *Mma*. Some things never change." Matanta laughed. "Only now Morag wants your man. I promise you, no one wanted Rodney and his slippers."

Gwynn also snorted a small laugh and I relaxed even more. Then she took my hand and I knew my bed was safe for the night.

"The next time she hangs on you," Gwynn said, "please, please, please knock her across the river."

I wanted to say that I didn't smack ladies, but even I knew the timing was wrong. "Got it." I slapped Matanta gratefully on the shoulder.

"*Mma en Rra*, I want you to know that Robert likes Morag. I don't. Not at all. But I like Robert. A lot. So we don't talk about Morag."

Gwynn gave me a victory smile that screamed 'I told you so.'

I held up my hands in defeat. "You win. I was wrong, you were right."

"And don't you ever forget it," Gwynn smirked.

"So, *Mma en Rra*, us three? We're a team? Or what?"

Before I could reply to Matanta, Gwynn leaned over and gave him a one-armed hug.

He yelped in pain as if he'd cut himself with the paring knife he was holding. Then he dropped to his haunches, holding his arm, eyes rolling in his head.

"Matanta," Gwynn cried, crouching down to help him.

Matanta leapt to his feet, laughing. "Ah ha! Fooled you. You thought you'd cut me! You're as easy to trick as that Pets."

Gwynn grabbed a carving knife from its cradle and started sawing viciously on Matanta's forearm. Shrieking with shock, Matanta pulled away.

"Ah ha! Fooled you," Gwynn laughed, holding up the knife, sharpened edge angled to the ceiling. "You're an even easier tease than that Pets." She handed him the knife, and skipped out of the kitchen. "I'm going swimming. Coming, Andrew?"

"Haven't you forgotten something?" I shouted after her. "I can't pole yet."

"*Gagona matata*." Matanta said, clapping me on the shoulder. "That means no problem, Andrew *Rra*. I will pole you both to the swimming hole."

"Done." We shook on it. "But first I have a job to do. Follow me."

I led Matanta to the notice board in the reception area, where one of Rodney's offensive signs was pinned. This one read:

STAFF BANK ONLY OPENS BETWEEN
11:00–12:00. MON-FRI
DON'T BOTHER ASKING FOR HELP AT ANY OTHER TIME
BECAUSE YOU WON'T GET IT

I slapped a drum roll onto the desktop, and then pulled the sign off the wall. Matanta took it out of my hands and shredded it into tiny pieces.

Kekgebele, who had been sweeping the floor, dropped his broom and darted past us, headed for the laundry, probably to tell the rest of the staff that today was the day all the signs came down.

CHAPTER 29

Linda, George, and Herb gathered at the bay, dressed and ready for our swimming expedition. Hans, still wearing his battle fatigues, stood at attention, watching us. "Aren't you coming?" I asked him as I tucked my curls under my hat.

"And be eaten by ze crocodiles? *Nein*. I have told my wife we will not be swimming today."

"Mary is also too nervous to join us," Herb said with obvious disappointment. "I tried to persuade her, but she's adamant she's not swimming in crocodile-infested waters. I can hardly understand it. We haven't seen a single crocodile since coming here."

"We haven't seen the hyena either," George chirped, not very helpfully, "but we know he's here."

Matanta and Andrew joined us.

Matanta had swapped his khaki longs for a pair of khaki shorts, ready for swimming. I introduced him as our deputy manager. He turned his winning smile onto each person, shaking hands using the traditional African handshake. Andrew had packed a cool box with a few drinks for everyone, which Matanta heaved into the closest *mokoro*.

Like good hosts, Andrew and I waited until our guests were seated in their *mokoro*. Only then did we climb aboard the one Matanta had commandeered from an off-duty guide. I wondered if this constituted car theft, Okavango style.

As a show of respect, I suppose, Matanta waited for Lecir and Dylos to lead the way out of the bay. Then, with us reclining comfortably on our cushions like rich *lekgoa*, we headed upstream for our first outing as managers.

One of the primary attractions that brought people—including us—to the Okavango was the experience of reclining in a *mokoro*, while a man whose very being was tied to the ebb and flow of life in the delta, poled one rhythmically along tranquil waterways. Very little compared with gliding past intoxicatingly sweet water lilies, while ripples from the *mokoro* projected streamers of sunlight onto the golden sand below. At times, the silky water was so shallow I could reach down and run my fingers through the fine sand. Sublime.

We had not gone far up the main channel when Dylos, Lecir, and Matanta parked their *mokoro* against the reed bank, skirting a bronze-coloured sandbank.

The guests looked at Andrew and me. I could almost read their minds: who was going to act as crocodile bait and dive in first? I—naively perhaps—expected the guides to lead the way, but they settled back in their *mokoro* to wait. The noonday sun beat hot upon our shoulders.

Then, George, looking a bit like a beached whale in his swimming shorts, launched himself overboard. The other guests followed. I was also about to leap in, but Andrew grabbed my hand. I looked at him in surprise.

"Patience," he murmured, gesturing with his head towards Matanta and the guides.

They hadn't moved a muscle.

Understanding dawned and I settled back in my seat to watch Linda, Herb, and George frolicking in the water. Then a stab of guilt lanced me. How could I sit here in the safety of my little wooden boat, using my guests as crocodile lures?

I threw myself into the drink.

Matanta and Andrew followed.

Finally, the other guides joined us.

Now fairly confident it was safe, I lay back on the sandbank, allowing the bubbling water to massage away my Morag-induced tension. I was vaguely aware of Andrew handing around drinks, and I'm sure he offered me one, but I was too deep in relaxation to notice. Then I heard a distant, dreamy voice echoing my own mood.

"If I fall asleep, pick me up in Maun."

It was followed by a loud splash.

I sat up with a start to see Dylos swimming after George. He had floated off the sandbank and was heading downstream towards Scops Camp and—if he survived the perils of the river, which was unlikely—Maun.

Without looking up from where she was lying, Linda called out, "Crocodile din-dins are served. American tourist. Tender. Well-marinated and very juicy."

"But no lean cuts," George added, laughing at his own expense as Dylos pulled him back to safety. "And at least I'll have something to tell old Hans about when I get back."

Too soon, the guides and Matanta climbed out of the water and I guessed we'd tempted fate for long enough.

As our little flotilla returned to camp, we saw Hans pacing in front of the lounge. "Ah, zo," he said, as we pulled up onto the bank. "You have all returned alive. I said to my wife that maybe one of you would not come back."

Deep down, I think he was sorry he hadn't joined us.

At lunchtime, Hans made up for missing out on the swimming by being first in the dining room. We were all tucking into a fantastic lasagne when an excited babble from the kitchen caught my attention.

I went to investigate.

A small, noisy crowd congregated outside the kitchen door, where a young boy held court. It was clear from his waving arms and wildly dancing eyebrows that he was getting as much mileage as possible from being the centre of attraction. The increasing decimal level brought Andrew over to join me.

Robert broke away from the huddle. "*Rra en Mma*, this boy is saying there are *tlou* on the island down at Scops!" Robert waited for our reaction while Andrew and I exchanged puzzled glances.

"What are *tlou*?" I asked finally, when it was obvious no explanation was forthcoming.

"Elephant!" Robert breathed in delight. "Elephant down at Scops Camp."

"Are they there now?" Linda gasped.

It was then I noticed that all our guests had joined us, probably to find out what all the fuss was about.

"What are we waiting for?" Herb yelled. "Let's go." His half-eaten lunch forgotten, he turned, probably looking for Lecir, because Mary was welded to his side.

"Not so fast. Let's get more on this. To the radio everyone," Andrew commanded.

Typical. If were up to me, I'd have grabbed my hat and bolted down to Scops with the guests. Now we all stampeded to reception.

"110, 110, 638," Andrew said into the mic.

Scops Camp responded as if they'd been waiting for his call. Joan would have been pleased. "638, 638, 110. This is Englishman. Go ahead, Andy."

"E'man. Please confirm the rumours that there are elephant down at Scops Camp, over."

"So *that's* what they are. We looked them up in the guidebook, but that page is missing. It was eaten by the baboons." I heard Milly laughing in the background as E'man continued, "They've been here all morning, Andy. Right now, they're playing in the river in front of the camp. I'm sure if your *lekgoa* come, they'll see them."

"Let's go, let's go," Herb called. "Get into the *mokoro*, Mary!"

"I don't think that's wise," Andrew said, pouring water onto Herb's fire. "The elephant are in the river. *Mekoro* float on the river. Don't intentionally meet an elephant in the water, when on the water."

"Ah! Not a pretty picture," Herb said, grabbing Mary's arm. "Come, let's change our shoes." He, and all our other guests, rushed off to grab walking shoes, hats, and cameras.

I looked at Andrew, querying if he wanted to go, too.

He shook his head, his face a woeful. "With my fix-it list, I have to pick my outings carefully."

Leaving him alone in camp, even if it was my afternoon off, seemed a little cruel—even for me. So, just a tinge jealous, I watched the camp empty as guests, guides, and off-duty staff vanished to Scops Camp.

Several hours later, as the sun was losing its strength, I heard people lumbering down the path towards reception. Anticipating glowing stories of close encounters, I went out to meet them. But it was a weary, dispirited crew, which slumped down into the wicker chairs in the lounge, begging for cold drinks.

Nature had tricked them.

The elephants had moved on minutes before they arrived.

"We did see some palm trees pushed down and a whole lot of fresh dung," Mary said, as if that made it all worthwhile.

I grinned. "That must have pleased the guides."

"True," George added, perking up considerably. "Other people come to the Okavango to spot birds or animals. But Tau Camp guests come to see dung."

"Well, in that case, elephant dung is a lifer for me," Gretchen said, unexpectedly, beaming at everyone. She was referring to the quaint habit birdwatchers—called twitches—have of calling new bird sightings 'lifers'.

"Then we will just have to tick it off on our list." Hans took her arm, laughing with her as he led her back to their cottage.

* * *

Uninterrupted meals were becoming something of a rarity at Tau Camp as I discovered that evening. We were just savouring a rather sublime after-dinner syllabub—a very English dessert, this one made largely with cream flavoured with sugar and Cointreau—when a loud crash from the kitchen halted all conversation.

Herb leaned forward and grabbed my arm. "More waiter training? Or is it something else altogether?"

"The staff have gone, so I think this could be something else altogether." I motioned everyone to keep still while Andrew edged his chair away from the table and crept to reception to fetch his Maglite torch.

He beckoned us, and we sidled up to him outside the kitchen. Then, like villains in an espionage movie, we all scuttled around the back of the building. Our destination was a five-foot high anthill a few feet from the back door. We quietly scaled it.

Praying the reek of wood smoke coming from the still-gleaming donkey boiler to the right of the mound would hide my human scent, I peered out into the darkness. I saw nothing.

Then I heard a scuffle, followed by a grunt. No genet could have made such a guttural sound.

It had to be the hyena.

A ripple of excitement trilled through me.

Andrew switched on his torch, and in the beam, I caught a big black dustbin lying on its side outside the kitchen door. The sloping rear end and buckled legs of a spotted hyena protruded from its open mouth. A thousand imaginary ants stampeded through my stomach.

A collective gasp from the watching crowd punctured the air.

Even with his ears buried deep in the bin, the hyena must have heard us, because he pulled his head out. Glinting green eyes, set in a primeval head massively out of proportion to his sloping body, skewered us. He didn't like what he saw because he opened his maw, displaying yellow, bone-crushing teeth, easily the size of my pinky finger.

My excitement drained into fear.

Mary, kneeling next to me, dug her fingernails deep into my arm. As painful as that was, I didn't make a sound.

The hyena watched us for a moment more then turned back to the dustbin. His total disdain chilled me to the bone. Had he wanted to, he could have been up the anthill and onto us in seconds—and we would have been defenceless.

Andrew must have shared my concerns because he quietly, but firmly, indicated with his hand that it was time to leave. We backed off the anthill and returned to the dining room, leaving the hyena to his meal. It wasn't long after that we heard him crashing through the undergrowth as he headed back out into the bush.

It was with some trepidation that Andrew and I, now armed with walking sticks, went about the last chores of the day.

CHAPTER 30

Gwynn was on early morning call. I listened to her leave the cottage, and then rolled over to doze. It was going to be a hectic day, seeing off our current crop of friends and welcoming a new supply of guests. I needed some sleep if I was going to cope.

Friends.

My mind played sleepily with that thought.

Herb and Mary, George and Linda, even Hans and Gretchen had become friends in the short time we'd known them. I was going to miss them. Still, such emotion shouldn't interrupt much needed sleep. I was happily drifting off when I thought I heard someone speak.

"Sorry, my love, but I think you need to get up."

I groaned, ignoring the voice.

A gentle hand stroked my face, brushing my hair aside. Nice dream. . .this could get better.

"Droon, you need to wake up." The voice was more insistent now, the sound completely at odds with the fingers caressing my shoulders and back.

I ignored it.

The caress turned into a pinch. "Andrew. Get up. Now."

My eyes shot open in alarm.

Gwynn stood over me with her hands on her hips. "The blasted hyena has destroyed the kitchen. It could mean no breakfast for the guests. And if that isn't bad enough, that idiot Lesego hasn't shown up for work, either."

Swearing under my breath that the damn kitchen—and Lesego—

hadn't been buried in a concrete bunker when Sean built the place, I dressed and headed into camp.

This time the trip down the path was like walking through the debris field of the *Titanic*. I waded through chewed plastic lids, pot handles, a tangled bundle of string, the long green pole now used for propping the Hyena fridge door closed, chewed tubs belonging to chewed plastic lids, and several other unidentifiable items. Heart drooping, I stopped at the still-broken kitchen door and peered into the room.

The Hyena fridge, repaired for the third time yesterday, was fast approaching a write-off. The lining hadn't just been pierced, it was shredded, with a dozen jagged pieces of plastic scattered on the floor.

The oven had also roused his displeasure. The door was twisted so badly on its hinges, I wondered if it would ever close again. The shelf where the pots and pans usually waited gaped emptily at me. I'd have to get the maintenance team searching the island for them today or the kitchen couldn't operate.

My shoulders sagged.

I had so much to do, so much to fix, and I was getting nowhere—largely thanks to this damn animal that had decided to turn our kitchen into his buffet lounge.

"What do you two intend doing about the hyena? If this goes on for much longer, we won't have a kitchen left."

Oh no.

My stomach knotted. The last thing I needed now was Morag. But here she was, adding to my stress.

"We're not sure, Morag," came Gwynn's sugary reply. "What would you have done if the hyena had arrived while you were running the camp?"

"What I would have done is irrelevant, because the hyena *didn't* arrive while I was running the camp."

"Yes, I know!" Gwynn lunged forward, right into Morag's personal space. The hair on Hazel's back bristled, but Gwynn didn't seem to notice. "Maybe you should talk to Matanta about that. He has some interesting theories about hyenas—and people."

I didn't have the energy for this. Not now. Not today, with so much needing to be done. I pulled Gwynn to my side. "Okay, girls. None of this is helping." Hazel sat next to Morag, but didn't take her eyes off Gwynn for a second.

Morag flicked her hair over her shoulder. "Of course *she* isn't, Andrew. But if you need *me* to help you, don't hesitate to ask. I'll be in the dining room, waiting for the coffee." As she turned away, she called over her shoulder to Gwynn, "Oh, by the way, I noticed Tom going into your house. Perhaps you should go and see if your cat is still alive."

Using swear words I didn't even think she knew, Gwynn charged up to our cottage.

Days like this shouldn't be allowed.

I followed at a slower pace. When I arrived at the cottage, Gwynn was cuddling Woodie.

"Is she all right?" I asked, trying not to sound as irritated as I felt.

"There was a fight, but no obvious damage. Tom goes to Scops Camp. Today."

My clenched stomach now knotted. As much as I loved Gwynn and Woodie, this wasn't a fight we needed with Morag. I hugged Gwynn, hoping to calm her. "I get it. You hate Tom. And Morag. But please, not today. Not with the hyena and guests leaving and coming."

Gwynn sighed, and then bit her lip. "What's happening about getting her to Otter? Maybe she can take Tom with her."

"I'm doing everything I can. The old women are gathering the reeds, everything else that can be fixed has been fixed. All we need now is for Sepei to play along and send the rest of the maintenance supplies."

"Maybe on today's plane." Gwynn sounded almost evangelical. "Maybe she'll have space today."

"That's the spirit." I stroked Gwynn, and then Woodie. "I think we have a job to do."

"Keep the guests distracted while I get the water boiled for the tea and coffee." Gwynn darted down to do Lesego's job while I chatted to the guests.

Despite the chaos of the morning, Matanta and Robert presented us with a fine breakfast. It was scarcely over when we heard the approaching aircraft. Gwynn rounded up the guides and guests, while I collected the outgoing mail.

"I am so sorry to leave," Mary said as we headed up to the runway.

"Come, come, we must not be late," Hans snapped at Gretchen.

She hastened her pace.

As the pilot brought the aircraft to a noisy halt, Gwynn and I offered our hands to shake our goodbyes. Herb brushed Gwynn's aside and scooped her up in a big bear hug. The next thing I knew, we were both being bundled from person to person. I even got a hug from Gretchen.

But, sad as it was to see them go, the arrival of new guests meant there was little time for lengthy farewells. Gwynn and I walked over to meet the first Italians we would welcome to the Okavango.

The sight of them left me speechless.

CHAPTER 31

My first impulse on seeing the four Italians was to look for the film director and crew—or, more particularly, the wardrobe person. There had to be one. How else did people look so immaculately turned out when standing on a dirt airstrip on a tiny island buried deep in the lower abdomen of Africa? But without any obvious outside help, these two Italian couples managed it. Perfectly.

Both women were tall, with long, tanned legs, clad in ridiculously short khaki shorts. Their highlighted blonde hair was beautifully coiffured. Being rather short, dark-haired, and somewhat stubby, I was instantly jealous.

The men, gorgeous with their Latin good looks and sexy two-day growth, made Denys Finch-Hatton from *Out of Africa* look shabby.

I swallowed hard, suddenly aware of how casually dressed I was in my grubby kikoy, (I had succumbed to the lure, buying one from the camp curio shop), a faded T-shirt, and dusty sandals. My hair, although brushed, was a tangled mess, and it was days since my face had seen make-up. Like Sean and Sandy, or Milly and Kyle, I, too, had gone 'bush.' I pushed the humbling thought aside and held out my hand in greeting.

"The airplane was late," one of the men immediately complained in good Italian English. "The travel agent said we would fly from Maun at nine-thirty. It's now eleven-thirty, and we wasted all that time sitting at the airport."

"Well, things need to be a bit flexible here in deepest Africa," I replied in my best dealing-with-complaints voice. "The important thing is that you're here now, and I'm sure you'll have a wonderful time."

From their sour expressions, it was clear they considered me a rabid liar.

It was time for a distraction.

I waved my arms to include the guides into our circle. "Let me introduce you to KD and Jackson. They'll show you the delights of the Okavango." Smiling, the guides offered their hands for a traditional African handshake. "They'll also carry your bags."

It was then I saw the mountain of hand-tooled leather suitcases and carry bags standing next to the plane. My heart sank. I was surprised the plane had been able to get airborne. Try as she might, Sepei would been unable to squeeze a roll of toilet paper in with that lot, let alone a car battery. The guides, no weaklings, winced as they struggled to pack it all onto their backs. Once loaded up, we gave a final wave to the departing guests and walked into camp.

There was no friendly banter while we checked in the Italians, partly because the spokesman from the runway was the only one who could speak any English. It looked like a difficult few days ahead.

"Let's hope we get a late booking of people who can at least speak English," I said to Andrew. We had just returned to reception after showing them to their cottages.

"A mixture of English and Italian if we can be really picky. I must say, though, the two I took down really loved the cottage."

"Oh!" I replied in surprise. "My two didn't even blink when I showed them around."

"Mine waxed quite lyrical. I thought they'd never shut up."

I looked up at Andrew's deadpanned face and grinned. "They didn't say a word, did they?"

"Nope. All they did was flick the towels into the laundry basket, as if using a hotel towel would give them a nasty rash."

I laughed, and then bit my tongue. The Italians had sneaked up on us. Hopefully, their lack of verbal communication skills extended into auditory areas, too. Their faces remained dark and glum, so it was impossible to tell. After I showed them the bar, the four of them sat in the lounge, staring at each other with expressions of saint-like endurance.

For a moment, I thought about going to talk to them, but pushed the idea aside as quickly as it formed. I intended saving what little conversation I could muster with these people for important occasions— like meals, when we'd be trapped with them for a couple of hours.

Turns out, that was a mistake.

They suddenly huddled together for a brief, intense conversation. Then The Spokesman walked over to join us. "You said we're going to have to walk in the bush. Is this right?"

Andrew smiled brightly at him. "Your guides will take you out in the *mekoro*—the long canoe things down there on the bank—to visit

142

some of the other islands. From there you'll walk, looking for animals and birds. Is this a problem?"

I swallowed a laugh at Andrew's faked innocence. You didn't need 20/20 vision to know that this was indeed a problem—a big one, judging from The Spokesman's stony face.

"The travel agent didn't say anything about walking."

Andrew and I looked at each other, unsure of how to proceed.

"I'm sure you'll find walking most rewarding," I finally hazarded, although even I could hear how lame that sounded. The Spokesman didn't look impressed, either. I tried again. "You can really see things you wouldn't otherwise see from a vehicle—"

The spokesman had had enough. He slapped his hand down onto the reception desk. "I hope so, because we paid for game drives. And lions, too." He glared at me before turning back to his party to relay the bad news.

I shuddered to think what they'd make of our 'poop walks,' Tau Camp's unique answer to the boring old game drives, offered by camps to the north of us, where hungry lions hung out in numbers unheard of here.

Lunch, when it was served, turned out to be uncomfortable. Conversation flowed at the same pace, and with as much enthusiasm, as a fly doing the breaststroke through marula jelly. Our guests largely ignored us, as if they didn't approve of the hired help eating with them at table. I can't even say they had a jolly time together. So, it was a relief when they headed to their cottages to fortify themselves for their afternoon exertions.

Even though Andrew's early morning lie in had been a disaster, the rules of engagement said it was my afternoon to relax. So, leaving Andrew at the helm to deal with Storm Italy, I strolled back to our house to play with Woodie.

We had just settled together in the sun, when I heard the purr of an aircraft coming in from the south. Expecting no more guests today, I ignored it, until I realised it was on final approach to our runway. I ambled out onto the strip to find Andrew already there, standing in the shade. The heat radiating off the dusty white runway was killing.

"Maybe our prayers have been answered and it's a late booking," I said. "Although a bit of warning would have been nice."

"Maybe Morag took the call and didn't tell us."

My face flushed with irritation. "Why am I not surprised? I'll brief Impeleng to prepare a cottage."

"Wait." Andrew grabbed my arm. "It's not a 206. Too small for that."

We watched the little plane—a two-seater Cessna 150—touch down. Without fuss or fanfare, it rolled towards us. The pilot took off his head-set, shut down the engine, and climbed out.

It was Sean.

My lunch curdled. Then I remembered the difficult Italians and my heart imploded, too. Why couldn't Sean have come yesterday?

"Unannounced visits. That's a bit rough," Andrew whispered as we walked to meet him.

Sean shook our hands and handed Andrew a spirit level. "To level the fridges. Andrew, you asked me for it before you guys left."

"You didn't perhaps bring a car battery with you as well?" I enquired, hopefully.

Sean looked at me in surprise. "No. Should I have?"

I gave him my broadest smile. "It would have been helpful. But no matter. We'll survive."

"Good. I like survivors." Sean turned towards the camp.

As Andrew and I walked with him, I noticed his eyes darting around, taking in everything. I hoped his first impressions of our efforts were positive.

Once at reception, I offered him a sandwich for lunch. He nodded, and I escaped to the kitchen to brief whoever was there. When I returned Morag, Sean, and Andrew were sitting across from each in the lounge. My built-in friendship-detector antenna kicked into overdrive as I scrutinised Sean and Morag, but nothing from their body language indicated a close friendship.

Sean pulled a familiar piece of paper out of his jean's pocket.

Our begging letter for the staff salaries.

He waved it at us. "What were you lot thinking, sending me this?" His downturned mouth added to his pained expression. "I'm particularly shocked at the amount you are suggesting for Lesego, the waiter." He looked at Andrew and me, demanding answers.

We looked at Morag, expecting her to justify her proposal.

She sat, looking smug, saying nothing.

I scowled, and then ratted her out. Apart from anything, I wanted to see just how buddy-buddy she and Sean were. "It was Morag's suggestion to up Lesego's pay. She thinks he's a good waiter." Morag turned brittle eyes on me, but I ignored it. "And since the increases were apparently needed now, I left it to her judgment."

"But what do you think?" Sean demanded, without so much as a glance in Morag's direction. "You're the manager, it's your opinion that counts, not Morag's."

I'm ashamed to say it, but I started to gloat. "I don't think he's worth it, but we'd only been here for a day when we wrote the letter, so I acceded to Morag's prior knowledge of his performance. Turns out I was right. The guy was late for work today."

"Great." Sean now turned to Morag. "And you want me to give him more money?"

Three sets of eyes now focused on Morag. I could see she was embarrassed. This wasn't what she'd expected. For the first time since we had arrived, her back was in a corner. If she stood by her demand for more pay for a laggard like Lesego, Sean would think her over-generous with his money. But if she backed down, she'd lose face with us. I was fascinated to see what she'd choose.

Finally, she took a deep breath and said slowly, "He was sick this morning, that's why he was late. And anyway, what's one morning? It's the overall picture one must look at and I think he deserves it. He's threatened to leave if we don't increase his salary, and it would be a great loss to the camp."

"Morag," Sean said, barely veiling his impatience. "If I pay Lesego what you are asking, he will be the best paid waiter in Botswana. And we'll have set a very unhealthy precedent for every other useless waiter in the country. They'll all be queuing up to work here." So much for that special friendship.

Although by now Morag knew the kitchen was my department, she looked to Andrew for support. "You've seen him work. What do you think?"

I answered for Andrew. "I think Kekgebele is a better waiter."

Sean slapped his hand onto the table. "Forget it. I am not paying both Kekgebele and Lesego exorbitant sums of money." I wish I could say Sean looked angry, but his face was just mild—and determined.

Morag launched into a long narrative of Lesego's virtues, at the end of which, Sean still looked unconvinced. Finally Morag pleaded, "Trust me on this, Sean."

Sean sighed. "Okay, Morag, but tell him I expect him to be the best waiter in Botswana, not just the best paid." He picked up our wage demand letter again. "And these outrageous amounts for Robert and Matanta?"

This time Andrew and I threw ourselves into the debate, and together with Morag, we managed to persuade Sean to part with a little more of his cash.

Sean ran a tired hand across his face. "I can't believe I'm saying this right after giving out pay rises, but Matanta and Robert need some time off, or the government will be all over me for exploitation."

"Forgive our ignorance," Andrew said, "but why?"

Sean looked squarely at Morag. "I thought you'd have explained the overtime situation?"

Morag wriggled in her seat. "There's been so much going on, I hadn't got to it."

Sean shook his head, and turning to Andrew and me, said, "Staff are supposed to work for a month, followed by a week off. Because Seatla has been gone popping out babies, Matanta and Robert are way behind on their off. I doubt they'd complain to Labour, but I'm not taking any chances. Pick one, and tell him to meet me at my plane tomorrow morning. We'll fly out together."

"Robert," I said immediately. "We'll send him."

Sean attacked his sandwich.

I spoiled his lunch. "We have a hyena destroying the kitchen. And the baboons are a real menace too."

As to be expected, he didn't look pleased. But his answer surprised me. "I've told these people exactly what to do about the baboons, but no one will listen." He waved his arm as if to implicate Morag and all the previous managers who had ever set foot on Noga Island. "In the warehouse in Maun, I have twenty litres of whitewash paint—bought at great expense, I might add —for the purpose of getting rid of the baboons. I'll have it put on the next plane up here."

"Sean!" Morag shrieked. "You're not still on about that! It will never work."

"It will work," Sean insisted, glaring at her. "The trouble with you people is that you won't try my ideas. Andrew, I'm sending up the whitewash. Then I want you to lay an ambush for one of the baboons. It doesn't even have to be the alpha. Just wait at the top of the camp and when the baboons come in, throw the whitewash at the first one you see. The more paint you can get on him the better. I guarantee you that when the others see the white baboon, they'll get the fright of their lives. They'll leave the island and never come back."

Andrew's mouth dropped. He snapped it closed. Then he said, "I'm a little confused. How *exactly* am I supposed to get close enough to a baboon as he swings through the trees to throw whitewash at him?"

Sean looked crestfallen. Yet another manager had rejected his brilliant plan. "Well, that's it then. If you people don't want to listen to my suggestion, don't complain about the baboons."

"Hey, maybe I could use it on the hyena." Andrew laughed. "We got so close to him last night, I could have done some art-deco paint effects on him."

Typically, Morag, joined in laughing at Andrew's joke.

Even Sean smiled. Then he stood up, and I knew he had no real solutions to our problems with the wildlife. "Andrew and Gwynn, come with me. I want to go and look over the cottages."

We walked from cottage to cottage, excluding those where the Italians were staying, making copious notes on everything Sean wanted fixed, revamped, or replaced. Andrew now had months of work cut out for him.

Sean then pulled out the stock requisition sheet Andrew had sent to Maun the day before. "I take it most of this stuff is for Otter."

Andrew nodded.

"Forget it. Otter's not the priority. Tau is. Morag will just have to camp out here for a bit longer."

I could have burst into tears.

At the end of our walk, we found ourselves back in the lounge. Our guests had appeared for their afternoon activity. As expected, they were elegantly turned out. But it was not the perfectly cut khaki trousers or the tailored jackets worn over pure silk shirts that grabbed my attention. Neither was it the leather-trimmed pith helmets. It was the hundreds of pockets that really blew me away. Some large, some small, some rectangular, others square, pockets covered ever inch of fabric, all glinting with brass buttons.

I tried counting them, but the Italians kept opening and closing them, feeding them with sun block, hankies, sunglasses, miniature cameras, and guidebooks. I even saw what looked like a bandanna. I looked around at Andrew and Sean. It was obvious their wandering eyes were counting pockets, too.

But, unfortunately, not even all the shiny buttons in the world could brighten the Italians' moods. They remained as surly as they had been at lunch.

I glance at Sean, then walked towards them. "Are you ready for a nice long walk?"

The Spokesman didn't bother replying.

After seeing them off, I rejoined Sean and Andrew. "I'm afraid these four are going to be tough. The travel agent told them they would be going on game drives."

"It happens." Then, as if it were of little concern, Sean turned back to Andrew. "So what are you going to do about the lighting?"

Andrew's face paled at the sound of another looming maintenance project. In our few brief private moments, he'd explained the complexities of the camp lighting system to me. Two solar panels, which charged two large car batteries, supplied our electricity. From there, the current was drawn to power the radios and small fluorescent lamps in the cottages and kitchen. The system didn't work very well and the lights were as dim as candles.

I now allowed my mind to wander as Andrew launched into a discussion with Sean about current usage and voltage drops. Whatever Andrew said must have been good, because when I tuned in again, Sean was agreeing to purchase a new battery and a third solar panel.

This was turning out to be an expensive trip for him.

In exchange, Andrew offered to rewire the whole camp to reduce current loss. He would probably have to do this between three and four in the morning, because I had no idea when else he'd find the time.

Sean now turned his attention to the hot water supply. He pulled a sketch out of his pocket and, with some enthusiasm, slapped it on the table. It was a page torn out of *Farmer's Weekly* magazine.

"Andrew," he said, with a gleam in his eye. "There has been a revolution in donkey boiler design. Instead of placing two fifty-gallon drums side-by-side, the experts now say we use *three* barrels. Two next to each and one on top!" Andrew and I grinned at the excitement in Sean's voice, but he didn't notice. He patted his paper. "I want you to build me one of these!"

All amusement banished, Andrew snatched the page and studied the design as if seeing it for the first time. He looked up, a faintly wild expression in his eyes, "But. . .but this will take bricks, a fifty kilo bag of cement, water barrels. All delivered by plane. What about all my other stuff? There will never be room for it all."

"Piece of cake," Sean said, brushing away his objections with a sweep of his hand. "Sepei will get the stuff to you before you've wiped your eyes out."

Did Sean actually know what went on in the logistics department of his camps?

I shook my head, doing a quick mental tally of all Andrew's fix-it projects. In no particular order:

1. Clean up Tau's rubbish tip.
2. Repair the Hyena fridge. For the fourth time.
3. Build a hyena-proof door to the kitchen.
4. Fix the scullery roof.
5. Revitalise the runway sprinkler system, including rebuilding the water pump.
6. Improve the functioning of The Cupboard and the bar fridge.
7. Give eight cottages a thorough facelift.
8. Install a new solar panel.
9. Rewire the camp.
10. Build a new donkey boiler.

Oh, and not to forget Otter Lodge, more urgent than anything, if

Morag and I were to survive sharing the island.

I think if Andrew had been prone to panic, he'd have had a full-blown attack at that point. As it was, he was looking decidedly weighed down, so I wasn't sorry when Sean announced he was going to Scops Camp.

I looked at my watch. It was after five. "Will you be staying the night, Sean?" I asked, hoping he'd say no. Having my boss around with four horrible Italians didn't sound like fun.

"Yes," came the reply. "I don't mind which cottage, but number four is my preference."

He and Morag had barely left the camp when Andrew rushed over to the radio. "110, 110, 638."

"Hi Andy. What's going down?" It was Kyle.

"You mean *who's* coming down. Sean and Morag are on their way. Over."

"Sean? Here? Now?" Kyle's shock made me wonder what they were up to at Scops.

"On their way down the runway this very minute," Andrew replied.

"This is a joke, right? I didn't hear any aircraft."

"Kyle, you're too smart for me," Andrew said. "Nice try, though." He put down the microphone with a satisfied grin on his face.

* * *

Because Sean was around, Andrew and I decided to do the early morning shift together. Sean waited for us at the kitchen. "So where's this hyena you were telling me about?"

As perversity would have it, the kitchen was untouched, looking as neat as I'd ever seen it. The fridge was closed, the oven door attached to the oven, and the pots and few remaining Tupperware all in their respective places. It was uncanny.

"It must have gone," Andrew said, somewhat superfluously.

Sean shrugged and turned towards the path. "I'm going for a walk around the island. Tell Morag when she wakes that I've gone without her."

We waved him away and joined the Italians and their guides at the bay. If they had been surly last night when just contemplating the prospect of walking, they were now positively morose when faced with the actual activity. Less than an hour had passed, however, when I caught sight of two *mekoro* racing back to the bay, poled by very glum looking guides.

Not, however, as glum as the Italians.

Andrew and I walked over to meet them.

As the first *mokoro* entered the bay, The Spokesman burst out, "How can you expect people to go walking here for hours? We saw no animals. There are no lions, no elephants, no rhinos, no leopards, and no cheetah. All we saw were stupid birds and animal droppings."

KD parked his *mokoro* on the bank, and said quietly, "*Rra en Mma*, we saw zebra, giraffe, impala, letchwe, and tsesebe. All nice and close. We even showed them a black coucal." He now looked pained. KD was a bird fanatic and bumping into a black coucal was a rare and privileged sighting. It was clear KD considered his *lekgoa* Philistines.

By now, The Spokesman had clambered out the craft and was standing inches from Andrew's nose.

Andrew took a step back. "It seems to me you actually had a good morning's viewing. The problem is your travel agent sold you the wrong camp. She should have booked you into Savuti in northern Botswana. That's where you'll find vehicles, and elephant, and lion galore. Here, at Tau Camp, you're seeing what Africa looked like without engines, vehicles, and motorboats. Like it was before man messed it up."

The glower on The Spokesman face said he was unimpressed by this little speech. "We're leaving today. You must arrange for our bookings to be changed."

"Bring me your travel vouchers and I'll contact the Maun office," Andrew said. "I'm sure they'll do their best."

The four of them marched off to their cottages, presumably to change into something more suitable for breakfast. Moments later, The Spokesman appeared brandishing his paperwork. He didn't bother waiting for Andrew's radio call.

Just as well, because it was with a fair bit of moaning that Joan agreed to shuffle them onto the incoming flight. They didn't even get to eat the enormous breakfast prepared for them.

Moments after their plane left the island, Sean announced his intention to leave. Andrew and I walked with him to the strip, to find that Robert and Matanta had beaten us there. Robert jived and laughed, obviously thrilled to be off the island for a week. Matanta smiled stoically at Robert's joy, and I could feel guilt infusing my face. I'd acted hastily to get rid of Robert, thus overlooking my friend who needed the leave just as badly. But this wasn't time to show doubt or weakness. I plastered a satisfied smile on my lips, and offered Robert a farewell handshake.

Once in the plane, before Sean started the engine, he turned to us and said, almost as an afterthought, "You guys are doing okay. And Gwynn, last night's dinner was the best meal I've had at Tau Camp in years. You have some very happy chefs. Matanta is beaming."

Experience would teach us that that accolade from Sean was abundant praise.

Andrew and I stood together on the runway until his aircraft was a little more than a speck in the deep blue sky.

I grinned. "Sean's just given us our wings to go solo."

"Yes, I think we can say that our trial days are over."

CHAPTER 32

A week had passed since Sean's visit. I was alone at reception, doing my paperwork, when Morag singled me out for a private chat. I'd avoided being alone with her since Matanta's and Gwynn's assertions that she was after my body. I steeled myself for this engagement.

"You know Robert came back from his leave today?" she asked.

My grunt was non-committal.

"Well, he brought me a letter from Sean saying I'm in charge of running CIMs." When I didn't reply, she added, "Overnight safaris to Chief's Island which Sean sells as Chief's Island *Mokoro*-trails. Anyway, twelve Canadians are arriving in a couple of weeks and Sean wants me to take them out with the guides."

My adventurer juices began to bubble. I dropped my pencil and calculator and looked up at her.

"Sean says KD and I have to do a high-speed recon to find the best places to take them. I've already spoken to KD, and we're leaving tomorrow." Morag leered at me. "You can come too, if you like."

I cleared my throat, and then stuttered, "Um. . .nah. . .maybe some other time."

Cringing at her obvious disappointment, I escaped into the lounge, grabbed a topographical map, and some aerial photos of the delta from the bookshelf, and laid them across the coffee table.

"So where are you planning on going? Chief's Island is a big place." Actually, Chief's Island was a *vast* place, a bush-covered sand island stretching some one thousand square kilometres in the heart of the Okavango delta.

I shoved sleeping Tom off the sofa and sat. Morag sank down next to me, thighs rubbing mine.

I shifted a bit.

With a resigned sigh, she said, "The Canadians have booked a seven-night excursion, so we can go quite far, even by *mokoro*. . ."

The next thing I knew, we were being called for lunch. At least two hours had passed, spent doing what I love most: pouring over maps, plotting routes to places with strange sounding names. Still deep in conversation, Morag and I made our way to the dining room. The guests—six unmemorable couples and a family complete with noisy kid—had already assembled.

Gwynn gave me a deeply questioning look.

Realising how my morning must have appeared from her perspective, I wrapped my arm around her and whispered so only she could hear, "Good news. Morag's leaving us for a few days. And I'm doing all I can to help her on her way." Gwynn raised her eyebrows in yet another silent question. "Tomorrow, she's going on a camping trip." Then I added a warning. "So I'll be busy all afternoon helping get her stuff together."

Gwynn bounced off to pour the wine.

That afternoon, Morag and I assembled cooking grids, paraffin lanterns, tents, roll-up mattresses, and all the other gear needed for her trip. I left her to pack and went to raid the kitchen for some cooking pots.

Matanta was there with the usual stragglers.

"Hey!" he shouted on seeing me. "Waiters, scullery ladies, and everyone else hanging around here hoping for kitchen scraps—out. I need to talk to the Chief."

Half a dozen grumbling people vacated the kitchen.

I gave Matanta a quizzical look.

"*Rra*, after lunch, Morag waited for Gwynn to leave the kitchen before she briefed Robert and Lesego about the food for her trip. Again, without telling Gwynn, she told KD to bring Sam tomorrow. Gwynn found out Morag went behind her back, and now I think your wife is cross. Very, very cross."

I sighed. "Thanks for the warning. And who's Sam?"

"A guide." Matanta gave a dispirited head shake. "Difficult, difficult guy. He runs his own church and he doesn't let anyone drink alcohol. Or smoke. Or even have sex." Matanta now rolled his eyes. "And the stupid people here all still run to him like he's selling the good stuff. And then he charges them for the privilege."

"Sounds like he's onto something," I said, grinning at the ingenuity of some people.

"No, *Rra,* don't joke. When they get sick, he gives them enemas. Always the pipe up the bum. It doesn't matter if you have a headache or a broken leg, everyone gets the pipe."

Camp Tau seemed to have an unlimited supply of weirdoes. You honestly couldn't make this stuff up. "But you still haven't answered my question. Why does Morag want to take him on her trip?"

"He can cook. That's why all Tau Camp managers put up with Sam's trouble. And, believe me, he's trouble. But we keep him on for times like this, when we have a CIM."

My heart sank. "Thanks for the info."

"There's more, *Rra*. Morag told Robert she also wants him to go on the trip when the Canadians come."

This was just plain malicious. Matanta was scheduled to go on leave during that week, and I knew Gwynn would never agree to cancel his holiday. But if Robert went with Morag, what choice would she have? This could only lead to a full-blown confrontation between Gwynn and Morag.

"Gwynn knows this?" I asked with some trepidation.

"She does, now that I've told her. So you can guess why she's so pissed off with Morag. She says she's going to tell Morag to go to hell. And to stay there. For a long time."

"That's only if she beats me to it." I turned to leave the kitchen, but Matanta grabbed my arm. "*Rra*, let Robert go with Morag. I'm happy to work to help you and Gwynn."

"But you've worked seven days a week for three months now," I protested. "It's not fair to ask you to do more."

"Andrew *Rra*, when was life ever fair? I'm Torn Trousers—a survivor. Just like you and Gwynn. So let Morag play her games, but we'll stand strong. Our team." I started to say how grateful I was for his support, when his mouth split into a lecherous grin. "And, *Rra*, about Gwynn. . .I understand women. My advice is that you do everything Morag asks—for today. But tonight, it's Gwynn's turn. You must make love to your wife."

Make love to my wife? Did Matanta have any idea how exhausted Gwynn and I were come bedtime? He might be a survivor who went at every girl he saw with the cheerful abandon of a spring rabbit, but I had a few years on him—at last three— and come bedtime, I was shattered with tiredness.

Sanguine as anything, he continued, "And I promise you, when Morag gets back things will be different. Gwynn will be in charge here, and everyone will know it. No one will dare go behind her back to make deals with Morag again."

I was about to point out that, while I agreed in principle, the practice might be more tricky, but Matanta wasn't finished. "And when Morag gets back, you must help her start her guide school. If she still wants to get into your trousers after that, then you know for sure she really does want you."

"The guide school, fine. But I'd rather saw my own head off than let her anywhere near my trousers." Wearily, I took up the cooking pots he held out to me and headed for the door.

Before I stepped out into the bright sunshine, he said, "So *Rra*, don't forget. Tonight you and Gwynn mess the sheets."

* * *

Maybe it was because I planned a romantic liaison with my wife, but dinner dragged. By eleven o'clock, I was exhausted, largely from making small talk with dull people.

I stood up. "Who would like to learn something about the southern skies?"

There was unanimous approval from our northern hemisphere guests. Thrilled with the response, I mustered my energy, bounded to reception and grabbed a handful of Maglites. When I returned, the guests were donning pullovers against the evening chill. I handed everyone a torch, and then, like the Pied Piper trailing guests, headed for the runway.

"This is brilliant," Gwynn whispered, walking next to me. "I think I know exactly what you are planning."

"Not all of it." I smirked, thinking of my plans to tumble her.

On the runway, I asked everyone to switch off their torches to get eyes attuned to the dark. I sucked in the sweet air, heavy with the tang of wild sage. Croaking reed frogs played in harmony around us, while in the trees, a lone Scops owl called its dainty chirp. Above us, a billion ancient embers glowed, the Milky Way defined in all its dusty splendour.

"I swear I can hear the stars," one of the guests whispered. "I read somewhere that there are some places on Earth where they actually hum."

This was the most interesting thing to come out of her mouth in two days. But instead of breaking the reverent silence that followed her comment, everyone—including me—tried to hear the unhearable. After a minute, someone shuffled, breaking the mood. It was my signal to launch into my lecture.

"There we have the Southern Cross," I said, pointing to the magnificent constellation and its two pointer stars.

It took a moment for everyone to locate it. Then, to a chorus of oohs and aahs, I complicated matters by pointing out the False and

Diamond crosses, often confused with the Southern Cross. Warming to my task despite my exhaustion, I even gave the Coal Sack, a small area within the Southern Cross, where the sky seems devoid of all light, a mention. My story told, I stood back to watch if my plan for getting these pesky people to bed would work.

I smiled as the first guest yawned. Then another. Suddenly, they were all saying goodnight.

As the last couple ambled from the runway toward their beds, Gwynn leaned over and kissed my cheek. "You're a genius. Masterful. I swear, I thought they were going to stay up all night, and I kept drifting off. It was just a matter of time before I started snoring."

"Can't have that. You sound like a steam train in full snore."

Before she could hit me, wrecking the romantic mood before it even got started, I grabbed her arm and steered her back into camp to refill the bar fridge. Even though I'd levelled it with my new spirit level, the fridge only worked a little better. Clearly, more tweaking was required.

After locking the pantry, (still no materials to build a hyena proof door had been delivered), we headed for bed. My prayers shot heavenward that we'd find Woodie happy and safe, so we didn't have to spend half an hour looking for her. I was just too exhausted for that.

My prayer was answered. I let Gwynn cuddle the cat for a minute, and then, although bone tired, put my arm around her, pulling her close. Face nestled in her neck, I managed to murmur, "I want you."

When Gwynn said nothing, I nuzzled harder, cursing Matanta and his stupid plan.

I could feel she was somewhat surprised, but not necessarily displeased with my advances. My heart managed a little skip. If I played my cards right, I could get my conjugal duty done, and be fast asleep before I actually passed out. I pulled her towards the bed and slipped with her under the mosquito net.

Oh man! Did my pillow ever look inviting!

But, I steeled myself and kissed my wife, a long deep kiss that, in the days before working the long hours of a camp manager, would have been a prelude to a night of lovemaking.

Gwynn kissed me back with, I must admit, a little less enthusiasm than normal.

I put it down to tiredness.

It was then that I remembered the radio.

Wanting to cry, I broke away from her and said, "The radio? Is it off?"

"Yes," she mumbled, but I could see she was trying to cover up that she was already half asleep.

"Not the HF, the VHF. I saw the green light after supper, unless you switched it off?" It was the critical radio we needed for our Maun communication.

Gwynn shook her head, muttering through a yawn, "Joan will kill us if we have no radio contact tomorrow."

Body feeling like lead, I said, "I guess we have to go back down to reception to check it."

"Be careful," Gwynn replied.

"Is that your way of telling me I'm going alone?"

"Well done."

Talk about betrayal! Sighing like a mournful wind on a drab day, I picked up my Maglite and walking stick. Then, remembering my quest, I added, in my best sultry voice, "Wait for me. I'll be back before you know I've gone."

I stepped outside. The bed creaked as Gwynn launched herself onto the mattress. I guessed I should make this trip to reception snappy. I set off at a fast trot. The darkness was thick, the air still, and the night noises dim and distant as I made my way through the sleeping camp. At the end of the path, I could just make out the radio's gleaming green on-light. It hadn't been a wasted trip. I sped up. Mere steps away from reception, I heard a scuffle to my left.

An animal?

Not noisy enough to be a hippo, but too noisy for a genet.

I swung the torch around to investigate.

There, standing in the yellow light, no more than two yards away from me, was the hyena.

I sucked in a breath. All I could think was how *huge* the bloody thing was. Its head stood easily as tall as my waist. Although my body betrayed me by freezing solid, strangely, I wasn't afraid. Perhaps it was exhaustion taking the edge off my emotions.

Also fearless, the hyena looked directly at me. And then it moved forward, threat in every step. Just as textbooks said one should do in an animal charge, I yelled a deep-throated scream, and then swung the torch around to my face. With my other hand, I waved my stick high in the air. Unfortunately, the torch blinded me. Now, the first nips of fear bit into me—the hyena could see me, but I couldn't see it. The whole idea was intolerable, so I swung the torch back at the hyena.

The path in front of me was empty. The hyena had scarpered. The sound of crashing in the undergrowth was all that remained to prove that I'd almost been eaten by a monster-sized predator.

My heart started pounding so fast, I worried I was having a heart attack. It took me about five minutes before I calmed down enough to walk the last few paces to the radio. Even then, I had to wait for my hands to stop trembling before I could switch it off. I staggered back to tell Gwynn that I'd just scared off the scariest beast I'd ever seen.

She lay on top of the bed waiting for me. Woodie curled up beside her.

Then I heard her snores.

How the cat slept through it, I would never know.

I smiled down at my lover, unable to bring myself to wake her—and that, to me at least, was the truest declaration of my love.

After covering her and Woodie with the sheet, I stood wondering what to do. A bucket load of adrenalin still coursed through me. Sleep had fled. There seemed nothing else for it but to sit in my lounge, waiting for sanity to return.

So much for my promise to Matanta to mess the sheets.

CHAPTER 33

There was a commotion going on in the kitchen, but not the usual
friendly banter that accompanied early morning activities. Today, an
unfamiliar voice, harsh and acrimonious, cut above all the others. I went
to investigate.

A tall, scrawny stranger, wearing the familiar khaki guide uniform,
stood in the centre of the room. He was arguing with Kekgebele, who
should have been cleaning up the chaos wrought overnight by the hyena.

After scaring the life from Andrew—or so he had told me this
morning when I awoke— the blasted animal had returned during the
night to ravage the kitchen. If that wasn't insult enough, despite Hazel's
warning, the baboons had snuck in this morning, too. The day was
shaping up to be all kinds of horrible.

My attention was drawn back to Kekgebele and the interloper. If
Kekgebele radiated a quiet serenity, then this man pulsed with a
dissatisfied arrogance, as if the world owed him something. I stepped
into the middle. "We haven't met. I'm Gwynn, the manager. And you
are?"

"Sam. Morag sent for me. I'm cooking for her CIM."

The hair on the back of my neck stood, all my senses shouting at
me that Sam was not someone I could trust. That surprised me. Although
I'd run into a few troubles with Morag and Lesego—okay, and Robert—I
usually got along well with people. Also, I generally wasn't prone to rash
judgments, but something about Sam was decidedly off. I needed to find
out more. "You have a problem with Kekgebele?"

"*Em, Mma.* He won't make me tea."

My mouth gapped. "Tea?"

"*Em, Mma.* How am I supposed to go to work without tea?"

I waved my hands at the baboon faeces strewn over the counters and floor. "Maybe you do what all the other guides do—you have your early morning tea at home. Then, when you get back from taking the guests out, you have more tea with your breakfast. Or, in your case, today you drink tea when Morag says you can." They were leaving for their CIM recon today. Good riddance to both of them.

Sam threw up his hands. "*Matata, Mma. Matata.* This cannot work."

"Well, it's going to have to," a sharp voice said. I turned to see Matanta standing in the kitchen doorway. He glowered at Sam. "With the hyena and baboons, there's no room in here for guides as well."

Like a viper, Sam whipped round to face Matanta. "Are you saying us guides are like baboons? I will tell everyone you said that, and there will be trouble. You wait and see, Matanta."

Sam started for the door, but I grabbed his arm. "Stop! What Matanta means is that there is no room in here for anyone but the kitchen staff." I gestured to the chaos and filth. "The staff have big cleaning to do, and then they have to cook breakfast for the *lekgoa.*"

Sam seemed to consider what I was saying, but there was no way of gauging what he was thinking. He clicked his tongue and stalked out. Something told me we hadn't heard the last of Sam and his tea. Trust Morag to inflict someone like him on me.

I wasn't feeling very charitable an hour later when I joined her at the bay for her great send off. With only an inch of freeboard to spare, three *mekoro*, heavily laden with camping gear, stood ready for her adventure. Despite my anger, I watched in awe at the pure romance as the guides poled her and her small flotilla out into the river.

Casting aside my envy, I turned to hug Andrew—the Chief everyone was talking about, who'd singlehandedly driven the hyena out the camp. For all that his fame had spread far and wide this morning, my hero looked terrible. A drawn face highlighted his red-rimmed eyes. "Maybe one day it will be us," I consoled.

"As if we'd ever be so lucky."

He turned towards reception, but I grabbed his arm. "Go sleep. I'll handle everything."

"Have you seen my maintenance list?" Quite unnecessarily, given Andrew's irritating diligence, Sean had arrived unannounced a second time to check up on the progress of the maintenance effort. Apart from the spirit level, he hadn't loaded his plane with much needed maintenance supplies. My husband was feeling the stress. What really annoyed, though, was Sean's total lack of feedback on a job well done. It went a long way in explaining why all his management were so grumpy. Being under appreciated can do that to a person.

I decided to sow some cheer. "Well, if it's not going anywhere, then it'll keep until tomorrow. Go and chill."

"I wish. But I heard a couple of the guests moaning about warm beers, so I'd better go and give the fridge some love." He stumbled to the bar. "And then there's still The Cupboard to fix."

Unable to deflect him, I went to my favourite place in the whole of the Okavango.

The kitchen.

Matanta was waiting for me with an expectant air. He grinned, and then asked, almost coyly, "So, *Mma*, how was your evening?"

"Boring." I opened The Cupboard, winced at the smell, and wrote chicken on my dinner menu.

"Boring?" Matanta repeated, sounding surprised. "But Andrew. . .he's not. . .boring?"

"No, but the guests are."

"*Em*," Matanta said, as if that explained everything. "But after that?"

"I don't remember." I pinned my menu up on the board.

"You don't remember?" Now he sounded totally perplexed, and I wondered what was going on. He'd never expressed this much interest in my personal life before.

"I was sleeping," I said, eyeing him warily. "Andrew is the one who had all the fun chasing away the hyena."

"Crap."

Surprised—Matanta had never sworn in front of me before, at least not in English—I turned to face him. A scowl marred his usually handsome face. "*Mma*, that hyena has now crossed the line. It's time we did something about it."

"Just the hyena?" I laughed. "What about the baboons?"

"Okay, the baboons, too. But, *eish*, that hyena has to go. Now."

I leaned against the counter. "All suggestions gratefully received."

Matanta plucked thoughtfully at the straggly stubble on his chin. Then he declared, "We must send a letter to the Wildlife Department, telling them we need a permit to shoot some troublesome baboons. Maybe two. That will shock the rest of the troop enough that they'll give us some peace for a while. Then we must drag the dead baboons down to Scops. That way the hyena will follow the trail—and *she'll* become Kyle and Milly's problem."

She? The reference to Morag as the hyena was clear. I snorted a laugh. "Maybe the problem will go away on its own, now we have a CIM happening. Like it did the night Sean was here. The hyena was nowhere to be found."

Matanta grinned, clearly understanding my veiled reference to Morag's reluctance to morph into a hyena when the boss was around. Then his smile vanished. "But the CIM has to come back."

"True." I frowned. I could joke as much as I liked about Morag, but I already dreaded her return. I changed the subject. "You really think the Wildlife Department will agree to shooting baboons? And what about Kyle and Milly? We're trying to make friends with them."

"Okay," Matanta conceded grumpily, "so we take the baboons somewhere else then. But if we don't try with Wildlife we'll never know, will we?"

"And if we decide to do this crazy plan of yours, how do we get the letter to Wildlife?"

"Thekiso can take it. They have a camp not far from here, up river. And it would be good if we go soon, because they'll be visiting any day now to collect the park entrance fees." Noga Island fell just outside the Moremi Game Reserve, but the moment a *mokoro* entered the river, it crossed the border into the park. As part of their nightly tariff, each guest paid a park entrance fee. Once a month, the Wildlife officials visited camp to collect the loot.

I wasn't convinced about Matanta's plan, but I agreed to talk to the Chief about it.

When I found Andrew, he was sitting cross-legged on the floor next to the bar fridge, surrounded by warm beers, cool drinks, and wine bottles. Soot blackened his hands, which held a wire rod rolled with fabric. Both he and the rod smelled of mentholated spirits.

"Right now I am a gas mechanic," he said, by way of greeting.

"I see. And what do gas mechanics do?" I asked, instantly forgetting to talk to him about the hyena.

"They clean flues." He shoved the rod deep into the fridge's innards. "If the heating tube isn't clean, it can stop the fridge working properly." After rattling the rod around a bit, he yanked it out, pulling down a small cloud of black dust. "Next, I reset the flame. It's got to be dead centre or—"

"Or the fridge doesn't work."

"You got it." After fiddling with the burner for a few minutes, he dropped a plumb line down the side of the fridge. "Now for my new spirit level." He positioned the level on the fridge, eyeing it critically. "Hmm. . .I'm going to need some wedges."

I left him to it.

I saw him again at breakfast, looking very pleased with himself. "We should have cold beers in a few hours," he said. "I hope no one's thirsty before then."

An hour or so later, the air was split by the screech of a high-pitched engine. Guides and *lekgoa* passing the camp pulled their *mekoro* into the reeds edging the channel as the swell of a large motorboat hit them. I could hear them shouting something above the din as the motorboat swung into our bay. It sent the jacana scurrying. In a haze of exhaust fumes, it launched itself onto the bank.

"Wildlife," Matanta, who had appeared as suddenly as the motorboat, breathed to Andrew and me. "Like I said this morning, they're due a visit. Be very nice to them, *Rra en Mma,* because they are like the police here."

Andrew nodded and walked to the water's edge to greet the two khaki-clad men scrambling out of the boat.

The taller of the two offered Andrew his hand. *"Dumela, Rra,* Mishak. Wildlife." Mishak waved at Matanta, saying something in Setswana that I didn't understand.

Matanta translated. "Mishak is here to collect the park fees, and to talk about how things are at the camp."

Matanta looked at me pointedly. I remembered his plan to kill two baboons. As troublesome as the animals could be, I had no desire to start shooting them, so I said nothing.

Andrew decided to be hospitable and invited the two officials to join us in the lounge for a cold drink. They sat in the wicker chairs, leaving it to me to play barmaid. I opened the bar fridge and felt a rush of icy air. Smiling my appreciation at Andrew, I handed around some Cokes. Before I could give Andrew his, Mishak cracked his can open.

It exploded in his face, covering him in iced cold drink.

"Eish!" he shouted, leaping to his feet. "What you guys trying to do? Kill me!"

Andrew also sprung up, his tired eyes now wide with embarrassment. "Sorry, mate. The fridges are still a work in progress. How about some coffee?"

Amid much grumbling from Mishak, we headed for the urn in the dining room. Once everyone held a steaming cup, Matanta gave me another pointed look, and started speaking to Mishak in a mixture of Setswana and English. I caught the repeated use of the words 'hyena', 'baboons', and 'kitchen'. But what really got me worried was Mishak's ever-changing expression.

Finally, Mishak turned to Andrew, and, speaking in broken English, declared, *"Rra,* this is a place for animals, not humans! You cannot go round shooting the wildlife."

Looking a bit like a stunned catfish, Andrew opened his mouth to speak, but I interrupted him. "Sorry, Droon. Forgot to mention it.

Matanta suggested we get a permit to kill a couple of baboons."

Andrew frowned, muttering under his breath, "Pity you didn't tell me that earlier. We could have put a proper strategy together to persuade Mishak. Now it's too late."

"Breakdown in communication," was all I could think of to say.

I glanced at Matanta to gauge his reaction. He shrugged, but from his expression, I swore I could see an idea uncurling in his mind.

I was not wrong.

As soon as Mishak and his smelly motorboat left, Matanta said, "*Rra en Mma*, come to the kitchen. I have another plan for getting rid of the hyena."

Andrew snorted a laugh, quoting Baldrick from *Black Adder*. "You have a cunning plan."

Without access to the BBC, the joke was lost on Matanta. But he did poke at the chicken Kekgebele, who was undergoing chef training along with table clearing chores, was chopping into pieces for supper. "I reckon hyenas like chicken, especially in a casserole. Yes?"

"I imagine they do," I replied, wondering where Matanta was going with this.

"And I reckon they like it spicy. Yes?"

"Probably," Andrew added.

"Then let's give him a feast tonight. Spicy chicken casserole."

"You're not thinking of poisoning him, are you?" I said, aghast. "Chefs who play with poison are even scarier than hyenas."

Matanta gave me an evil grin. "Tempting. But no. I'm talking about English mustard, Tabasco, cayenne pepper, chillies—lots of them. Give him a meal that makes holes in his teeth. Then when he eats it, maybe he'll decide not to come back."

"C'mon, Matanta," Andrew said, in disbelief. "Hyenas chew airplane tyres and swallow spark plugs. They even drink hydraulic fluid. I'm not sure a little Tabasco is going to be a problem."

Matanta gave a dramatic sigh, and, quoting Sean for whom he'd worked for so many years, replied, "That's the trouble with you people. You never want to try my ideas."

Andrew and I burst into laughter.

"Okay. Why not?" Andrew said, finally gaining control. "We have a culinary date."

Just before dinner that evening, Andrew and I joined Matanta in the kitchen to mix our witch's brew for the hyena. My eyes watered and my breath caught from the reek of chillies and onions Kekgebele had spent the afternoon chopping. He looked high from the smell.

Matanta, seemingly immune to the fumes, grabbed the mustard

powder, Tabasco sauce, and a bottle of Bitters, which he emptied into a metal bowl, holding a generous helping of the *lekgoa's* dinner. He stirred it up with the onion and chilli mixture. Finally, in an attempt at *haute cuisine*, he added a bay leaf to the top. "So the hyena will know he's come to a top class establishment."

"The plan?" Andrew asked, holding his nose.

"After my shift, I'll leave the bowl on the floor, near the door," Matanta replied. "Just don't stand on it when you lock up."

During dinner, we told our guests about the hyena. It was with great anticipation that everyone went to bed, eager to know what the morning would bring. But when Andrew and I went to lock up the kitchen, we were astonished to see that our bowl had already been licked clean. Unseen and unheard, the hyena had crept into camp while we sat at dinner, not twenty paces away.

It was a frightening thought.

Perhaps the next person who bumped into it would not get off as easily as Andrew had.

Andrew still managed to crack a joke. "That casserole's gonna hit him hard when he takes a dump."

Maybe it was exhaustion, or nerves, or just my childish love of toilet humour, but I burst into uncontrollable giggles.

Smiling patiently, Andrew took my arm, and led me to bed. We'd just settled in the blackness under our mosquito net when we heard a blood-curdling animal yowl. It came from the runway behind our hut. This was followed by a manic yelping, which slowly faded into the distance as the animal raced off into the bush.

"That's him. He's just taken a crap," Andrew said, with some satisfaction.

He fell asleep to the muffled sound of my giggles.

CHAPTER 34

Despite our casserole, the kitchen was trashed in the morning. Muttering about the bloody wildlife—hyenas in particular—I left the staff to handle the mess and went to my office on the runway. I was in the final stages of assembling my bastardised water pump, and all it needed was a throttle lever, which I'd fashioned out of a steel bracket. Feeling the calming effects of the autumn sun on my back, I whistled as I fitted it. Then I poured some petrol in the tank.

The moment of truth had come.

Would the damn thing work? Or would it be like all my other maintenance projects at Tau—an exercise in pushing rocks uphill? There was only one way to know, so I gripped the starter cable and pulled.

Nothing happened.

I wiped sweat from my eyes. Even though we were edging into winter, the sun had changed from warm to unpleasantly hot.

I ripped the cord again.

Still nothing.

Another wrench of the cable and I heard a splutter. I yanked for the fourth time and was rewarded with a throaty lawnmower-like roar. It was so loud, Thekiso, working on the other end of the runway, came running to inspect it.

I immediately got him working.

Singing my maintenance praises to the birds and letchwe, he wheeled the pump down the strip to the narrow channel at the far end. I joined him, stepped into the water, and sloshed about, until we got the pipe submerged. We were ready for spray action.

This time the pump started on the first pull.

Okay, I admit, I shouted with joy when great arcs of water sprang up all along both sides of the runway. Trouble was, most of them were spraying in the wrong direction. No point in watering the grass on the side of the strip. That wouldn't dampen the sand, stopping it from blowing away when planes landed. That may sound crazy, but the constant chaffing of aircraft tyres on a sand strip ploughed ruts, which made rough landings. The sand helped keep things smooth.

Undeterred by this minor setback—it was Tau Camp, after all—I turned the pump off. Thekiso and I walked the length of the strip again, adjusting the sprinkler heads. Another walk back to the pump, and we had water spraying on the runway for the first time in months.

I was quietly gloating on my successful morning at the office, when I spotted Gwynn standing outside the camp, waving her arms. She looked even more dishevelled than usual. Leaving the pump to run itself dry, I took a slow victory walk up the runway through the spray. I was soaked to the skin by the time I joined her.

"Nice." She patted my wet shoulder. "Cool too." I could hear both envy and pride in her voice. That always made everything worthwhile.

"So, what's so important you had to pull me out of my board meeting?" I asked, shaking water out of my hair.

"We have guests coming in."

I swallowed my irritation. "We always have guests coming in. We run a lodge, unless you haven't noticed."

"It does describe the high turnover of people."

Guessing there was more to this than Gwynn just peeing on my parade, I opened my hands expectantly, waiting for an explanation.

"Joan forgot to mention that we have two boatloads of very rich, very demanding French aristocrats dropping into camp today. Just when I'm low on supplies, too. The only things I've got enough of are some very over-ripe fillets, and a couple of green oxtails."

My euphoria evaporated like spray mist before the sun.

"When are they arriving?"

"No idea. Like I said, they're travelling by motorboat. They left Shakawe three days ago. Joan reckons they should arrive sometime today."

"Crap," was all I could think of to say. Then, realising that wasn't very helpful, I added, "Shit."

"I sent Alfred to the village to call some guides."

My heart sank. Alfred, my maintenance *medala*, had only two responsibilities: collecting wood for the donkey boilers, and then building fires in the donkey boilers. No wood. No fire. No heat. . . I think

I've mentioned this somewhere before. Anyway, if he wasn't here to gather wood, everyone would be having cold showers tonight. Not what demanding French aristocrats who've spent three days living in a boat would appreciate.

Hiding my frustration at Gwynn's interference in my department, I said, "Why him? Why not Olutuswe?"

"He's fixing a blocked toilet in number six. It actually overflowed onto the guest's slippers."

I sighed. "Okay. Good call in sending Alfred. What do you need me to do?"

"Nothing. Just thought I'd share the pain."

With my day spoiled, I left the runway with her and headed for the kitchen. My stomach grumbled its protests when I caught the smell of cooking. I'd skipped breakfast and lunch was still a couple of hours away. I filched a piece of fruitcake, while Gwynn and Matanta argued over what to cook for supper. Matanta was all for the oxtail, but Gwynn won, insisting the fillet was less likely to poison us all.

Thanking the culinary god who kept oxtail off the menu, I headed to the bar fridge to grab a Coke. It was the perfect temperature. Smirking at yet another maintenance triumph, I cracked the tab.

Unfortunately, the profoundly satisfying first fizz was lost under a roar coming from the bay. It sounded a bit like my new water pump, except in stereo. Our French guests must have arrived. I chugged the Coke down, belched, and then joined Gwynn at the bay in time to see two sleek, silver boats beach onto the bank. Our eight new guests and their guide disembarked.

Funny, but it doesn't matter how dirty, windswept, or sunburned some rich people are—they still manage to exude disdainful arrogance. Or at least this lot did. What was even more impressive was that, with the exception of their guide, none of them could have been younger than seventy. That says something for French stamina.

Gwynn must have shared my sentiments about our new guests, because she mouthed, "I'm anticipating a rough few days with these old coots."

We went to greet them.

They all spoke perfect English, a talent they put to good use by immediately asking for lunch. I guessed a Coke and a piece of fruitcake wasn't going to cut it here. Gwynn smiled a fake smile—she was getting good at those—and went to cadge an early meal out of Robert and Matanta, while I did their paperwork.

Their haughty superiority followed them to the dining room.

As far as I could see, the only good to come out of their arrival was that they scored me a pre-lunch run of quiche and salad to fill the gap left by the fruitcake. While chatting with them, it was clear they had 'done' the water and had no intention of leaving the camp during their three-day stay.

One old matriarch even asked if we had any deck chairs, so she could park off while the waiters supplied her with a steady flow of grog. I was about to say all the deck chairs had gone down on the *SS Normandie*, but thought better of it. Instead, I led her to a wicker chair in the lounge. It had the advantage of being close to the bar fridge. Only problem was, waiters were not acceptable procurers of hooch for these French aristocrats. Turns out only camp managers really knew how to pour white wine. So, it was very late in the afternoon before Gwynn and I managed to escape for our cherished family time.

As we ambled along the runway with Woodie trailing behind us, Gwynn said, "Did you know Matanta is a *sangoma*?"

I snorted my disbelief. Matanta may have been many things, most of them good, but he sure as hell didn't strike me as a man with mystical talents.

"Honestly, he says he can throw the bones to communicate with people's dead ancestors. He's offered to do mine. Not that I think any of my dearly departed would have too much to say to me."

"So when's the show happening?" I asked, to humour her.

"Soon. He says he's waiting for the perfect moment. Something to do with the moon, apparently."

This I had to see. "Call me when the moon's in place."

"You'll be the first to know." Gwynn stopped to watch Woodie.

She had slumped lethargically down onto the sand. She and Tom seemed to have worked out some kind of truce that allowed him continued occupancy at Tau. He owned the front of the camp, where he got regular table treats, prime spot in the sun on the sofa, and endless cuddles from adoring guests. Definitely the loser, Woodie huddled in our house, her boredom broken only by a short evening promenade on the runway. It wasn't much of a life for her, and, despite her resolute silence on the subject, I knew Gwynn was eaten up with guilt over it.

"That's strange, she's usually so active on her evening walk." Gwynn scooped her up and Woodie nestled in her arms like a baby— whose purring could probably be heard down at Scops Camp.

All was at peace in my world.

Until I heard the high-pitched whistle of escaping steam.

I swore.

Having lost a few hours today when he went to call the guides for the French, Alfred had tried to make up for it by over-stoking the fires in the donkey boilers. All he'd achieved was to turn them into geysers Old Faithful would envy. I knew from bitter experience that once the airborne display of steam and noise was over, the barrels would quickly refill with cold water.

No one—not even the French—would be having hot showers tonight.

CHAPTER 35

One of the benefits of running a lodge like Tau was the guests. Meeting a plane with new arrivals always provoked the odd flutter of navel butterflies. Would the people we had to share our home and dining table with be pleasant?

Out of today's plane jumped a scruffy man with a broad American, if I could guess, Californian accent. He greeted me with a firm handshake, like he really meant it. I immediately considered him a welcomed addition to the French.

His name was Joe Camp. I remember him because he wasn't in the least bit camp, and he immediately demanded not to be treated like a tourist. He wore an invisible barrier, warding off tourist platitudes like he would a swarm of bees.

While doing his paperwork, he told me he was a film director living in Hollywood. Well, he was wearing brand new Ray Bans. And he sported the coolest Nikon camera and lenses I'd ever seen. So maybe he was telling the truth.

"I'm here to see Africa," he enthused. "I mean *real* Africa. And I was told this is a good place."

And it was. I just hoped he would have some good game sightings.

We appointed Jackson as his guide. On the water's edge that afternoon, Jackson stood at his *mokoro* and started giving Joe the 'if you see a lion, you must stand still' speech.

Joe was having none of it. "Look, my man Jackson. I appreciate all this tourist stuff, but I want to see some animals up close. Can we go now?"

Dumbfounded, Jackson stepped on board and pushed his *mokoro* and Joe out into the river.

Around five o'clock, Gwynn and I walked to the front to welcome the guests returning from their afternoon excursions. There had been the usual sightings of kudu, wildebeest, zebra, and a distant elephant. KD's group managed to get a good look at a Pels fishing owl, a real surprise, and something neither of us had yet seen. I made a note of its whereabouts in the camp diary, used to record noteworthy events, daily temperature, and animal sightings. Sean liked to look at it when he visited the camp.

Come six o'clock, we were beginning to get worried. Joe and Jackson had not come back. This was the first time a guest had not returned on time, and we were clueless on what to do about it. We paced up and down at reception, remembering the story of the Belgian mercenary Karomona had got lost with in the bad weather.

The sun had almost set when a lone *mokoro* appeared on the river. A dishevelled Jackson poled Joe furiously towards the camp.

Once landed, Joe was a changed man.

He hugged Jackson, and handed him two hundred dollars. Then he slammed his Nikon on the reception desk. It had been smashed. His big lens followed. Its front bits were dented.

"Best day ever!" Joe gushed. "Spent the day up a tree, with a buffalo snorting down below. They charged us and we had to climb for our lives. Did you know that? When a buffalo chases you, you have to climb a tree! And fast."

Then he hugged me, too.

I now understood Jackson's bemused expression. Joe's hug was as firm as his handshake.

"So that stuff wasn't bull after all. Good man, Andrew. I'm gonna put my camera on a display for all to see. This is what really happens in Africa!" Joe then pulled out his wallet again, and handed me a hundred dollar tip. "Go buy your lady something nice. It's not for the staff. It's for you."

That was the first and last monetary tip we received at Tau Camp.

CHAPTER 36

Sadly, Joe left. Even more sadly, the French were still with us. Tonight was their last Tau dinner. Robert and I stared into the depth of The Cupboard, where two fillets and a couple of oxtails, our last remaining meat, lay congealing in their own slime. Somehow, all of Andrew's attempts to get the freezer working had failed. It really was ready to be pensioned off. But having given the French fillet steak on their first and second nights here, I could hardly dish it up for their third. The problem was, anyone eating that oxtail would probably spend the next week hanging over a toilet. In a hospital.

"Maybe today, *Mma*, Sepei will send us supplies," Robert said, with an air of hopelessness.

I shook my head doubtfully. "Only one plane coming in, and it's filled with Scops Camp *lekgoa*."

"No *lekgoa* for Tau?"

"No." I whistled glumly through my teeth, and then joked, "I suppose we could always do a tuna bake."

Robert snorted his disapproval, hoicked the oxtail out of The Cupboard, and plunked it down onto the counter. We stepped back, retching.

"I'll radio Sepei again and plead with her," I said, holding my nose. "In the meantime, give that oxtail a decent burial."

"And if the plane is too full for stock, *Mma*, what then?" Robert asked, tossing the oxtail into a bucket.

"I'll beg some meat off Milly. Let's just keep the dinner menu open until further notice." Sensing his disapproval, even though we both knew the situation was entirely out of my control, I changed the subject. "So what do you know about Matanta's bone throwing skills? Is he really a *sangoma*?" Robert's face instantly went into lock-down, but I pushed on. "I thought Karomona was the only *sangoma* on the island."

Robert pulled himself up tall and replied, stiffly, "*Mma*, I cannot talk of such things. It is forbidden."

I was about to protest that Matanta didn't seem to mind talking about his skills, when we heard the screeching of cats—a sound that had been blessedly absent for the last week or so.

Robert and I dashed out the still-broken kitchen door in time to see Tom chasing Woodie through the camp.

A wave of fury hit me.

After weeks of hiding out in our cottage, Woodie had finally plucked up the courage to look for me at work and Tom had savaged her.

Again.

By the time I reached home, Andrew had the first aid kit out. "A gash on the side of her face. It looks bad," he said, dousing her cheek in water and disinfectant. She was too beat up to even struggle.

I slapped the *letaka* wall. Hard. "That's it. Tom leaves today."

Andrew handed me the cotton wool and the trembling Woodie. "I'll tell Thekiso to punch some holes into a cardboard box. As soon as we catch Tom, he can pole him down to Scops."

By the time I'd finished medicating Woodie, Tom had been evicted. Aside from protecting my own cat, getting rid of that menace seemed like my first real triumph at Tau Camp. I finally felt like the manager. So, it was with a tiny spring in my step that I headed for the airstrip to meet the incoming flight.

The booking sheets promised an Islander and I was hopeful Sepei had squeezed some Tau stock aboard. Andrew's face lit up as the pilot unloaded wooden poles needed for fixing the scullery roof and building the kitchen door, some bricks for the new donkey boiler, and even a bag of cement.

I wasn't so gleeful. There was no meat. Not even a lousy sausage.

So, with dinner looking decidedly shaky, I headed for the radio to call Milly.

It squawked to life as I reached reception. "638, 638. This is 110." It wasn't just 110 calling, it was Milly.

I wondered if she was radioing to moan about being saddled with Tom. To pre-empt that, I grabbed the mic and said, "Milly! How's Tom doing?"

"Tom?"

"The cat."

"He's here?" With the mic still keyed, she yelled, "Kyle! E'man! What do you guys know about a cat?"

"Last time I saw him, he was mauling a rat under the bar," I heard Kyle yell back, sounding as if he was on the other side of the camp. Things were definitely a lot more casual down at Scops Camp.

"Seems he's having a grand time," Milly said. "When do you want him back?"

I shoved my guilt aside. "Never. He's all yours."

"Cool. The rats have really been getting on top of us."

I let go of a breath I didn't know I'd been holding. "Great. Now I need to ask you a favour."

"Seems like you've had your favour for the day," Milly interrupted. "And anyway, I called you. Do you have any spare condoms? Kyle and I could really use some down here."

I swallowed hard, but that didn't stop my voice from squeaking, "Condoms? Um. . .actually, Andrew and I. . .well. . .we tend to use—"

"Not condoms," Andrew shouted into the mic. "And when the hell do you guys even find the time or energy for it? Share the secret."

I covered my face with my hands. What was the matter with these people—my husband included? Didn't they know that everyone in the Maun office could hear our chatter?

Milly was laughing hysterically when she came back onto the mic. "Not for us, you idiot. Kyle and my sex life died the day we started running this camp."

"Then for who?" I croaked as Andrew cracked up laughing next to me.

"Our staff. They seem to have both the time and energy. They've been going at each other like rabbits. Now everyone has some horrible disease. It's the pits."

"And you know this because?" I asked, wondering if I really wanted the answer.

"Because I've had a line of them here today, all wanting to show me their tackle."

"How nice for you. But we're clean out of condoms."

A new voice entered the fray. Joan in the Maun office. "I'll have Sepei send you up a couple of crates of rubbers, Milly. Verity will also let the district doctor know that her services are required. And, Andrew, just in case you're feeling left out, I've news for you, too—Tau had a cancellation, so after the French leave tomorrow, you and Gwynn have an empty camp." I could hear laughter coming from the staff in the Maun office. "Use the time wisely."

"Tau has an empty camp! That's not fair! What about Kyle and me?" Milly moaned before Andrew and I had even finished our jubilant high five.

Then we heard Kyle say, "Leave this to me, Mill, I'll burst their bubble. An empty camp huh, Andrew? Remind me, didn't someone once mention something about a volleyball tournament?"

Andrew grabbed the mic from my hand. "The challenge stands, Kyle. Prepare yourselves for a thrashing."

"Right on," Kyle shouted triumphantly into the mic. "You Tau wusses be here tomorrow night and we'll see who gets the thrashing."

Before Andrew could respond, the mic crackled.

"Sorry to be a kill-joy, guys, but I'm doing my best to rustle up some late bookings for tomorrow," Joan said.

Andrew's face fell, but maintaining a professional edge to his voice, he said, "Of course, Joan, guests are the top priority, but how about a cut-off time?"

"Meaning?" Joan barked.

"Three o'clock tomorrow afternoon we turn off the radios. If you haven't told us about a late booking by then, the volleyball tournament goes on as planned."

The radio went silent for a full minute and I could picture Kyle and Milly on the other side of the island, waiting, breath held, just like Andrew and I were. Finally Joan spoke. "Deal."

A joyful ululation broke out behind us. I swung around to see Matanta and Robert leading the rest of the staff in an impromptu dance.

Robert broke away, jived over to Andrew, and slapped him a high-five. "*Rra*, the team, leave it me. By tomorrow I'll have us some champions."

Everyone cheered.

Whistling Elgar's *Land of Hope and Glory*, Andrew started towards Robert. I grabbed his shirt. "Not so fast. I think we have a problem." He looked at me like I'd sprouted a moustache. "You forget that Joan, Verity, and Sepei are not the only people working in the Maun office. Sean is there too. Maybe even Sandy."

Andrew's eyes widened with understanding. "Oops." He grabbed a piece of paper and a pen and scribbled a note. "This may save our lives." I read it before he shoved it into the mailbag to go out on tomorrow's plane.

Dear Sean

I would like to inform you of an upcoming event. For the smooth operation of the island, I have decided that our relationship with Scops Camp and their staff is in need of improving. Hope you don't object, but I have planned a Tau versus Scops volleyball game at Scops on Friday late. Milly will provide a simple meal for all team players. We will only do this if Tau Camp is empty. Please let me know if this is okay.

Regards
Andrew

It would arrive in Maun too late for Sean to object. Grinning like a cat, Andrew bounced off with Robert and Matanta for their first team talk.

Oh, and by the way, I think the French enjoyed the fillet—doused in a red wine sauce to mask the rancid smell and flavour.

* * *

An empty camp. I hardly knew what to do with myself once the French left. Then I saw Kegkebele and Lesego dragging the kitchen table out onto the lawn.

"And now?" I asked.

"No *lekgoa* means spring cleaning," Matanta said, from the kitchen door. He stepped aside, allowing Petso, holding a bucket and a mangy-looking brush, to pass. "Pets, you scrub that table until your hands bleed."

Petso bobbed something that looked like a curtsey, and attacked the table as if her life depended on it.

Making a mental note to check on her in ten minutes, I poked my head into the kitchen. Matanta wasn't kidding when he said they were spring cleaning. Betty was on her knees, scrubbing out the oven. Kekgebele slopped a cloth across the grimy shelves in the steel grocery cupboard. Shining the stoves had fallen to Lesego. Robert had the unenviable task of sanitising the belly of The Cupboard—or rather, trying to. Even Matanta was down on his knees, grinding his way through the grease build-up on the concrete floor. I grabbed a cloth and joined in, swabbing down the other two fridges.

My staff's cheerful banter—most of it about the upcoming volleyball game—made it the best cleaning experience I'd ever had. Then it struck me that one voice was notably absent in the chatter.

Lesego.

I stopped what I was doing to watch him trail a handful of steel wool across the gas burners. He wasn't even breaking the crust on the leftovers from the French guests' breakfast. At this rate, we'd need a couple of months of empty camps before he'd dragged his way through the midden caked on the stove. Yet again, I saw the glaring contrast between him and everyone else. To add to my frustration, he had been late again for work this morning, leaving me scrambling around making tea when I should have been coddling guests. "That's hardly going to get the job done," I said. "Put some muscle into it."

Lesego let his steel wool plop back into his bucket. "I'm a waiter,

177

not a scullery girl."

Robert swung his soapy cloth into Lesego's face. "If *Mma* and Matanta can scrub until their fingers drop off, then so can you!"

Fingers drop off? An image of Petso with bleeding hands shot before my eyes. I was supposed to have checked on her, and at least an hour had passed. I flung my cloth down and dashed outside, leaving Matanta and Robert to deal with Lesego.

Uniform wet with sweat, Petso still scrubbed away at the counter. Any more rubbing, and the melamine would flake away. I sent her into the kitchen to show Lesego how it was done. A couple of hours later, we all agreed there was nothing left to clean or polish.

You want to know a depressing thing?

All our work hadn't make a jot of difference. No one visiting would ever suspect that seven people had spent the morning scrubbing the ancient surfaces, cracked concrete floor, and broken appliances. If Sandy arrived, she would probably tell us to start over.

It was time to do something life-affirming.

I went to find Andrew. He was messing around with the electrics in the dining room. "Radio's been nice and quiet this morning," I said.

He looked up from his wiring. "Don't speak too soon."

"Joan wouldn't really send us a late booking? Or would she?"

"Empty camps are bad business. Everyone knows that."

I sighed. "Maybe we should just turn the stupid radio off."

Andrew's head jerked up, and he glared at me. "I said three o'clock, and I stand by that."

Huh! Why did he always have to be so noble? I gave the bay in front of the camp a disgruntled stare.

"By the way, I've something to show you. Come." Andrew tossed his tools down on the sideboard.

I followed him across the room. He pointed at the rolled up *letaka* blind and my heart skipped a beat. Woodie! Praying she'd plucked up the courage to come into camp, I lunged forward.

Andrew grabbed my T-shirt. "Easy. You'll frighten each other."

Not Woodie.

I stepped forward more carefully this time.

A bright black eye, set in an iridescent green face, hatched with black markings, stared out at me from the rolled up blind. Then, a startlingly blue forked tongue flicked out, smelling the air.

"Jeez!" I jerked back, bashing into the table as a lissome body sailed out of the *letaka* towards my face. "It's a bloody boomslang! Are you crazy? We can't have that thing living in here." (Boomslang—tree snakes—are deadly poisonous, even if they are a bit reticent about attacking people.) That said, there was nothing retiring about this guy. He was as angry as any snake could be.

Andrew smiled. "Relax!" Then the idiot put his finger out and stroked the snake on the side of the head.

Its mouth shot open, and it reared back, hissing at him.

At that point, I almost wet myself. I opened my mouth, but no sound came out.

So Andrew said, "See that blue tongue with the black tips?"

I managed a nod.

"It's a major tell, distinguishing this little beauty from a boomslang." Andrew sounded way too calm, especially as his fingers were still trying to tickle the snake under the chin. "He's a spotted bush snake. I'm going to call him Spotty."

Still keeping my distance, I objected, "But we already have a Spotty. The hyena."

"So? We also have a bat called Moriarty and another bat called Moriarty. They live next to our toilet. Or have you forgotten? I'm just going for consistency."

Andrew had spent too long in camp. He needed to get out more. I took his hand and gently pulled him away from Spotty. "How about asking Matanta to teach you to pole?"

CHAPTER 37

Gwynn was right. I was suffering from cabin fever. When we arrived here in March, the water level had been low. Now, in mid-winter, it was at its highest, and we hadn't left the camp for weeks to enjoy it.

It was time to organise myself some transport.

But before I could risk taking a *mokoro* out into the delta, I had to learn to pole. Gwynn suggested asking Matanta to help me, but like all men, I have this independent streak that stops me from asking for directions. I headed for the bay where, happily, one of the guides had left his *ngashi*—the stick used for poling—in his *mokoro*. That was equivalent to leaving your keys in your car's ignition. Silly boy.

A quick glance over my shoulder told me I was alone. Without hesitation, I kicked off my sandals, hopped onto the *mokoro*, and dug the end of the *ngashi* into the mud at the bottom of the bay. Then I did what I'd seen a dozen or more guides do—I pushed off hard.

With a beautiful burst of speed the *mokoro* shot backwards. Only problem was, I was no longer on it. Suspended in the air, hanging at the top of the pole, it took me a few seconds to figure out what had gone wrong.

Then—splash!

I'm not sure what you'd call the opposite of a belly flop—back flip, maybe? That implies a certain grace, which was sorely lacking from my manoeuvre. Not that the semantics really mattered. I was just as wet, either way. If that wasn't humiliating enough, the treacherous mud released the *ngashi* and it came thumping down onto my head. Swearing loudly—but refusing to be undone by this setback—I grabbed the stupid stick and waded over to where the *mokoro* bobbed against the reed island separating the bay from the main channel.

The water was deep here. Climbing onto a boat moored in the middle of the lake isn't a challenge for the undetermined—especially when the current is working to sweep you and the boat to the hippo pool downstream.

A grunt from said hippos focused my mind, lending speed and accuracy to my boat-boarding skills. Now I just had to master the art of poling—and snappily, too, before the current whipped me into the main channel.

So, *ngashi* in hand, I took up a poling stance—picture an Egyptian hieroglyph of man-holding-long-stick. Remembering my hard-earned *ngashi* placement lesson, I lowered the pole into water until it gently bumped against the bottom. Delicately, smoothly, I pushed against the pole until something amazing happened.

I moved. With the boat. Forward. The way I'd planned.

So I did it again.

Pure magic.

One embarrassing fall, a bit of follow-up logic, and I had this poling down pat. I was a born natural.

Until I tried to turn.

I've never tried negotiating a London bus round a postage stamp but, hell, it couldn't have been harder than trying to convince this six-foot long, carved out tree to go right. Or left. Finally, after an hour of trying everything I'd seen the guides do, I admitted defeat.

It was time to call in an expert.

I hopped out of my beleaguered boat, grabbed the prow, and towed the bloody thing back onto the bank.

Praying Matanta wasn't at Robert's volleyball practice, I skulked to the kitchen.

Practice—if they'd even had one—was over. Matanta, Lesego, Robert, and Kekgebele were draped over the kitchen counter, sharing a joke that had them all cracked up.

Feigning oblivion to the water dripping off me, I said, "Hey, Matanta, sorry to drag you away, but I could use your help with something." I cleared my throat and added, "In the office."

The laughter rose a few decibels, and then Matanta turned to Lesego and Kekgebele. "You two, go move the reception desk, because from now on the Chief will be doing his paperwork in the bay."

What can I say? Someone must have seen me. We lived on a tiny island, and news—especially the embarrassing kind—travelled fast.

Refusing to be deterred, I grabbed Matanta, and headed for the water. We gathered a small audience, come to witness my first lesson in *mokoro* turning. Trouble was, from my vantage point on the bank, Matanta's lesson consisted of him doing exactly what I'd been doing.

Only he was successful.

I shook my head. "Matanta, you must teach me. Showing me isn't enough."

"Because you aren't watching closely enough, *Rra*. See what I do." Without appearing to change his stance, Matanta slalomed the *mokoro* across the bay to the bank. "Now you try, and I will tell you what you are doing wrong."

That could work, so I swapped places with him. Half an hour later, I admitted defeat, again. Matanta had probably learned to push a *mokoro* before he could even crawl. Everyone born in the Okavango had. No one in Matanta's twenty-odd-years of existence had ever asked him how he did it. I suppose it would be like asking someone to teach you to walk. Where do you even begin? I wasn't sorry, therefore, when Gwynn pushed through the crowd, gesturing at her watch.

"It's ten to three. Joan hasn't called with any late bookings," she shouted. "It's looking good for volleyball, so I suggest you guys call it a day. Our players need to get their team colours on."

She didn't have to speak twice. My audience dumped me, running towards the laundry to dress for the match. I couldn't help feeling a little deflated. Here I was thinking my *mokoro* lessons were fascinating, but all they were actually waiting for was the signal to ditch camp. I let them go and joined Gwynn at reception.

Her hand hovered over the radio off-button. I looked at my watch. Five minutes to go. The temptation to flick the switch was unbearable, but Joan and I had a deal. I gestured to my sodden clothes. "You wait here while I go and change." A few steps towards the edge of reception, I stopped. "And no cheating."

Gwynn stuck her tongue out at me just as the radio cackled into life. "638. 637."

Joan.

My heart plummeted.

Gwynn scrunched up her face, eyes tight shut, as if not seeing the radio would stop it from squawking.

I picked up the mic. "Go ahead, 637. Joan, please tell me this is a courtesy call, inviting us to enjoy our volleyball game."

"'Fraid not," came Joan's curt voice. "I have two Germans flying in for Tau Camp on an otherwise empty plane. Gwynn, expect stock. They land at 3.15."

So that was the end of that.

I opened my mouth to acknowledge Joan's transmission, when she added softly, "Andrew, what you do with the Germans is your business."

Decisions. Decisions.

Gwynn and I looked at each other for a full minute, saying nothing.

Then Gwynn said, "What German wouldn't enjoy a delicious African barbecue, followed by a night walk to check out the stars?"

"Especially if you kick the event off with a trip down river by *mokoro*. There are some guides hanging around for the volleyball match."

"Wouldn't kill one of them to do some poling."

Easy for Gwynn to say, she'd never poled a *mokoro*.

"It would be the perfect start to the perfect holiday."

"Isn't that what the travel brochures would say?"

I flicked the off-buttons on the two radios. "You get a room cleaned, and I'll fill a cool box with drinks for their trip down river."

Twenty minutes later, our three fridges were bulging with food, and Kurt and Wilhelm were on a *mokoro*, headed for Scops Camp.

The party had already started when Gwynn and I finally walked into Scops. Someone had set up a couple of speakers, blasting the campsite with Bob Marley's *Buffalo Soldier*. It seemed appropriate.

A crowd—the two teams?—clapped and wailed as Robert and Kyle knocked a volleyball back and forth over a net slung between two palm trees. The court itself consisted of a patch of grey sand, peppered with rough grass.

With a marked disinterest in volleyball, Matanta, holding a beer can, stood off to one side. He leered at one of Milly's prettier staff members. She leaned in closer, giggling at something he said. Clearly, his night was sorted.

Back on the court, Robert smashed a serve, sending Kyle scrambling. Smelling potential victory, I punched my fist into the air.

I could have saved the energy.

The ball sailed clean out of the demarcated court area and lodged in a palm tree, far off to the right. Robert was supposed to be our star player. The first inklings of doubt assailed me. Was it possible Tau Camp could be whipped? The humiliation would be worse than my little episode in the river.

I called to Kyle, "You're taking this seriously?"

"Oh yes. You will be thrashed." Like a monkey, he scrambled up the tree to get the ball.

How could I not have noticed how athletic the guy was?

I cleared my throat. Then remembering Englishman was supposed to be pathetic at ball sports, asked hopefully, "I take it E'man's on your team?"

"For sure," came the reassuring answer as Kyle lobbed the ball back to Robert, who fumbled the catch. "E'man. Be a team player and hand my friend a beer."

Now I knew we were in trouble. I cracked the tab on the can, putting the open bit to my ear to hear the fizz, and then reverted to what I do best—humour. "Brilliant goal, Kyle. Listen you can hear the crowd cheering."

A German-sounding guffaw pulled my attention away. Kurt and Wilhelm propped up one end of the bar.

"*Wunderbar!*" one of them—I'm not sure which—shouted, waving a beer can at me. "Four hours ago, we were in a bar in Windhoek in Namibia, and now we are here, in a bar in the Okavango."

"*Ja,*" added the other one. "And thanks for the beers for the river. We drank them before we even reached the camp."

I looked at my new German friends with profound respect. I'd put at least ten beers in that cool box, and it was only a fifteen—twenty, if one goes at a crawl—minute boat ride to Scops.

The sharp trill of a drill whistle rent the air. Milly calling us to order. When no one listened, she yelled at the top her lungs, "Scops Camp! Tau Camp! Get your teams on the court. Now."

No one dared disobey.

I took up position behind Robert—he was a lot bigger than me, so I figured he'd protect me from too much ball damage—and sized up the competition. Apart from Kyle, no one looked particularly menacing, so I relaxed, stepping out to face the first ball.

Milly blew her whistle again and the Tau World Series Challenge was on.

Robert, our team captain, shouted orders no one listened to, and— even with Kyle's moral guidance—Scops Camp cheated openly. It was a total blast, the way team sports should be played. But in the end we had to succumb to the inevitable—Scops Camp beat us by about 700 points.

Sweating and grinning, Robert bowed gracefully to Kyle, and went to grab Matanta—who was grabbing the pretty girl. Robert dragged him away from her, over to the glowing coals in the barbecue. Together, they cooked a succulent fillet steak in mustard sauce. From Milly's kitchen came a salad and a huge pot of *stywe mealie pap*, a crumbly, tasteless corn porridge much beloved by all in southern Africa. All except me, that is. *Pap* is usually served with a tomato and onion *bredie* (an Afrikaans word for stew, also not beloved by me). The meal may not have been the best ever prepared on Noga Island, but it probably ranked high among those served at Scops Camp.

I tipped my glass to Gwynn, toasting the day's success.

"It's not over yet." She gestured at Kurt and Wilhelm, singing raucous German drinking songs at the bar. "We still have to get them home."

True.

It was my turn to drag Matanta away from his two girlfriends—he'd added another girl to his arm since dinner—this time for a quick discussion on travel logistics.

"You go first, *Rra*," Matanta said. "Gwynn and I will come after you. With the Germans." His eyes flickered to his girls, draped around a palm tree, waiting for him.

"So you can finishing making out with Hot and Sultry?" I demanded.

"No, *Rra*," he said, with faked indignation. "I'll catch them later. But we need someone to chase the animals off the runway. And what happens if the hyena is in the camp?"

"And I'm that idiot?" I asked, aggrieved, although I knew he was right. Someone—preferably someone sober—had to make sure it was safe before we took our unsuspecting *lekgoa* home.

Gwynn obviously agreed, because she said, somewhat callously, I thought, "Get the kettle boiling, so we can offer Kurt and Wilhelm some coffee when they get there."

So, orders in hand, I picked up my Maglite, checked its operation—it looked very dull—and headed for Tau. I had not gone far when it dawned on me that I was a lone, suburbanite, white man, walking on a moonless night, along a footpath deep in the African bush with only a twelve-inch torch to protect me. That was also about the time I discovered the major flaw in our plan.

I hadn't had nearly enough to drink.

All my faculties were working faultlessly, including the ones used to distribute fear. So, it didn't matter how hard I tried to blot out the cloying darkness and scary noises, my over-wrought mind happily filled in the blanks. Elephant. Hyena. Maybe even the odd lion. Who knew? Not me, because I could barely see my hand in front of my face.

I wish I could say I walked swiftly, but weeks of elephant depredation on the Scops Camp side of the island had taken its toll. The path was littered with fallen trees, which had been easy to negotiate during the daylight when Gwynn and I had walked to Scops. Now they were like bear-traps, waiting to ensnare me in twisted vines and broken branches. My shins were skinned raw by the time I finally caught the glow of the pale runway sand. Almost home. I took a deep breath to calm my hysterical heart and started jogging.

My relief was premature.

The most horrifying sound I had heard since coming to the Okavango rent the air. Even though I knew exactly what it was, my mind slammed down in denial. I swung around to face this nemesis, my torch beam about as useful as a hammock on a desert island with only one tree.

Still, in the pale beam, I saw IT.

A hippo, as heavy as a locomotive, stood about fifty paces away from me. Only difference is that, unlike locos, hippo are bad tempered and unpredictable. But, thankfully, they also have poor eyesight, so I switched off my torch.

Heart pounding—its sound was drowning out my footsteps, which were drowning out everything else—I ran a short distance into the grass on the side of the strip and crouched low. I had no idea what to do to warn Gwynn and Matanta, so I sat for a while, to think.

The hippo continued munching on the grass opposite me.

Then I heard a less common bush sound: an off-key German drinking song. The broken lyrics continued for a time, gradually getting louder. They were punctuated by violent swearing. One of our new friends must have been tripping over the fallen trees. I choked back a laugh. By the time Gwynn and company reached the runway, the singing was operatic in tone, if not quality.

Then my blood froze.

Gwynn and Matanta had obviously not seen the hippo. Given the interest it was paying them, it was just a matter of time before it charged. Someone, maybe even my wife, could die.

I stood, about to scream a warning, when the singer, striving for a particularly high note, let out a strangled screech. The hippo yelped like a frightened puppy, and then dashed off into the water on the other side of the strip.

I could have cried with relief.

Laughter took over as I watched Kurt, our singer, stumble his way up the strip. It was only thanks to Gwynn's arm slung around this waist that he was still standing.

Wilhelm wasn't doing nearly as well. He was out cold. If Matanta hadn't been dragging him, he'd have fallen by the wayside somewhere along the track.

"Did you hear the hippo?" I asked, when they got within earshot.

"Yes, but we got lucky," Gwynn replied. "Wilhelm's snoring frightened it away."

CHAPTER 38

The morning after the volleyball match started slowly. Understandably, Kurt and Wilhelm didn't stir until breakfast. Once at the table, they made up for lost time by cracking their first beers of the day. A couple of lagers later, they both looked positively radiant. Okay, slight exaggeration, but good enough for Kurt to say, "We came to the Okavango to do some fishing. The lady in the Maun office said you have rods and tackle we can use."

Andrew's eyes brightened. He loved fishing, but never caught a thing. "I'll get you fixed up with some kit after breakfast. Any particular fish on your list?"

Wilhelm burped, and then said, "Tigers, of course. That's what everyone comes to the Africa to catch."

"They are the best fighters," Andrew agreed, "but I think you're being a bit optimistic. I haven't heard of anyone pulling a tiger this far south in the Okavango." Kurt and Wilhelm deflated visibly, so he added, "But I'm pretty sure you'll hook some bream. If they're a good size, bring them back. The chefs will cook them up for you."

"Then let's get the party started," Kurt downed his beer and thumped the can onto the table. We had offered him a glass, but what can I say?

"*Ja,*" Wilhelm added, "Andrew, you must come with us. We insist."

Andrew turned to me with his hands held up in mock defeat. "The word of a guest *is* law."

"Huh," I snorted. "And I suppose you want me to supply the bait for this goof-off?"

"Some of that fillet steak that came in yesterday would do nicely."

I left a very smug Andrew and his new buddies to tackle up.

Once they and the guides had poled out of the bay, I ambled to the kitchen to prepare the menu for Morag's up-coming CIM trip with the twelve Canadians. She was due back today from her recon, and I wanted to be ahead of the game with my planning to avoid any unnecessary conflict.

I was deep in thought when Matanta said: "I think it's time. You are ready, *Mma*."

"For what?" I looked up from my notes to see Robert leaning against the prep-counter. "Shouldn't you be off duty already?" I asked him. He had done the breakfast shift, which had just ended. "You know the Canadians are coming. Then you're out in the bush for a week with just Sam to help you cook. You should grab some time away from work while you can."

"A meeting with your ancestors." Matanta crooned, before Robert could reply. He swung a black leather pouch at me. "I've brought my bones."

His *sangoma* bones! Finally. This was definitely more interesting that my human resources interview with Robert, or Morag's menu. I plunked my clipboard down, and joined Matanta and his bones at the prep-table.

Matanta fondled his pouch lovingly. "My great-grandfather started collecting them. When he died I—" He stopped, looked at me, and then at Robert, and said indignantly, "And what about me? He and Sam are going out to have a holiday in the bush with the *lekgoa*. I'll be alone here in the kitchen doing everything. And I haven't left this camp for over three months."

He was right. But thanks to Morag's and Andrew's insistence that Robert go on CIM, there was nothing I could do about it, so I poked a finger at the pouch. "Tell me more about these."

Matanta yanked the bag away so quickly, you'd think I carried some sort of finger plague.

"My bones are sacred. No *lekgoa* is ever to touch them." He glared at the other staff who had drifted over to watch. "And no dirty little Motswanan fingers are to touch them, either." As one, our entire complement of waiters and dishwashers took a step back. "Now. Silence. Everyone."

You could have heard a cockroach fart in the laundry.

Then Matanta closed his eyes and started chanting. An eerie, almost manic sound, it made the hair on my arms rise. I wasn't the only one in his thrall. The other staff shuffled closer, belief and awe alight on their faces. Finally, with a showman's flourish, Matanta tumbled the contents of the bag onto the counter. A collective gasp went up around me, and I realised, with some surprise, that I had been part of the chorus.

"Study the bones," Matanta intoned. "See how they lie. Hear what the ancestors tell you."

So I did, leaning in for an even better look. Even though I had only seen *sangoma* bones in pictures, these looked like the real deal: odd-shaped, bleached-white animal bones, small stones, and seed-pods. There was even a rusty nail.

Matanta waved his fingers over a particular knobbly bone. "The aardvark speaks." He paused. I opened my mouth to ask what it said, but he lifted a flat hand to silence me. "Your days at the camp will be long." He flicked a camel thorn tree seed pod with a fingernail. "Your husband is a good man. He will become a great chief of many." Another pause. Then he rolled one of the pebbles. "Treasure will find you here." Yet another pause, longer this time.

I waited for more.

Still, Matanta stood with eyes closed, as if deep in conversation with an unseen world. Then I heard a muffled guffaw coming from behind me. I looked over my shoulder to see Robert, spluttering and shaking, as he propped himself up against the stove.

A thought began to dawn. I glanced furtively at the other staff. They were holding their breath, looking pained, clearly at the end of their self-control—and their acting skills. My flush of humiliation started at my forehead, roared down my face, past my throat, and was half-way through my stomach when Matanta burst into raucous laughter.

"You fell for it, *Mma*," he screeched. "You thought you got me when you pretended to cut my arm off, but now I've got you back. Never, ever play with the master." The swine then dropped down onto his haunches, holding his sides with laughter. Moments later he was up on his feet, hand scattering his 'bones' across the prep-table. It was then I noticed the marked resemblance between the aardvark bone and the oxtail I'd consigned for burial.

It was mortifying.

All I could think was to pat Matanta on the arm before making a rapid escape. Cowardly, I know. By the time I reached reception, my humiliation had given way to laughter.

And respect.

Matanta was good. No doubt about it. But I had to be better. And I knew exactly what I needed to do to achieve that honour. When I was finished with him, Matanta would be crying real tears of real pain while the rest of us laughed. I rubbed my hands gleefully, wishing Andrew were back from his fishing trip so we could put my plan into operation.

Lunchtime saw the return of the fishermen. Kurt was the only one dragging in a fish. I'm not exaggerating when I say 'dragging.' His catch was well over a yard long, with a head about as thick as a rugby player's thigh.

"Congratulations, a barbel," I said, tweaking the whiskers protruding from the monster's flattened nose. "So ugly, only their mothers can love them. I thought you guys were after bream. No one is going to eat this thing."

"And that is where you're wrong." Andrew stuck a hand into the fish's gills to help Kurt with the weight. "Alfred specifically asked me to bring him back a barbel if we caught one."

"What on Earth for?" I asked, unable to grasp why anyone would want this almost prehistoric looking bottom-dweller.

"For lunch." Andrew grinned at my revulsion. "Yes, I know. Amazing. Apparently he loves the green flesh and muddy taste."

It takes all types, I guess. But then who was I to argue when Alfred's barbel sounded—and looked—just like some of the high-class meat decomposing in The Cupboard? So, while he cooked his delicacy over an open flame in the laundry, Andrew and I sat down to lunch with our guests.

I immediately told them about Matanta's trick on me.

"That should not go unchallenged. Matanta will be running this place if you guys aren't careful," Kurt joked, half-warningly.

"With a beer in one hand, and a girl waiting for him in every cottage," Wilhelm added.

"That's why I have a plan," I said. "Only problem is that it includes Robert. He might not play along with me because of—" I covered my mouth with my hand, and coughed under my breath, "Morag."

"Hmm. But he may do it for me," Andrew said, eyeing me thoughtfully. "Tell me what you have in mind, and I'll see if I can bring him over to our side." Clearly, he also saw the opportunity this presented to break some of the ties between Robert and Morag.

"You mean the dark side." Kurt cracked open another beer, little understanding the depths the office politics he was wading into.

By the end of lunch, we had fine-tuned the plan for bringing Matanta to his knees, and Robert onto the dark side.

Then, almost as if she knew we were plotting against her, Morag and her small flotilla of *mekoro* sailed into the bay. My lunch—a delicious coronation chicken with rice salad—turned to acid in my stomach as her dark pall stretched across the camp.

Reluctantly, I followed Andrew to the bay to welcome her home. That didn't stop the mantra 'only two more days and she'll be gone again' from racing through my mind as I listened to her babble on endlessly about her adventure.

CHAPTER 39

It had been a hectic day and it was only eleven in the morning. Our new Canadian guests sat in the lounge—far away from the smoke billowing from Kurt and Wilhelm's enormous cigars—watching me, Morag, Robert, Sam, and the guides load up the *mekoro* for their CIM. Things were running late and their departure was now a couple of hours behind schedule. Feeling the pressure, I wedged a pile of camp chairs into a *mokoro* when Gwynn appeared. She looked worried.

"Woodie's face has exploded."

I dropped the chairs. "What?"

"She's got a huge bulge on her cheek. She needs a vet."

Timing, why did it always suck?

I sighed, running my hands across my face. The logistics of getting her to a vet in Maun, treated, and then returned to us were complex. Then a thought struck. Did they even have vets in Maun who dealt with domestic pets? It seemed unlikely.

While I was musing, Morag lashed out with a sharp, "How do you propose doing that, Gwynn? The pilots won't take kindly to having a yowling cat on board. Neither will the Maun office."

Gwynn's fists clenched and she opened her mouth to reply. I got in before she could fire off a shot. "The pilots are great; they won't mind helping out. And it's Verity's job to look after the camp managers. Gwynn, give Maun a call."

I listened with half an ear as Gwynn spoke to Joan. Call complete, she came back to the bay, looking even glummer than before. I tossed down the bag I was manhandling and waited for an explanation.

"She leaves today at four. Joan will take care of it all for me." I gave Morag an I-told-you-so glare, but Gwynn wasn't finished speaking. "Problem is, she's going out on an unscheduled incoming flight."

Morag forgotten, I faced Gwynn. "Who's flying in on it?"

Gwynn sighed. "Sandy. Her baby. A couple of nannies. Sandy's friend. And the two boys. The noisy ones we met at Sean's house."

So, it was finally happening. A visit from Sandy. The temptation to join Morag on her CIM was almost overwhelming. I suppressed it and the scream of frustration threatening to explode from my chest. Emotions on a tight rein, I turned back to the *mokoro* I was supposed to be packing.

It seemed Gwynn wasn't finished dispensing bad news. "Don't forget we have a plane arriving in five minutes. More Italians."

Italians? Just what I needed. But right then, I didn't care. I wriggled a cooler box into the *mokoro*, and grunted, "Handle it." I hoped my temper cooled off by the time they arrived.

It had, and I caught my first glimpse of our three new Italian guests at lunch. One of them, a round, almost bald man in his mid-sixties, chatted to Wilhelm as he helped himself to a huge plate of spaghetti bolognese. I thought it brave of Gwynn to offer pasta to Italians, and was about to make a witty crack about it, when she grabbed my hand, pulling me to one side.

"That's Giuseppe," she giggled, pointing to the balding man. "When Kamanga met him on the runway, he gasped, and then scurried off to find a wider *mokoro*."

I could see why. Giuseppe could have gone in his creased chinos and polo shirt to a costume party, called himself a beer barrel, and no one would have been any the wiser. I stepped over to him and extended my hand in greeting.

"Ah!" he enthused in a lilting Italian accent, and then planted a kiss on each of my cheeks. My proffered hand fell limply to my side. "You must be Andrew, our charming hostess's husband. Delighted to meet you." He bowed. "Call me Giuseppe." He waved a pudgy arm at the equally barrel-shaped, sixty-something chap standing next to him. "And this is Guido. The beer king of Italy."

I swallowed hard, wondering if Giuseppe was cranking my chain.

But Guido also bobbed a bow, and then winked, his eye almost disappearing into the folds in his face. "In my past, Giuseppe, in my past. Today, I find myself in good company. My friend Giuseppe, here, was the pasta king of Italy."

I looked at the third Italian. In contrast, he was so skinny he could have crawled through a piece of macaroni without touching the sides. He smiled an even thinner smile. "My friends have recently retired from the

Beer and Pasta Associations in Italy."

That made sense, if looks were anything to go by. "And you?" I asked.

"Franco." He, at least, didn't kiss me, and instead, held out a hand for a shake. "I? I am nothing."

"Ha! Nothing but a liar," Giuseppe declared, slinging an arm around my shoulder. "Franco is a prosecuting attorney. By necessity, he does a lot of work in Sicily."

The Mafia! This should make for good conversation around the dinner table. I turned to Franco. "I bet you've met some real charmers."

Robert De Niro would have envied his shrug. "Guilty or innocent, they're all scum. When God designed hell, he had those guys in mind."

An unpleasant vision of four other perfectly turned-out Italians floated before my eyes, and I couldn't help asking, "Are you sure you guys are from Italy?"

Giuseppe laughed, and then turned to his friends. "I think our host has had a bad experience. Tell me, where were the other Italians from?"

"Rome."

"Ooh!" came a collective moan of commiseration, and three sets of hands pointed skyward.

"Next time you order Italian, make sure it comes from Milan." Giuseppe grinned down at the spaghetti spilling off his plate. "Now, time for a product test."

I heard Gwynn groan, and I smiled. It was my turn to spread the pain around. As I poured the wine, I watched Giuseppe taking his first forkful of Matanta's best. After slurping in the noodles, he chewed, rolling them around in his mouth, then his eyes closed and his face lifted. Rubbing his fingers together, he finally breathed, *"Bellissimo."* Having decent guests in camp was certainly going to help when Sandy arrived.

CHAPTER 40

Sandy. I had just got rid of one witch and now, if what I had been told were true, I was expecting another. This just wasn't fair.

Remembering how Sandy had tormented Barbara, after lunch, the staff and I gave the kitchen a thorough scrub down. Not that it made any discernible difference. It still looked as grimy and rundown as always. I braced myself for Sandy's ire.

The sound of the approaching Islander grew loud in the sky. Heart heavy with worry about my job and my cat, I packed up Woodie for her trip into Maun. She slumped in our wardrobe, her right eye lost in the livid, plum-sized ball growing out of her face. I instantly felt guilty. If I'd spent more time with her, I'd have found this sore before it exploded into an abscess. But, off-duty time was a luxury, and I usually spent it catching up on much needed sleep. Aching over my neglect, I gently eased Woodie into her cat box—she was too sick to even protest—and headed to the runway to meet the boss's wife.

The Islander touched down at exactly four o'clock. I knelt down and whispered comforting words to Woodie while the pilot taxied to a stop. The door flew open, and I left Andrew to greet Sandy and her brood. My whole focus was on getting Woodie safely on board.

I handed the pilot the cat box. "Wes, no more free Cokes, ever, for as long as you draw breath if anything happens to my cat between here and Joan's loving hands."

"Joan's loving hands? Crikey, Gwynn have you actually met her?"

"Okay," I admitted. "She can be a little crusty, but she's promised to take care of Woodie. That makes her my new best friend."

Wes took the cat box. "You're about as deep as a teaspoon." I grinned to hide my tears. Wes must have seen a glisten or two, because he crushed me in a one-armed hug. "If it goes pear-shaped with Joan,

Woodie can spend the night at my place. I'll get her to the vet for you."

I brushed away a tear, gave a tremulous smile, and then steeled myself to face Sandy.

Andrew joined me, his face a picture of incredulity. "She came in an Islander," he groused, "but she's got so much junk, Sepei couldn't even squeeze a ball of *mabinda* twine on board. Have Sean and Sandy no idea of the daily struggle we have with stock?"

I could see why he was so indignant as a veritable mountain of suitcases, baby cots, high chairs, a couple of tricycles, fishing gear, and a crate load of toys sprang up on the runway.

"How long is she staying for exactly?" Andrew demanded, now looking decidedly panicked.

"Unknown," I whispered, moving over to greet her. Pity Morag wasn't here to keep her entertained—and out of my hair.

"I trust you've organised a guide?" came Sandy's opening salvo.

"Two. We thought you would double up with one of the boys, while your friend—" Name unknown. "Um. . .went out with your other son."

Sandy rolled her eyes. "I only wanted one. Send Lecir home."

I looked over to where Karomona and Lecir stood politely to one side. Lecir's face crumpled as Sandy spoke. The guides freelanced and only got paid if they worked. I felt so sorry for him, I pointed to the mound of luggage. "A Coke in exchange for helping us shift this lot into the camp."

He answered by heaving the baby cot and one of the tricycles onto his shoulders.

"That's mine!" one of the boys, the eldest one with a faced blurred by freckles, wailed. He was about six.

"No! It's mine," his little brother bellowed back, showing a mouth missing a whole lot of teeth.

"S'not," Freckles yelled, shoving him in the chest.

The little guy reeled onto the strip. All credit to Toothless, he wiped off his tears, and leapt to his feet. His little fists were clenched, ready to pummel Freckles. Freckles' fist shot out first, and Toothless landed in an ungainly heap.

I looked over at Sandy. Standing with her friend, she seemed oblivious of the Noga Island Featherweight Championship being staged two feet from her nose.

Just then, her baby, cradled in a nanny's arms, let rip an almighty scream. Anyone would think it had been stung by a bee. The birds in the trees stop chirping, mid-song. Some took flight. Even the baboons, watching the plane from across the strip, bolted back into the bush.

So *that* was the answer to the baboon problem. Bring a few babies into camp.

I wondered if it would work on the hyena. The laundry ladies would be only too happy to oblige for an experiment. I was always sending their babies, sneaked into the camp just as the guests were heading off for afternoon naps, back to the babysitters camped out at Otter Lodge.

But for all that Megaphone's scream silenced a few square miles of Okavango bush, it had little effect on her fighting brothers. Or her mother, who still seemed oblivious to all her kids' antics.

Toothless now planted a kick on Freckles' shin, making him squeal. Freckles lunged forward, for what he probably hoped would be the *coup de grace,* a finger in the eye. Karomona swooped in. He scooped Freckles up, swung him onto his shoulders, and started for the camp.

Toothless immediately wailed for someone to carry him, too.

It was going to be a long and trying visit.

* * *

Sandy had been in camp for a full day. It felt like a week. Although she'd complained about the lighting in her cottage, I was still to hear anything from her about the rest of the camp, housekeeping, and catering. It was like balancing on a guillotine, waiting for the blade to fall.

But, despite my tense anticipation, her only priorities seemed to be to ignore her children's bad behaviour and consume vast quantities of gin and tonic.

She and her friend—still unnamed—commandeered the lounge, spreading sun hats, magazines, clothing, swimming towels, and shoes across every chair, sofa, and table surface, making it impossible for any other guests to find a comfortable seat. Every time I sent the waiters in to clean up, Sandy sent them packing.

She was not my only frustration.

I had yet to hear anything from Joan about Woodie's health, even though I hadn't strayed more than five feet from the radio since the plane had taken off. Had Woodie made it to the vet? Could the vet do anything to help her? When would she be home?

Unable to stand the suspense, I finally radioed Joan.

From her tone, I quickly surmised that she had been avoiding me. "Letter about your cat is in the mail," she said. "Should get it on the next flight."

"The next flight? But that's tomorrow. What's happening now?"

Joan keyed the mic and I heard her sigh. Then her voice softened into despairing kindness. "Gwynn, if your cat had been a cow or a goat, the vet may have been able to help."

My stomach imploded and my knees trembled. "What are you saying? Is she. . .dead?"

"Not yet. It's just that the local vets don't deal in Siamese cats. But they do know enough to predict that her abscess is life threatening."

I slumped down onto the ochre-coloured concrete floor in reception. "What do I do, Joan?" Never before in my life had I felt so isolated, so cut off from all that mattered. It took me a moment to remember to take my finger off the mic key so Joan could reply.

"If it were my cat, I'd send her to Johannesburg." Joan's voice sounded as if it was coming from a great distance away. It was. So far away from all help, all hope. "Is there someone I can send her to? I can have her on a plane tomorrow."

I rubbed my face, vaguely aware of tears streaming down my cheeks. "Will she survive until then?"

"Who knows? Give me a number to call in Joburg, and I'll get it sorted out for you."

So much for Joan being crusty. She was now my life-line, my true best friend. I mumbled off my parents' home number, while my mind grappled with one thought: Would I ever see Woodie again?

As if she could read my mind, Jean said, "Bringing a city cat into the African bush probably wasn't the smartest thing you could do."

I wasn't about to argue, even though the African bush had nothing to do with Woodie's plight. That was all Tom. Her abscess was the result of one of his attacks. I left reception, headed for the privacy of my cottage, where I planned to sob into my pillow until lunchtime.

I had only taken a couple of steps when my foot squelched down into something mushy and foul-smelling. I looked down—and swore. A stark naked Toothless, toy airplane in hand, sat in the dust next to a urine puddle. It had a strategically placed turd perched in the middle of it. The poop I had just stood in.

Cursing Sandy and her children for further ruining my day, I took off my soiled shoe, and hobbled to the laundry to find a member of the maintenance team to do a clean-up job of the offending dung pile. I could just picture one of our charming Italians or Germans falling unsuspecting into the same trap.

By the time I'd cleaned my shoe, supervised the poop disposal unit, tracked down a nanny to put some clothes on Toothless, and placated Wilhelm and Kurt about the vile smell wafting into the lounge from his indiscretion, where they were smoking their equally vile cigars, it was time to serve the midday meal.

Thoroughly ticked off with life, I joined Matanta in the kitchen to help put the finishing touches on lunch.

He flicked a tired-looking dishtowel at a fly and said, "Only six more days until Robert gets back from his CIM. Then I go on leave." He stretched, clicking his neck, as if releasing bottled tension. A miasma of exhaustion hung over him.

My own worries forgotten for a split second, I felt guilty about the trick Andrew, Robert, and I had concocted to play once Robert got back from the CIM. But then I remembered the oxtail bones, and my heart turned to flint. "Counting the days, huh?" I asked innocently, waving my hand at another fly, intent on the crabmeat salad.

"*Em, Mma*, you have no idea." He eased the salad onto Kekgebele's tray. "My friends and I are taking a motorboat from Maun to Jugujugu."

"Where?"

"Jugujugu? It's a few hours upriver. We're going to spend the week eating, drinking and sleeping—" he leered "—with girls. Lots of girls."

"Better not let Meshu hear about that. Or Impeleng."

Matanta gave me cocky smile. "Both my sweet girlfriends will be safe at home with their babies."

"*Your* babies," I corrected, as Kekgebele carried the tray out.

"Details, *Mma*. Details."

Why did I like this guy so much? When all was said and done, Matanta was a complete dog when it came to women. He just did charming so well. I changed the subject. "I guess you wouldn't want to miss your leave."

His face paled at the thought. "I've dreamt about this trip for months. Getting all my friends together at the same time has been a big *matata*. But you know me," he rubbed his palms together, "I'm Torn Trousers. I can scheme things."

I slapped him on the back, hiding my smile at his cockiness crashing and burning when Robert returned in six days' time. "I'm sure you can. Now, I better get everyone eating this crab salad before the maggots start crawling out of it."

Shuffling leaden feet, I made my way to the dining room just as Karomona's *mokoro* slid into the bay. He and Freckles had been out fishing. Somewhere along the way, Freckles had lost all his clothing. He jumped out of the *mokoro* butt-naked. Squealing with delight, he scooped something up out of the bottom of the boat.

A small dead fish covered in ants.

Lovely.

Before I could suggest he throw it back into the water to feed the wildlife, he bolted into the dining room, where the guests and Sandy were assembling.

I opened my mouth to protest, but Andrew sidled up to me and grabbed my hand. "It's Sandy's problem, not ours," he whispered in my ear.

"But these are our guests," I whispered back, watching the Italians and Germans shooting askance looks in Freckles' direction.

"Correction. They're Sandy's guests. She and Sean own the place, remember?"

Although it burned my butt to see a naked kid parading around with a smelly, dead, ant-infested fish in the dining room, Andrew was right. Through clenched teeth, I invited everyone to help themselves to the food.

Plate in one hand and glass of wine in the other, Sandy took Andrew's and my chair at the head of the table. Hope sprang up in my bosom. Maybe she would use that elevated position to discipline Freckles.

How could I have been so naive?

Fish firmly clutched, Freckles clambered up onto the table right between the seated guests. After giving us a quick flash of his anus, he sat gazing into space, one hand absentmindedly fondling the wrinkled skin on his scrotum.

Giuseppe's knife and fork dropped from his hands. He jerked back in his chair, and folded his arms across his chest. Face aggrieved, he turned to stare at Sandy.

She took another sip of her wine, between chatting with her friend.

I now had little trouble believing the guest report about Sandy that Barbara had shown us so many months ago. What little respect I had for the boss's wife vanished in a puff of smoke.

She couldn't leave quickly enough.

This was the first of three Sandy-and-kids visits we endured. Sadly, none of them got any better. She never did comment on the camp, the cleanliness, the staff, or our relationship with Morag. It was as if all our efforts, both good and bad, were for naught.

CHAPTER 41

After four days of torment, Sandy finally returned to Maun, leaving a bitter taste in our mouths and a dread in our stomachs for her inevitable return.

The Italians and Germans left, too. Giuseppe's parting words seemed pithy: "You have a beautiful place here, Andrew, and the best intentions of running it well. But with such a boss! She flushes the wonder away with her excrement." Harsh words from a man who did nothing but gush praise for even the tiniest pleasure.

Now the camp was empty while we awaited the return of Morag and her twelve Canadians. They were expected at any moment.

Gwynn and I took advantage of the respite to enjoy the winter flood. Despite being the dry season, winter in the Okavango means rising water levels. News from the towns further north said the floods were looking good, and might even be better than recent years. We had nothing to compare it to, but that didn't mean that we couldn't enjoy the bounty the waters brought.

At breakfast, I'd spotted hundreds of birds, mostly giant white egrets and herons, lining the channel outside the camp. The water boiled with the rise and fall of countless fish. The barbel run had begun, and the birds were feasting.

As ugly as they were, barbel had an extraordinary defence against drought. They'd dig themselves into burrows in the drying riverbed. Once hidden, they created a protective slime cocoon around their bodies. They could remain in stasis for years. When rains returned, they emerged from their slippery hibernation to swim and spawn. As the floods arrived, they swam vigorously into every expanse of the delta.

With no guests to host, Gwynn and I commandeered a *mokoro*, and, using my still mediocre poling skills, I pushed us out into the channel. The water was black with fish.

"Are you going to stick your hand in?" I asked, knowing how squeamish Gwynn was about barbel. I lowered my hand into the seething mass to make a point.

Face contorted with disgust, Gwynn dipped her hand in, too. "Ugh, it's so slimy," she moaned, quickly pulling away. "This is a sight best enjoyed from a distance. Ideally with drink in hand."

She had a point. I love fishing and fish, but even I had to admit that the fish bumping my hand were gross. To add to the creepiness, a forest of tendrils—the barbels—rose to the surface. The white gums of countless gaping mouths gulped at the air. I grinned at her. "And to think the water for that drink would have come straight out of the river—home to all these fish."

"Disgusting, when you think about it."

I sat back in the *mokoro* and got some splendid photos of the pristine white birds stalking their prey.

* * *

It was show time.

Robert and the rest of CIM crew headed down the river towards camp. The flight due any moment would take both Matanta and Morag to Maun for their leave.

Gwynn kept shooting me cryptic smiles as Matanta paced the bay. He had dumped his uniform in favour of a cool pair of jeans, a brightly coloured shirt decked with palm trees, and a pair of sparkling white Nikes. Mirrored sunglasses, perched on top of his head, completed his ensemble. His packed bag lay at his feet.

I felt for him. Despite his snazzy clothes, he looked shattered from working non-stop, both day and night, for over four months. For the last week, all he'd spoken about was his planned boat trip to Jugujugu with his mates.

Still, he was the master prankster who gave no quarter with the endless jokes he played on everyone. Although none of the other staff knew of our plan, I guessed it would have found instant support if they had.

Matanta let out a girlish squeal. "I see them! I see them! Right on time." His hips did a twisty sort of dance. "Let the party begin." He swept his hand around to give me a high-five.

"I'm happy for you," I said, my voice betraying none of the mirth bubbling under the surface.

Then a thought struck. It had been almost ten days since we'd hatched our plan with Robert. Would he even remember? I gnawed my lip, wondering how I could jog his memory. For that, I needed Matanta to leave, so I could have a private chat with Robert. But judging by the way Matanta was prancing around the edge of the bay, that wasn't going to happen. I was about to suggest to Gwynn that she distract him, when the flotilla of *mekoro* turned off the main channel and surged into our little lagoon.

Too late for any diversions.

So, ignoring Morag and the Canadian guests, my eyes locked on Robert. Focused on climbing out of his *mokoro*, he didn't acknowledge me.

Matanta rushed over to shake Robert's hand. "You're back. Now I can go." Again that hip shimmy he did so well.

Robert didn't take Matanta's proffered hand. Instead, his face collapsed into a deep grimace of pain.

He'd remembered!

I smiled, holding my breath.

"Matanta," Robert said in a quavering voice. "The CIM. . .it was tough. I'm a camp chef, not a bush chef, and my back. . ." Both hands rubbed his lower back. "It's buggered from sleeping on tree roots. Man, they killed me." His voice quivered some more, and even I wondered if this was an act, or if his pain was real. "I'm sorry, Matanta *Rra*, but I need the doctor. I have to go to Maun today."

Matanta's face blanched. There was only one available seat on the aircraft, as he well knew. His hand shot up to rub his hair, bumping his sunglasses off his head. They tumbled into the water. He didn't even notice. Then his fingers tugged at his straggly beard. "Painkillers, maybe?" he pleaded. "Booze?" His eye caught Sam, the enema-giving-trouble-making-cooking-priest-guide. "Pipe up the bum?"

"Sorry, man, but I can hardly walk." Robert punctuated his words with a slow, painful hobble up the bank. He was putting so much heart into his display, I couldn't help but wonder how many times Matanta had caught him in practical jokes. "I promise, Matanta *Rra*, I will only be in Maun for one day. I'll get an injection and be on the flight back tomorrow."

Matanta's eyes seemed to spin in his head. "That doesn't help me. My boat leaves this afternoon. I can't hold up my friends. They also only have a few days before they have to get back to work." They must have been desperate for this holiday if they were all willing to risk being on the river in the evening when the hippos were at their most aggressive.

Robert threw up his hands.

Matanta let out a long, tired sigh, and then turned to stare out north, in the direction of Jugujugu. A thousand emotions washed across his face. Finally, shoulders sagging, he muttered, "Your health comes before my leave. Take my place on the flight." Despondency bleeding from every pore, he lumbered back to the kitchen.

Robert turned to Gwynn and me and winked. Then he called out to Matanta. "Be a friend and help me to the runway. I can hardly walk."

Matanta paused mid-step, and I wondered if he'd tell Robert to go drown himself. But he turned, managed a tired smile, and came back to sling his arm around Robert's broad shoulders. "Bob, if you lost a few kilos—like about thirty—maybe your back wouldn't give you so much trouble, and roots wouldn't be such a *matata*."

Robert moaned painfully—probably to hide his laughter.

I picked up Matanta's bag and slung it over my shoulder. Smiles firmly suppressed behind faked worried frowns, Gwynn and I walked behind Matanta as he part-carried, part-dragged Robert to the airstrip. The short journey through the camp took so long the Cessna had already touched down when we arrived. Tears gleamed in Matanta's eyes as he helped Robert towards the open door. Matanta was about to heave him up into the seat when he stopped and looked around.

"Your bags?" Matanta asked. "What are you going to wear in Maun? You can't go dressed in this." He poked a disparaging finger at Robert's soiled uniform. "No girl will even look at you."

"Girls? Is that all you ever think about?" I dropped Matanta's bag at Robert's feet.

Matanta's eyes widened and his hands—supposed to be holding Robert upright—flew into the air. "No, Andrew *Rra*! There are limits. Even for me. I'll give up my leave for him, but Robert is *not* wearing *my* clothes in Maun."

Without his support, Robert stumbled, falling onto his knees. He cried out in agony as if the impact had crushed every bone in his back.

"*Eish!*" Matanta moaned. "I'm sorry. You can have my clothes. Anything."

Robert caught my eye and, from the mirth threatening to boil over his face, I guessed this joke had just about run its course.

Gwynn stepped right into Matanta's personal space. "About the oxtail bones you threw for me." Matanta looked at her blankly. "And the time you told Andrew the camp had an electric winch for unblocking toilets so he didn't need to use his hands—"

"Forget that," Robert interrupted. "What about the time you told me my father had died when he hadn't, and I stole a *mokoro* to go to

Maun because there was no place on the flights for me? The Wildlife guys wanted to lock me in jail and you were going to let them!"

Matanta's eyes widened, perhaps with dawning understanding.

"Well, gotcha," Gwynn said, grinning.

The usual crowd of laundry and scullery ladies, maintenance men and guides standing at the strip—who had all been victims of Matanta's pranks at some point—burst into cheers, laughter, and clapping. They had got the joke, even if Matanta was still being a little slow to catch on.

He turned to Robert. "So your back? It's fine?"

"Never better. And make any more cracks about me needing to lose weight, and I'll skin you and feed you to the hyena."

A slow smile spread across Matanta's face. Then he dropped to his haunches and his shoulders began to shake with laughter. Finally, rubbing tears from his eyes, he clapped both Gwynn and me on the backs. "I must learn a lesson from this. I don't know what the lesson is yet, but I do know one thing."

"And that is?" I asked.

"I'm afraid of you both."

"And me?" Robert demanded. "It was my acting that made the magic."

"Pff," Matanta snorted. "You're just a lump of lard."

CHAPTER 42

Like Matanta and the rest of the staff, we needed time off work, too. In terms of our contract with Sean, after every three months worked, we earned a ten-day break. As we had to pay for our flights back home, if we chose to go there, any break needed to be well thought out.

As it turned out, my brother, Simon, made the first decision for us. Just prior to our three month mark in June, a letter arrived announcing his wedding. It was to take place in Johannesburg, six weeks after our first break was due.

"What do you think?" I said to Gwynn after reading it to her. "Do you want to take our break now, or wait another six weeks so we can throw confetti at them?"

"Would it be churlish if I said I wanted to throw something heavier and far more painful?" she asked.

I understood how she felt. We were both exhausted from three months of solid work and the prospect of adding another month and a half wasn't thrilling. Also, I had been writing my 4x4 vehicle guidebook in my spare time, such as it was, and the lack of sufficient electrical power to run my computer was a constant frustration. I planned to buy my own solar panel and battery during our leave to power my Mac. That would have to wait, too. Still, he was my brother and family was important. So I said, "Another six weeks probably won't kill us."

Gwynn snorted.

I knew she wanted to go home to check on Woodie. From the last two letters from her mother, we'd learned that she'd had had a couple of operations to drain her face. For days, it had been touch and go. Post-ops,

Woodie's recovery, punctuated by flares of infection, had been slow. Gwynn was now on tenterhooks to hear if the latest round of antibiotics had kicked in. Letters took a painfully long time to reach the Okavango Delta.

I expected her to comment on Woodie, but instead she said, "I guess it all depends on who we have in camp." I knew she was referring to Sandy and her bunch because a day didn't pass when we didn't dread the announcement of another visit. Gwynn grabbed the clipboard with the booking sheets and started flipping through them. "All clear. Unless they come unannounced again." Her teeth gnawed the inside of her mouth. "But that can't happen because we're chock-a-block full for the next six weeks. Not a spare bed for anyone." She sighed and then clunked her forehead with the clipboard. "Why oh why did Simon plan his wedding so badly? And why did Woodie have to get sick?"

"She's having the best care possible," I said, hoping she'd agree to extend our time. I really wanted to be at the wedding.

Gwynn glared at me.

"Hey," I said. "Look at the bright side. A full camp means no room for Morag. She'll have to stay at Scops."

The tiniest grin crossed Gwynn's face. "Where she can plague and torment Kyle and Milly. Oooh, I do like full camps."

"She'll have to come here during the day to run her school," I warned.

Morag had started the guide school Sean had employed her to run. The lessons on bird identification and animal lore took place at Tau Camp, an attempt, I think, by Sean to impress his guests with his progressiveness. She had asked me more than once to pitch in and help her teach the guides, but I had declined. The joy it would have given me wasn't worth the strife it would have caused.

"Yes," Gwynn agreed, "but if I juggle my day carefully, I won't have to see her until lunchtime. Even I can probably cope with only seeing her for an hour a day." Obviously now feeling magnanimous, she conceded, "Write and tell Simon we'll be at his wedding."

And that's how we got rid of Morag and Hazel for a while. And ended up working eighteen hours a day, seven days a week for five months straight. The only thing that made that kind of insanity possible—and pleasurable—was the wonder of our ever-changing world.

About a week after my letter had gone off to my brother, I was sitting in reception working on my paperwork when Gwynn stormed in, looking wild-eyed and breathless.

"Where's my 24mm lens?" she gushed, "I need to take a photo of an elephant."

I rolled my eyes. Ever since I'd met Gwynn, I'd been trying to teach her photography—I even went so far as to buy her a fancy camera. She never got past the basics, but this was pathetic, even for her. Without bothering to look up from my work, I said, "You don't use a wide angle lens to photograph elephants."

"You do with this one." She grabbed her camera bag from under the desk and bolted from the room.

This I had to see. I chucked down my pencil and followed her to cottage number eight—and almost soiled my underwear. An elephant the size of a small house stood no more than ten paces away from us. It eyed the nuts in the palm trees overhead.

"Good lens choice," I muttered. "Now get the shot before he stomps on us."

I heard Gwynn's camera click and pulled her back a few steps, only to hear a trumpeting coming from behind. I spun—and looked right up at a beetle-black eye set in a wrinkled grey cheek. My heart— already beating like a jack hammer—attacked my rib cage.

We were surrounded by elephants.

I was plotting an exit strategy that wouldn't get us charged, crushed, or leaned on, when I heard a scream coming up the path. Again, I pivoted, this time to see Matanta racing towards us. Back from his leave, he had more energy than a nuclear warhead.

"*Tlou*," Matanta shouted at the top of his lungs. "In the camp. Everyone come, see."

His shouts emptied the laundry and kitchen of staff. Even a few guests joined in to witness the arrival of our first elephants.

The elephants, clearly offended at having their morning spoiled by noisy tourists, snorted a bit, but didn't hang around. Feet pounding, they broke cover and headed out of the camp, back onto the runway. There they stopped and looked at us.

Matanta grinned at me. "Ever touched an elephant's butt, *Rra*?"

"No. You?" I asked, grinning at him.

"Me neither. But I'm about to."

Before I could think of how to stop him, Matanta burst into a sprint towards our little bachelor herd. I can't even begin to imagine what the elephants thought about this mad man running full tilt towards them. But, whatever it was, they weren't hanging around to find out. They took off across the runway, skidding to a stop at the line of trees our baboons lived in.

Who knows what Matanta had been smoking—his mattress maybe—but he raced after them. As three of the four elephants fled into the bush, Matanta reached out a hand to flick a retreating tail.

It was an affront which elephant number four would not forgive. Ears pressed hard back against its enormous skull, he turned and charged straight for Matanta.

Laughing like the village idiot, Matanta wheeled round and raced back across the runway with the elephant at his heels. Everyone— including Gwynn and I—scattered as the wild pair approached the camp.

Matanta burst through the trees onto the pathway leading to our house—and the elephant stopped. Trumpeting furiously, it kicked up a cloud of dust before prancing back across the runway to join his mates.

I smacked Matanta on the side of the head. "Are you stupid? I need a chef tonight!"

Sweat pouring down his face, he laughed triumphantly and held his hand up in the air. A few strands of coarse elephant tail hairs blew in the breeze. "All my life, I've wanted to do that. Now I can die happy." He kissed his fingertips and then opened his hand, letting the hair blow away in the wind.

"Whatever floats your *mokoro*, Matanta," I said, rolling my eyes.

CHAPTER 43

The arrival of the elephants was timely because we had a group of guests in camp who were passionate about another of Africa's treasures—the rhino. These folk, a mix of seventeen Australian and English cricket lovers, were here to support the Save the Rhino Foundation. The idea being that they paid a bucket load of cash to the charity for the privilege of spending a few days in the bush with a cricket hero. The man in question: David Gower, one-time English cricket captain who led England to victory in the Ashes cricket tournament against Australia. The Ashes were an annual series of matches in which England and Australia each sent fifteen fleet-footed, nimble-handed sportsmen to do battle.

The term Ashes was first used after England lost to Australia on home soil back in 1882. The next day, the *Sporting Times* carried a mock obituary of English cricket which concluded that: "The body will be cremated and the ashes taken to Australia." A few weeks later, an English team set off for a series in Australia. Bligh, the English captain, vowed to return home with the ashes. His counterpart was equally as determined to defend them. At the end of the tour, the Australians awarded Bligh a small terracotta urn as a symbol of what he came to claim. Almost a hundred years later in the early nineties, a fancy trophy entered the fray. England and Australia have been waging cricket war over it ever since. Cricket being the only team sport I'm even vaguely interested in, this was my chance to, if not join the Balmy Army, at least be a stupid English supporter.

It was their first day in camp. We had long since finished lunch but, despite Gwynn's imploring eyes and the waiters' vain attempt to evict us from the dining room, we were not budging. David Gower had us rapt, listening to a ball-by-ball account of his winning innings that had sent the Australians limping back to the dressing room, and took the Ashes trophy back to England.

He stopped to sip his drink, giving Phil, the tour organiser, the chance to ask, "Is there anywhere we could set up a pitch for a game of cricket?"

A rumble of approval rippled across the table.

I snorted a laugh. "You've just landed on it, but the outfield needs a mow. Did you bring a bat?"

His eyebrows shot up. "Ah! I knew there was something I forgot to pack."

"Anyone else?" I asked, looking around the table. Seventeen heads shook in unison. Man, this lot was unprepared. And I really fancied playing cricket with David Gower. It was something I could tell my grandkids—if Gwynn and I ever got to have sex again. I stood up. "Leave it with me. I'll devise something."

"Oh, and a ball as well," Phil added.

I glared at him. "Now you really are pushing it."

"We have absolute faith in you, mate," one the Australians said. "In fact, so much so, I think we should start dividing up the teams."

"Surely that's obvious," David said. "It's the English against the Aussies."

"Are you sure that's wise?" I asked over my shoulder as I headed out to find something we could use to hit one of Hazel's many chewed tennis balls Morag had left at the camp before moving to Scops.

My steps took me to a clump of palm trees in the centre of the camp. One of our visiting elephants had nudged a tree, knocking down branches. I selected a nice sturdy one and headed for my workshop. Bow-saw in hand, I cut off the fronds and then used my Swiss Army knife to carve something that looked a bit like a bat out of the soft wood. All it needed was black insulation tape around the handle to take the edge off the spiky grip. Then it was back to the dining room, where the guests still occupied the chairs, making Lesego's life difficult. A roar of approval greeted my offering and, again in unison—had they been practicing?—our guests headed straight for the runway. After making sure no planes were due, I set two camp chairs up as wickets.

Then the game was on.

In all honesty, it wasn't that different from the volleyball match. Nobody was doing much of anything but laughing at the pitch and joking with David, who was being altogether childish. No teams. Just mucking about. However, I am proud to announce that, while I have the hand-eye coordination of a silkworm, I scored a run, and got bowled out by the great David Gower.

Back in the dressing room—the anthill next to the strip—I had an idea. It led me to the bar, where I selected a small whiskey bottle, the type they serve on aircraft. After ditching the Scotch, and removing the label, I filled it with ash from the evening's campfire. Trophy complete, I presented it to Phil that evening at dinner.

Instantly recognising it for what it was, his face split into an enormous grin. With an almost childlike agility, he leapt up onto his chair, and declared, "Gentlemen, order!"

Everyone stopped talking and looked at him.

He held up the bottle. "Tomorrow we play for the Ashes. England against Australia."

A roar of approval went up and glasses chinked all around.

In all this excitement, I was the only one looking concerned about my ancestry. I'm was a mixed breed. My father was a New Zealander, my mother an Australian, and I was born in England, although I grew up in South Africa. That pretty much covered the entire English-speaking cricketing world. But I really wanted to play on David's team.

Tugging on my beard, I hazarded, "Even though my mother's Australian, I was born in Kent. So would you mind if I—"

"Happy to have you on my team, Andrew," said David.

"But that means he's with us," Phil, also on the English team, moaned. The Australians started laughing—they'd seen me play. "Didn't you say something about your mother being Australian?"

"I'm as English as you are," I said to Phil. "And that's it. All negotiations are closed."

* * *

The following afternoon our Ashes match began. To everyone's shock and surprise, David made me captain of our team. We won the toss and elected to bat. David opened our innings, but just played silly buggers, acting like a little kid, missing the ball at every shot. He obviously needed some coaching.

I stormed up to him, doing my best serious captain act. "David, for heaven's sake, I thought you were supposed to be this great batsman. I've been billing you as our secret weapon. Now grow up and hit the bloody ball for once."

"Yes, sir. Sorry, sir," he said sheepishly, and then began what must surely be one of his most memorable innings, albeit witnessed by only a dozen or so people. His next swing was a beautiful cover drive. One of the Australian fielders sprinted through low scrub to catch it.

I cupped my hands and yelled, "Watch out, there's a dirty great snake living there."

The fielder stopped dead in his tracks and the ball sailed over his head. "Is there?" he shouted back in alarm.

"No," I shouted back.

There was hysteria around the England camp as we collected a quick six runs, putting us ahead on the scoreboard.

The Aussies set their collective jaws and the bowler fired another ball at David. David's left hand swung out, and the bat connected perfectly with the ball, sending it far into the outfield, headed for another six runs.

But this time the tennis ball hit an anthill and bounced.

I—and the rest of the English team—watched in horror as it flew directly to the Aussie wicketkeeper's outstretched hands.

David was out for four.

It all fell apart after that and the Australians won convincingly.

That evening, while the boys recounted their losses and victories, David and I huddled in the CIM room. I had suggested that he autograph the bat as a gift to the Man of The Match. Trouble was, the polished finish of the palm bark was proving impervious to ink. We were about to give up when I spotted a dusty bottle of typist correction fluid sitting on the shelf.

"Your best signature, please," I said, handing him the half-hardened paintbrush.

I held the bat as he painted a wobbly signature onto the front surface. He grinned at me. "As much as it pains me to say it, I think we need to give the award to an Australian. The one with the dodgy leg who still managed to score a few runs."

"But they won," I moaned.

"Isn't that always the way?" David said, clearly feeling my pain.

The recipient of the bat and the bottle of Ashes teared up and had to be handed a table napkin to mop his face as David made the presentation over dinner.

Now if only all guests could be like these. Star that he was, David was a gem to have in camp. To make good friends so quickly, only to have them taken away again, was one of the difficult-to-get-used-to parts of the job.

And, as we were soon to be reminded, not all guests become friends so easily and left with such regret.

Enter the Fox party.

CHAPTER 44

Fox Family Adventure Tour: Alaska, Himalaya, Rocky Mountains, Chile, Kenya, South Africa, and Botswana. Or so claimed the itinerary blazoned in bold capitals on the T-shirts worn by our seven new American guests. Father Fox, a very rich Californian, had a penchant for splurging exotic travel destinations on his wife, two daughters, and their spouses. He even paid for a professional guide.

The air thick with West Coast twangs, Andrew and I showed them and their guide to their cottages with instructions to meet us at the dining room for lunch in half an hour.

Not even five minutes passed when Paul, their guide, hunted us down at reception. Andrew and I were arguing over which of the women was wearing the most expensive jewellery. I was making a case for the faux redhead with the gold-and-diamond choker the size of a bulldog collar when Paul cleared his throat. He looked troubled.

"The Fox family want to leave. Now."

"Whatever for?" I asked. "They haven't even had lunch." Not even with the best hearing in the world could they have heard us gossiping about them. And even if they had, it didn't warrant bailing out before the first meal had been served.

"They say if they see another bug they'll go crazy."

Andrew raised a quizzical eyebrow. "Then what the hell are they doing in Africa? There are more bugs in this reception area than there are animals in the San Diego zoo."

Paul sighed. "Of course there are. I know that. You know that. I thought they'd know that. Apparently, I was wrong. Please, whatever you do, don't tell them I've told you this, but honestly, I've had it with these people."

"But surely they encountered bugs in Kenya and South Africa?" I demanded, refusing to let this go. "Unless their T-shirts are lies."

"Oh no, the South Africa bit is true. I was there with them. We stayed at a top game lodge and the women saw a few moths. They didn't stop moaning about it." Paul ran a hand across his face. "Anyway, bottom line is, they want to leave now. By charter, if necessary."

Andrew moved to pick up the mic. "So where is this bug free utopia I'm supposed to be sending them to?"

"Sandton City, in Johannesburg. And they want me to go with them." Paul sounded even more pained. "Like they need a guide to show them around a five-star shopping mall and hotel."

Andrew patted him sympathetically on the shoulder and called Joan.

"I saw this coming when I met them in Maun." Her sigh was the identical twin to Paul's moan of frustration. "The father kept yapping on about how adventurous his daughters and their lawyer husbands are, but all I could see was a bunch of spoilt Americans." That was harsh, even coming from Joan. "Andrew, make sure they understand that there'll be no refund on the Tau Camp accommodation. That has to be made clear before I waste my afternoon rescheduling things."

"They know that," Paul said. "I've already had this discussion with Fox senior."

Andrew relayed the message and Joan let out an even more tired sounding oomph. "Okay. Leave it with me, and I'll see what I can organise."

I noticed Lesego slouching at the kitchen door with the lunch tray. "Paul, why not persuade them to at least get their money's worth by having lunch before they go."

"Make sure the wine flows, particularly in my direction. I need fortifying." Paul clamped his professional guide smile onto his face and went to negotiate with his clients.

We and our guests were just settling down to lunch when the radio squawked. I let Andrew handle it while I topped up Paul's wine. He returned a few moments later, looking glum. "Sandton City is fully booked. Some huge international convention in Johannesburg. The only rooms Joan can find are at the Milpark Holiday Inn." He slid a piece of paper with a rather large looking number scrawled on it in front of Father Fox. "And here's the quote for the charter flight."

Father Fox brushed it away as if it were of no consequence. "Holiday Inn?" His face crinkled with distaste.

"'Fraid so," Andrew said.

The Fox family exchanged disgusted looks, but it was left to Father Fox to handle the negotiations. It reminded me a bit of the *Godfather*, how they all—even the sons-in-law—deferred to him. I suppose that came with the territory when you held the purse strings.

"What's Milpark like?" Father Fox demanded.

Andrew cleared his throat and broke the bad news. "You won't want to stroll about the shops unless you like stepping over homeless people sleeping in urine-scented doorways."

The daughter with the gold and diamond dog collar actually choked on her wine.

I stepped into the fray. "Even if we have elephants and hyenas wandering around camp at night, you'll be much, much safer sleeping here than you'd be locked in a hotel room in Milpark."

Andrew grimaced at me, clearly questioning why I was working to hang onto these people. I wasn't sure, except that I felt offended that they sported those loud T-shirts but didn't have the guts to handle a few moths. I wanted to see them live up to all that hype.

"Tell your travel agent to keep looking," Father Fox instructed.

The whole table stopped to listen while Andrew relayed that message back to Joan. Once he'd reappeared, one of the girls—this one with gold earrings about the size of Ferris wheels—asked where the drinking water on the table came from.

"The river," I answered, pointing at the water sparkling darkly as it rippled passed us in the channel.

Earrings smiled at me like I was a small, dumb child needing humouring. "No really, where does *this* water come from?" She held up her glass. "It's quite sweet."

"The river," I repeated, with just the right amount of small-child inflection in my voice. I saw Paul smile, but he quickly buried his face into his wine glass before anyone else could spot it.

I had answered this question countless times, but I wasn't in the mood today. Not with these people who couldn't appreciate the magnificence of this place because of a few lousy bugs. Also, I was tired, and desperately in need of some leave. I should never have agreed to postponing my holiday for the wedding.

Father Fox, clearly agreeing that I was too stupid to live, leaned across, and said slowly, "No, what Gail means is. . .where does the *drinking* water come from? A borehole? Flown in from Maun?"

As if we had space on planes to fly in bottled water. I rewarded him with my brightest smile. "Like I said, it comes all the way from the river."

Father Fox hissed in a breath and then forced a sick smile. "You can't possibly get the drinking water straight from the river. So, please, let us in on the secret. We promise not tell anyone." He now winked, poking his tongue out at me as if we were cohorts in some evil scheme.

Andrew came to my rescue. "Maybe I can explain it better. You see, it's like this. . ." He picked up the water jug and emptied its contents over the atrium plants. Then he kicked off his sandals, and walked out of the dining room. Without pause, he waded out into the bay up to his thighs and scooped up a jug of water. He was loving this. Bloody show-off. I wished I'd thought of it. Back in the dining room, dripping water on the clean floor, he filled his glass and then topped up mine. We clunked glasses as if they held the finest Champaign—it tasted almost as good—and each took a gulp.

"It comes from the river," I said, making a point of smacking my lips. Yes, childish, I know, but what can I say?

To a man, our guests pushed their water glasses away.

Paul smiled, lifted his glass, and said, "That's why I drink wine."

Only Andrew and I knew he was joking.

Then a thought struck. We had just given them another reason to leave. Dang, I wasn't going to see them beating off swarms of moths tonight.

Andrew refilled their wine glasses, and asked, innocently, "So, why *exactly* do you want to leave? Is it because of—"

"Snakes!" Dog Collar burst out. "We hate snakes. We saw one at the lodge in South Africa and I almost died."

"And this place looks like there must be a thousand snakes here." A tear actually welled in Earring's eye. What was her name again? Gail.

I felt awful for being so ungracious. To make up it, I leaned over and patted her hand. "Please, don't let that stop you enjoying an amazing place. We hardly ever get snakes here."

Apart from the black mamba in that English lady's cottage a few weeks ago. She was a real star about it. Didn't even flinch when she heard it was Africa's deadliest snake. Evicting it had been a real challenge. Thekiso and Olututswe still paled when anyone mentioned the word 'snake'.

And not to mention the little spotted bush snake—Spotty—who had taken up residence in the *letaka* blind, right here in the dining room. We only saw him occasionally, but he was around.

And the Cape cobra, living somewhere in our new scullery roof. He popped out every few days, sending me and the kitchen staff diving for cover.

Oh, and what about the boomslang hiding in the tree outside number two?

Okay, so we got the occasional snake. Nothing to get worked up about.

"And the odd ones who do visit are usually harmless," Andrew added, lying through his teeth.

For a moment, the girls and Father Fox look half calmed.

Andrew nodded his assurance. As he did so, a tiny movement above Gail's head caught my eye.

Spotty.

The darling little beastie.

And what perfect timing, too.

Andrew guffawed, telling me he'd seen the snake.

Exercising every bit of self-control to stop myself from laughing, I stared at Gail, desperately trying not to look above her head.

It was hopeless.

As if he knew exactly what was going on, Spotty slowly unwound himself until his elegant green body hovered a foot above Gail's and her sister's heads.

Ten thousand years passed.

Gail must have sensed something, because she suddenly looked up, directly into Spotty's bright eyes. Her face contorted and a horrific screeching tore from her throat. She leapt to her feet, sending her massively heavy chair skittering across the floor.

The rest of the Fox family, Father Fox included, screamed.

But Dog Collar shrieked the loudest. She tore from the room and ended up down at the bay.

Plates spun off the table, and the jug, still full of water, toppled, soaking Mother Fox as the rest of the family scattered out the door. They huddled together a few feet from the dining room. Mama Fox, the slowest of the bunch, yelled at son-in-law-number-one for bumping into her. He didn't stop long enough to reply. Robert, Lesego, and Betty charged in from the kitchen to see what all the fuss was about.

Rescuing this situation seemed pointless.

Once silence descended and hell composed itself, Andrew shouted, "I told you, most of the snakes that visit us are harmless. Now watch this."

That got some of their attention. Even Dog Collar, down at the water's edge, took a step closer.

Offended at the reaction to his grand entrance, Spotty had recoiled into the blind, leaving just the tip of his tail sticking out. Andrew gave it a tug. Spotty reared his head out of the reeds and opened his mouth, showing a maw devoid of fangs. Even in my mirth, I understood at least some of the Fox family's shock, having been a tad taken aback myself when I first saw the snake.

"Meet Spotty, our resident dining room snake," Andrew said, so calmly you'd think he was introducing his mother. "Harmless and very cute."

It seemed to work.

The Fox family settled down enough to gather in the lounge. In truth, I don't think a stampeding herd of elephants could have gotten them back into the dining room. Paul and I carried the wine bottles and some clean glasses to them, and then joined them while Andrew spoke to Joan on the radio.

The news was bleak.

Johannesburg was over-run by convention-goers. The only hotel available remained the Holiday Inn. After a heated discussion, Father Fox announced that he and his lot had decided to stay. Funny, it seems there are things in the world more terrifying than snakes: homeless people sleeping in urine-scented doorways.

During their four-day stay at the camp, the Fox family covered the entire spectrum of human emotion. After the initial horror and panic, no meal started on time because they were always late back to camp, delayed by some new marvel discovered while out on their walks. Dinners filled with belly-numbing laughter went on deep into the night, only ending after exciting walks down the runway to see the lechwe and impala and to soak up starlight. When the time came to leave, none of them wanted to go. For a while there, it looked like they would miss their flight. So charmed by the wonder of the Okavango, we almost had to lift them bodily onto the plane.

Just goes to show that one should never judge a person by their T-shirt.

The day after the Fox family left, Andrew and I took our much needed holiday.

CHAPTER 45

Home at last.

The Cessna's door opened on the Tau strip after our ten day break and I reeled back in my seat. The overpowering scent of spring flowering acacias hit me like humidity at the seaside.

Our visit to Johannesburg for the wedding had been more stressful than relaxing, thanks to snarled traffic and the pressure to see too many people in too short a time. It was good to be back in our little backwater.

September was the loveliest time in the Okavango. While the water was receding, it was still not too low for a *mokoro* to get about. Animals roamed everywhere, and the birdlife was at its most plentiful. I had hoped to see the camp diary filled with interesting sightings during our absence, but the last entries, posted by Morag, read: *Andrew and Gwynn on leave*, followed by, *Andrew and Gwynn are back.* So, I drew a smiley face.

It seemed while we were away, the hyena had left as inexplicably as it had arrived. The kitchen had definitely benefitted from his absence. Still, nature abhors a vacuum, so he had been replaced by a bachelor herd of young elephants. Too old to be mothered, the youngster would have been kicked out of their matriarchal family herds to fend for themselves until old enough to mate. Like naughty teenagers everywhere, trouble followed them.

Elephants in camp, we quickly learned, were far worse than hyenas. Now it wasn't just hazardous walking around the camp at night, but during the day, too. These obstreperous giants had taken a marked fancy to the palm trees growing in the centre of the camp. Every day we watched in fear as yet another tree fell victim to their craving for juicy palm hearts. Too often, they'd fell a tree, sniff at the leaves, and then move on to wreck something else. The destruction was astounding. It really was just a matter of time before someone—other than Matanta, who deserved it—got charged by an angry elephant, or a cottage got flattened by a falling tree. Either way, the chance of someone losing their life was good.

In a futile attempt to protect the guests, we implemented a rule that no *lekgoa* was to walk around the camp without their guide. I don't know how having a guide at their heels would help against a falling tree, but it made us feel a bit better.

It did mean rumbles of rebellion from the guides, though, largely stirred up by Sam.

Sam.

Matanta had been right; the guy was bad news. A day didn't go by when he didn't agitate for tea and other food privileges. Thanks to months of full camps and a rash of CIMs, he worked regularly, casting a pall of discontent over everyone —especially, Lesego.

Given everything, it peeved me one morning to arrive in the kitchen for my early morning shift to find no waiter—or, more specifically, no Lesego. He had been late the last three mornings, maxing out my patience. It didn't help that we had a camp full of guests, and not all of them accommodating.

I put the kettle on to boil for the early morning coffee, and started clearing the brandy glasses off the dinner table. Our guests included six South Africans who liked drinking deep into the night. Last evening we'd tried the walk-on-the-runway-to-see-the-stars routine, but it hadn't worked. They had returned to the table to dent the brandy bottle. As hosts, we had to keep them company. Now I was tired as well as peeved.

So, I wasn't in the best of moods when Lesego finally appeared after the guests had left for their morning walk. Worse, he was dressed in a pair of dirty jeans and a Lusaka Football Club T-shirt. His gear looked as if it had spent the last month lying in the bottom of a *mokoro*. He even had a Walkman on his belt and headphones strung around his neck.

"You're late," I said unnecessarily. "And where is your uniform?"

"Dirty, *Mma*. I need another one."

"You already have two. One for the wash and one for the back."

"I don't have time to wash clothes. I have a life."

Fury nipped at my self-control. Oh to deck this guy! But I forced myself to take a deep breath. "This is the fourth time you've been late this week." He shrugged, like it didn't matter. "And because you've had your three letters of warning, I can now legally fire you." I managed to resist rubbing my hands together. Only just, mind you.

Lesego thrust his jaw out at me. "You can't fire me. I'm the best waiter in the camp. Sean told me this when he gave me my salary increase."

"Sean told you this?" I asked, disbelief haemorrhaging into my voice.

"Of course. He gave me a salary increase and not Kekgebele."

"Ah," I said, understanding dawning. "Correction. He gave you an increase so you could *become* the best waiter—not just the best *paid* waiter. Surely Morag told you this?"

"Morag said nothing like that to me." Why wasn't I surprised? "And Sean gave me that money, so that means you can't fire me," Lesego added with quaint logic.

Andrew and Matanta joined Lesego and me at reception and I quickly brought them up to speed. Matanta grinned, looking positively Machiavellian. It was no secret that he and Robert had little tolerance for Lesego's laziness and lack of team spirit. Even Andrew cracked a smile.

"You know the Chief can fire you now?" Matanta chimed, echoing my words.

Lesego crossed his arms, hugging his chest. "Only Sean can fire me."

"Not so," Andrew said, in his best official voice. He reached over for a pen and paper and started writing Lesego's letter of dismissal. He signed it with a flourish, and then fished around in the cigar box under the desk where we kept the petty cash. After counting out Lesego's severance pay, he handed the money, the letter, and a pen to Lesego. "Sign. And then you're out."

Lesego backed away, hands now held out defensively in front of him. "No, *Rra*. I can't sign this. Only Sean can fire me. I'm his waiter."

Andrew opened his mouth to argue but Matanta beat him to it. Gushing Setswana—I caught the odd phrase, mainly telling Lesego how useless he was—Matanta grabbed the money and letter, and frog-marched Lesego down the path leading out of the camp. Once at the runway, he shoved Lesego hard, sending him spinning away. The handful of money and the letter followed, fluttering in the breeze until finally landing at Lesego's feet.

"Don't come back!" Matanta shouted, turning to the camp to get breakfast started. Feeling somewhat shell-shocked by his uncharacteristic display of violence, I stumbled to the kitchen, listening to him mutter. "Useless, the man is useless. A waste of a good black skin."

For all that we were all pleased to see Lesego go, I had added another *matata* to my list: who was going to serve breakfast this morning?

Me? I don't think so. I had been a waitress once, working in my brother's restaurant. I was so pathetic not even nepotism could save me.

My brother fired me after my first shift. I think dropping a burger on that lady's lap had been what clinched it. . . Anyway, I needed a plate carrier, and fast.

Just then, Petso sashayed into the kitchen to start her shift, singing at the top of her lungs. Before I stopped to think it through, I yelled, "Hey, Pets, see me in reception."

Her face fell as if she'd just been caught stealing the petty cash.

I put a reassuring arm around her shoulder. "How would like a job as a waitress?"

For a moment there, I thought her eyes might actually pop straight out of her head. Then she skipped, swinging her arms. "*Emmm, Mmmmmma.*"

I was unlikely to get any more conversation out of her. I felt good about my decision. Petso had a smile as big as Africa. Just that made her preferable to the surly Lesego. She was also eager to learn. While in practice I couldn't wait tables to save my life, I did know the theory of how it was done. Between the two of us, we'd manage. I just wished we had more amenable guests than the South Africans to experiment with.

Ah, well, this was Tau Camp; one couldn't have everything.

Leaving a pile of dirty dishes for Betty to handle when she arrived for her shift, I led Petso to the dining room to teach her how to set the table. We were just finishing up when our South African guests arrived back from their morning outing.

If Lesego was surly, then this lot seemed absolutely morose. Even the guides looked. . . I sucked in a breath. Belligerent, that was the only way to describe the set of their jaws and their hooded eyes. Worse, they shifted restlessly on the bank while their *lekgoa* struggled to climb—unaided—out of the *mekoro*.

I hurried over and asked the guests, "How was your morning?"

"*Bleerie* awful," Koos shouted. He was the same profile as a Mann truck, pulling a fifty-nine thousand gallon tanker. "These boys of yours are *bleerie* useless. All they did was shout to each other in their language and smoke. We saw no animals."

The other guests rumbled their agreement, punctuated with more Afrikaans swear words.

I was so not in the mood for this. I called out to Andrew, working on his paperwork in reception, to spin his 'Chief' magic.

He took one look at the guests' faces, and strode over to KD, our head guide who should have known better. "Care to explain?"

KD had the decency to look down at his shoes.

Dylos, also part of the crew, wasn't so shy. He barrelled towards Andrew. "We need a *kgotla* to talk about this."

Andrew winced. *Kgotlas* were long, drawn out meetings, sometimes spanning days, where problems were aired and, hopefully, solutions found. "You need to apologise to your *lekgoa*," Andrew said instead, masterfully dodging the *kgotla* arrow.

The South Africans folded their arms across their chest, waiting expectantly.

"No, *Rra*," Dylos insisted. "Talk first and then say sorry afterwards."

Like a rugby scrum, the three South African men joined shoulders and edged towards the guides. I clearly read their intent: the guides were about to be taught a short, sharp lesson about back-chatting the management.

"Um," I stuttered, grabbing the closest guy's arm. "Let's let Andrew sort this out while the rest of us have breakfast." I tried pulling him away, but he was built like a brick privy and I couldn't budge him.

"*Ag*, no man, Frikkie," his wife said, coming to my rescue. "Listen to Gwynn now, and come and have breakfast." She glared at Andrew. "Just you sort these boys out before we have to deal with them this afternoon."

"Don't worry," Andrew said. "I'll be on your afternoon outing to make sure it goes as it should." He now glared at the guides.

KD wasn't the only one to look shamed. Having the manager tag along to monitor their behaviour was no small matter. Jobs were on the line here, and they knew it.

What had gone wrong today?

As I invited the guests to tuck into their bacon and eggs, I decided it must have been something in the spring air that had everybody riled up. The temperature—soaring to a cool 107 degrees at ten in the morning—was doing nothing for my mood.

My next concern was whether Andrew's *mokoro* driving skills would be up to the challenge of keeping up with guides. His poling had definitely improved since his first lesson with Matanta, but the last time he'd taken me out, he had ended up in the water again. Maybe because I'd laughed myself silly, there had been no further offers of Andrew-propelled *mokoro* trips.

Oh well, the day had started off badly. Who said it couldn't end that way? Especially if a *kgotla* was part of the planning.

CHAPTER 46

As much as I didn't want to sit through a *kgotla*, the guides made it clear that I didn't have much choice if I wanted them to show up for the afternoon outing. So, while Gwynn placated the guests over breakfast, I led them to the laundry to talk. Morag saw us. Maybe figuring that the guides were her baby, she joined me.

"This should be interesting," Morag murmured. "I've been hearing mutters about this for the last few days in the guide school."

"Would have been nice if you'd mentioned something."

"I'm not the manager here. And anyway, if you'd accepted my invitation to help me run the school, then you'd know."

That didn't warrant an answer. We both knew I had a camp to manage, a thousand maintenance projects to complete, and a wife who took exception to Morag hankering after my flesh. Even after all this time, she never missed the chance to touch me. I shoved the distressing thought aside and sped up, entering the laundry at a trot.

Sam waited for me, and it suddenly all made sense.

He was a regular pupil at Morag's school, but I guessed discussions on bird calls and plumage were not what had brought him here today.

I grunted a greeting and sat down in the shade on a sawed-off palm stump. Once everyone settled in the circle of protest, I called the meeting to order. My eyes fixed on Sam.

But Sam was a wily chap. He gestured to Dylos to speak.

Even before Dylos opened his mouth, I knew I would be hearing Sam's words. He didn't surprise me.

"*Rra*," Dylos said, "it all starts with the morning tea. How can you expect us to go walking with *lekgoa* when we have no tea?"

"Yes," Karomona added. "The *lekgoa* even have rusks. We must too."

This was rich. I wanted to say that when you pay hundreds of dollars a night for bed and board, you could have early morning rusks, too. But I didn't. Instead, I countered with, "We sorted the tea problem out weeks ago. I agreed to give you a cold drink before you went out with the *lekgoa* instead of tea after you came back." Shortly after Sam had returned from his first CIM, he had begun campaigning for early morning tea again. It had caused so much hard feeling that I had agreed to replace the guides' breakfast tea with a cold drink to take out on their morning walk. It had seemed a small price to restore peace, but maybe all I had done was open the door to more trouble.

Discontent rumbled through the circle, confirming my suspicions. Still, I wasn't concerned. We'd had *kgotlas* before, and I understood how the system worked. This party wouldn't end until everyone had their say.

Also, I knew Sam well enough to figure that the morning cold drink was a red herring. So, as I listened to a litany of complaints about nonsense, I kept waiting for Sam to bring up the real issue. My tiny patch of shade had given way to full sun when he finally spoke.

"*Rra*, the real *matata* is not about the cold drinks. It's about our lunch."

I resisted the urge to roll my eyes. "Lunch?"

"*Er, Rra*. It does not help for us to only eat at lunchtime. We are hungry before then. You and the *lekgoa* have a big breakfast. We just have a cold drink and sandwiches. We need our lunch. Especially now that we have to protect the *lekgoa* from the elephants in the camp."

"So what do you suggest?" I asked, running out of patience with this. It was blisteringly hot. In fact, I'd heard earlier on the BBC World Service that Maun was the hottest place on Earth that day. It was supposed to clock a miserable 116 degrees F. I was feeling every degree of that. All I wanted was a pre-lunch swim to cool off. But for that, I had to get the guides back on board, because Gwynn and I could hardly sneak off, leaving our guests behind.

Sam stood to explain his solution. "The scullery girls must cook us our meals when we need them. We, each and every one of us, will go and ask for our lunch when we are hungry. And then they must make it."

I snorted a laugh as I pictured Gwynn and the chefs agreeing to that demand. "Betty has enough to do without spending her morning cooking guides' lunches."

"Petso must help her," Dylos said, to a murmur of agreement.

"Petso is now a waitress. Lesego no longer works here," I replied.

Morag, sitting next to me, sucked in a breath. "What's happened to him?"

"Fired. This morning." I sighed. "It's been quite a day. And he might not be the last." I said that last part loud enough for everyone to hear.

Some of the older guides shifted in their seats. I expected Morag to complain about the loss of her favourite, but instead, she left the laundry. I hardly knew what to make of it, but had no time to worry, because Sam was back with his next salvo.

"Then let us guides cook our own meals in the kitchen."

That was an even worse idea than having Betty at the guides' beck and call. I gave a definitive headshake. "Not happening. This camp is here for the *lekgoa*. They pay your salaries, and I'm not risking their meals because you can't wait until one o'clock for lunch. You are not children." I stood. "That's my decision. The *kgotla* is over. Guides on duty, get your *ngashi's* because we're taking the *lekgoa* swimming." Without waiting for a reaction, I left the laundry.

Gwynn was waiting for me at the kitchen with an expectant look.

"Tell the guests to get changed. We're all going swimming," I said.

"Thank goodness. I'm dying here." She flapped her T-shirt, exposing her stomach, as if that would help cool her down. Then she kissed me. "Whatever magic you're weaving, don't stop doing it."

I raised a quizzical eyebrow. She put her finger to her lips, and tiptoed into the kitchen. Puzzled, I followed. Morag stood on the beer crate in the scullery, helping Betty wash the breakfast dishes.

You could have floored me with a bacon rind.

Gwynn cleared her throat, and then said hesitantly, "Morag, we're all going swimming. Care to join us?"

Now I knew for certain that the world had gone mad.

"Are you going?" Morag asked, without bothering to face Gwynn.

"Wouldn't miss it for anything," Gwynn replied, her smile looking just a tad strained at Morag's rudeness.

"Then I wouldn't come. For anything."

I sighed, a peaceful, happy sigh. My world—that seconds before had shifted on its axis—had righted itself again. All was as it should be.

Leaving Gwynn to fume, I headed to the bay, fully expecting the guides to be waiting for us.

It was my turn to be disappointed.

Swearing under my breath, I stomped back up to the laundry.

None of the guides had moved off their sawn-off palm logs.

I stopped at the entrance to assess the situation before speaking.

The older guides still wouldn't look me in the eye. Yet, there they sat with the firebrands who had no such qualms about staring me down.

Sam stood and faced me. "No one is going swimming until you agree that we can make our own lunch."

Insanity stalked the camp once more. I could feel the world teetering on its axis again. What was with this day? Maybe it was the heat.

I put my hands on my hips, and let out a long breath, counting slowly to whatever number is supposed to stop one from losing one's temper. I'd reached about a million before I realised it wasn't working. "And if I refuse?"

"Then we go on strike." Sam turned to the waiting guides and, like a conductor leading a discordant choir, waved his arms, chanting, "Lunch or strike. Lunch or strike. Lunch or strike."

The younger guides got to their feet and started to *toyi-toyi*—a highly politicised protest dance youth in South Africa's townships had used during their fight against apartheid. Not a scene I ever thought I'd see under my watch at Tau Camp.

A thousand doubts assaulted me. I had been sweating before, but liquid now gushed from my body. Had I been too lenient with the guides? Should I have been a racist prat like Rodney? What could I do to save this situation?

Before I could conjure any answers, our three South African guests—the built-like-a-brick-privy-sized guys—chose that moment to poke their heads into the laundry. The towels slung across their hairy shoulders said they were ready and waiting for their promised swim. To a man, their eyes widened as they summed up events.

Then their faces hardened.

They, too, had watched scenes on South African news reports where *toyi-toying* crowds threw rocks at police, or necklaced people. Necklacing: the charming practice of placing a burning vehicle tyre around a victim's neck . . .

Frikkie stepped into the laundry, cracking his knuckles threateningly. "Having some trouble, Andrew?"

Inspired by Sam, the guides' chanting rose a few decibels.

Frikkie's eyebrows rose proportionately.

This couldn't end well.

I grabbed Frikkie's and Koos's hambone-sized biceps. "Beer. We need beer. *Uys koue bier.*" Ice cold beer, I added for emphasis in my best Afrikaans. Hoping their mate Piet would follow, I steered them out of the laundry, down to the bar.

Piet did. Deflected by the promise of a cold lager, they and their wives gathered around the fridge. Still, their conversation was filled with all the dire things they would like to do to the 'boys'—a phrase I hate when applied to black men, any men, in this kind of context.

Feeling my world slip away, I went to the radio, and took a deep breath, dreading what I was about to do. But there was nothing for it, so I keyed the mic.

"637, 638."

Joan's voice crackled back at me. "Go ahead, Andrew."

"Is Sean around?"

"Stand by."

Moments ticked away, and then Sean greeted me. "Andrew, what do you need?"

"Guides have gone on strike." Best keep it short and to the point. If he wanted details, he'd ask for them.

"It's Sam, isn't it? I knew this day would come."

I nodded; then remembering he couldn't hear a nod, added, "Affirmative."

"Fire the lot of them. I'm sending you a motorboat with a new guide. They'll be there tomorrow morning."

Before I could say how radical that was, Joan spoke. Sean was already on the phone organising the boat. I dropped the mic and buried my face in my hands.

Why, why, why had it come to this? With the exception of Sam, I liked the guides. All of them. There had to be a solution that didn't include the wholesale carnage Sean proposed.

A gentle hand stroking my shoulder pierced my misery. "Matanta has an idea."

Forcing a smile, I turned to face Gwynn and Matanta. "Of course he has."

"*Rra*, get rid of Sam and the problem will go away."

"What about CIMs? He's the cook."

"What's wrong with me and Robert? One of us can go along to cook. We've proved already that it can work."

He had a point. With Sam out of the picture. . .I swung around and scooped up the mic. "637, 638."

"Andrew."

"Joan. Message for Sean. I'm firing Sam. All the other guides have to reapply for their jobs. Anyone who still wants trouble will go with him."

"I'll relay the message, but the motorboat is already organised. Might be too late to call it back now."

Man, that was quick. Why couldn't I get a roll of wire that fast?

"No problem. I'll park it somewhere safe in case we need it."

I dropped the mic and turned to see a mischievous glint in Matanta's eye.

"A motorboat at Tau?" He rubbed his hands together. "Did I tell you how great Jugujugu was?"

Matanta always knew how to bring a smile to my face. I slapped him on the back. "Hold that thought. I have a troublemaker to fire."

Back in the laundry, they were all there, talking among themselves. By and large, these were fair-minded people. Talk reasonably and be fair, and you'd gain their support. It had worked before, and I reckoned it would work again.

I didn't sit down. "Sean does not pay my salary if the *lekgoa* don't come. If the *lekgoa* are unhappy, they won't come. The trouble is, if my salary is taken away, I'll get very upset, and I'll do something about it. Like find some guides who won't chase the *lekgoa* away."

No one said a word.

Kamanga stood, stared over at his colleagues and then walked out. He was one of the oldest, most experienced, respected guides. A few weeks before, he and his guest had been stampeded by a herd of elephants. Risking his own life, Kamanga had ensconced the guest safely under a bush before seeking shelter for himself.

Everyone else stayed quiet.

Everyone else except Sam who ranted a little in Setswana.

Matanta, standing at my right, didn't translate, but I didn't like the tone. Voice hard, I said, "Sam and the rest of you, what are you going to do?"

Sam stood, shouted something, and sat back down. The rest of the guides looked down at their hands and I sensed that the mood had shifted.

It was time to go for the kill. I fixed my eyes on Sam. "There's an easy solution. You are fired."

Sam hissed in a breath. I looked around the circle, stopping to drill each man with my eyes. Shifting in their seats, no one met my gaze. I knew it wasn't necessary, but I added, "Anybody who wants to go with Sam, leave now. The rest of you, take the *lekgoa* for a swim. I am coming with, and you had better be smiling."

And they did, and they were.

CHAPTER 47

Andrew handed me beers to replenish the supply in the bar fridge, depleted by the South Africans. The dust had settled on the guides' strike, but we remained jittery as we went about our chores that evening. In one day, we had lost both Lesego and Sam. Sure, they were troublemakers, but if a strike could happen once, it could happen again.

Morag appeared. She spoke hesitantly. "Perhaps we've all been at fault."

Morag admitting fault? It had to be the hot night air that hung languid and heavy over us all. I jerked my head out of the fridge and stared at her.

"We've neglected the staff village," she said. "Maybe if we'd been more in touch with what happens there, the guides would not have been so inclined to follow Sam."

The staff village was on a neighbouring island, a distance of about thirty minutes by foot and *mokoro*. Andrew and I were yet to visit it, so yes, maybe Morag had a point.

"When do you want to go?" I asked.

Morag kept her eyes fixed hopefully on Andrew. "Tomorrow?"

He shook his head. "I lost almost the whole day today, thanks to the strike. Sean could drop in at any time to inspect his precious new donkey boiler. Given that we haven't even dug the foundations yet, I have to focus on that." His voice hardened, as if brooking no argument. "Why don't you two go tomorrow? You can report back to me on anything I need to get involved with."

Morag looked over at me and sighed—a pained one, filled with self-sacrifice and stoic endurance. "All right, for the good of the camps."

So, that was how Morag and I ended up going to the staff village together.

We left soon after breakfast the next morning with Karomona at the helm of our *mokoro*. Like the day before, it was stinking hot, the kind of heat that usually had me cowering under the leafy canopy covering the camp. I hoped to make this visit short and to the point.

Arriving at the village was a bit like beaching on a foreign shore. We landed on a small muddy bank from where a dozen pathways wandered into the trees. Karomona picked a well-trodden one and led the way.

It quickly became apparent that his pathfinding wasn't really necessary. Paper wrappers, plastic packets, broken shoes, tin cans, bottles, and rotting *mekoro* littered the winding trail. My eyes widened and my jaw dropped with each step I took into this midden. The guides, so strict about even the smallest piece of litter in the delta, obviously didn't care about the mess in their own village. It shocked me rigid. They, especially Karomona, loved bringing their *lekgoa* here. I couldn't imagine what the guests must have thought of this dump.

"I think we could do with a bit of clean up here," I said to Morag, who had her hands filled with the rubbish she'd collected.

"Order some extra black bags, and I'll arrange for some of the kids to do a litter blitz," Morag said. Then she frowned. "I might have to motivate them, though. Maybe both Scops and Tau could donate some cash."

It seemed outrageous that the kids would need to be bribed to clean up their own living space, but I guessed Morag was right. "We can pay them ten tebe for every bag collected." That was equivalent to a couple of U.S. cents.

We reached the first line of houses. Constructed from mud and thatch gleaned from the surrounding bush, each house consisted of one small room, with perhaps a second, used for a bedroom. Ablution facilities were non-existent, except for a communal long-drop toilet in the centre of the village. If the residents wanted to bathe, the women had to carry water from the river.

Despite the depressing air of neglect, each yard was swept, with nary a trace of litter. Rickety fences, made from sticks, demarcated individual ownership. The absence of junk in the gardens exemplified the concept of Not-In-My-Back-Yard beautifully.

Part of the problem was that the village wasn't recognised by the government as an official settlement. These people had gathered here because work was available at the nearby camps, and not just Sean's, either. The government believed the camp owners were responsible for providing facilities, while the camp management considered it the job of the administration. Stuck in the middle, the people living here had fallen into a bureaucratic hole.

Perhaps that explained some of their lack of pride.

Morag and I walked in silence as Karomona led us through his world.

We stopped to watch a huddle of woman, sitting under the palm trees, weaving baskets from palm fronds. Their snotty-nosed, butt-naked babies and toddlers crawled about in the dust at their feet.

The baskets ranged from large Ali-Baba designs to small bread trays. Each featured beautiful, geometric triangles, diamonds, or zigzags in muted colours of natural cream, dusty pink, beige, sooty black, ochre red, and donkey brown.

The women brought their wares to the camps to be sold for pennies to rich *lekgoa*. We used their baskets for everything from serving bread to collecting laundry. I even had a private collection going in my cottage that I intended to take home when I finally left here.

Basket making, it turned out, was a time consuming labour of love.

"These women," Karomona began in his heavy pidgin English, "they collect the palm leaves. Lots and lots of leaves. They walk far, very far each day for leaves. Then, they must find the colours for the baskets."

It took me a moment to realise he was talking about plant dyes. My eyes widened in admiration at the effort. My mother was a mad knitter who loved to spin and dye her own wool. She, too, would forage for plants to naturally dye her yarn. So I had some insight into the effort it took to find enough raw material to dye a project of any meaningful size.

"It takes months and months to make a single basket," Karomona finished.

How the women found the time, I would never know. Like in most parts of Africa, they performed the bulk of the work in the village. As if to prove the point, a couple of women carrying ten gallon drums of water on their heads trudged past us—and a group of idle men, shading themselves under the trees. The men didn't even look up from their card game.

Karomona continued his tour.

"Now we visit our chief," he informed us. "His name is Monnapula. He has no English. I speak for you."

I didn't know the village had a chief. I risked mentioning that fact to Morag.

She surprised me by answering. "You are as in the dark as I am."

We quickened our pace, eager to meet this man—and to get out of the heat into the shade of his home.

Karomona stopped at a house no grander than any of the others. He ushered us in. Although the staff called Andrew chief, I had never met a real chief before, so I wasn't sure what to expect. It just wasn't what confronted me in Monnapula's perfectly swept yard. I was about to proffer my greeting when I stopped short.

A wizened old man sat hunched in the grey dust. The stoic, unhappy resignation on his dark face said that life had not been kind to him. A skinny, wrinkled woman, his wife I assumed, clucked as she went about her sweeping.

I noticed his foot. It was bandaged with the filthiest piece of cloth I have ever seen. Grey from the dust, green pus oozed through it from whatever wound it hid.

An acrid, vile smell hit me.

But even as my stomach threatened to launch my breakfast, my heart went out to him. Monnapula, no great chief, just a sick old man, seemed to sense my interest. He sprang into action, ripping at the bandage.

Horror and nausea washed over me as the bandage unwound. His lower limb was ulcerous, rotten, and, even to my non-medical eye, beyond repair. What could have reduced a human being to such a pathetic state of pain and neglect? All thoughts of a quick escape from the village fled my mind.

Morag and I exchanged horrified looks and then I rounded on Karomona. "Why hasn't he seen a doctor?"

"We can't get him to the plane. Too heavy to carry." Karomona's answer summed up the problem of the staff village's ambivalent place in the Botswanan social structure. No government doctor would visit here. I thought of the wheelbarrow in Andrew's work shed back at the camp. Would it work as wheelchair to get Monnapula to the airstrip? Would Joan book him a seat on a plane? She had to. I would fight Sean and his tight wallet to the death over this.

"How long has he been like this?" Morag asked, her words gagging in her throat.

"A long time. Many, many months."

"He needs to get to the hospital." I smiled reassuringly at Monnapula who listened without understanding to our discussion about him.

"*Lekgoa* medicine—no good," Karomona said emphatically. "This chief, he has a bad spirit. A Bushman, he came here, two, three years ago. He wants to be chief. So this man," Karomona pointed one of his mangled fingers at Monnapula, "he fight with the Bushman. But the Bushman is too strong. He sent the ancestors to curse Monnapula. His leg go bad, and there is no medicine that can fix it."

An expletive, aimed at telling Karomona exactly what I thought of his evil spirits, danced on the tip of my tongue. I swallowed it. I was here to help, not mock other people's beliefs. Instead, I said, "Tell him I will be back here tomorrow with medicine and clean bandages."

As Karomona translated, I watched Monnapula's face blossom with relief. He grinned a toothless smile at his wife. Her face streamed with tears. It steeled my resolve to help get him to hospital.

Once back at the camp, I called Maun, determined to fight Joan for the next available seat on the plane.

I did her a disservice.

After her kindness to Woodie, I should have expected Joan's prompt reply, "The next available flight out is his. Get him to the runway, and I will have a vehicle waiting at the airport to transport him to the hospital."

Tears pricked my eyes as I said my thanks.

"And, Gwynn," Joan added. "Where there is one man in need, there may be more. Ask around the village. If anyone else needs help, let me know, and I will send in a plane, if necessary."

"What about Sean?"

"Let me worry about Sean."

The next morning, I went alone to the village with Karomona. This time I was armed with anti-septic, clean bandages, some pain relievers, and a couple of pairs of surgical gloves.

Monnapula was thrilled to see me. With much tongue clicking, he galvanised his wife into fetching clean water. Eyes darting at all the attention, she set about boiling a large, black, three-legged pot. The fire could not burn fast enough, so she fanned it with a wing collected from some large raptor. A cloud of black charcoal dust wafted into the sky, only to settle on our supposedly sterile water.

As I waited for it to boil, I looked around the house and courtyard. A few threadbare blankets, obviously someone's bed, lay crumpled on the sand under a lean-to, built next to the main hut. A black and white goat lay sleeping peacefully on them.

The sound of babbling people caught my attention. A crowd had gathered to watch my ministrations. I hoped I didn't embarrass myself by throwing up all over Monnapula. If anything, the smell wafting off him was even worse than yesterday.

With the water just cool enough to touch, I swabbed Monnapula's limb and foot. Putrid skin peeled away under my fingers as pus oozed from open sores the size of oranges. I knew my face was as green as the pus.

Despite my stomach's objections, I pressed on doggedly, with lots of encouragement from the old man. Seemingly oblivious to all pain,

Monnapula poked and squeezed at his limb in an effort to remove as much poison as possible.

After what felt like a day, but was only an hour, he and I re-dressed his leg in a fresh bandage. I left him with instructions to keep the bandage clean—a hopeless dream, given that he spent his day sitting in the dust. Promising I would return to do it again the next day, I returned to camp.

It was Matanta who finally brought me news of the other sick and disabled in the village. After another radio call to Joan, an Islander arrived at Tau Camp to collect Monnapula, and three elderly ladies crippled with arthritis.

As long as I live, I will never forget our guests' faces as an entourage of well-wishers wheeled barrows filled with the sick and infirm up the runway to welcome the incoming plane.

It was some months before Monnapula arrived back at the camp. Despite Karomona's protestations to the contrary, he was in good health, but with an amputated foot.

There was another positive spin-off from Monnapula's adventure in the Maun hospital, though. He'd obviously told all who would listen of the plight of other infirm villagers. It didn't take long before a deputation of social workers arrived. This brought to light a mentally disabled woman, two blind children, and a paraplegic. This time, the government footed the bill to ferry them into Maun for treatment.

CHAPTER 48

I wiped the sweat off my face with my sleeve and stared in disbelief at the calendar in reception.

Unfortunately it didn't lie.

Today was the 15th of September. Andrew's birthday.

I had forgotten. I immediately blamed the guide strike and my meeting yesterday with Monnapula. Combined with the incessant, brain numbing heat, those events were enough to make anyone forget anything.

Dragging my flagging energy together, I lumbered to the kitchen. If it was hot outside, then it was scorching in here, and all the staff suffered. To add to their woes, the camp was full to capacity with our six South Africans, five Canadians, and a party of six English folk. Even with Seatla back from maternity leave, the chefs had their hands full.

Still, I knew Matanta wouldn't fail me. I sidled up next to him at the prep counter and crooned, "Feel like making me a chocolate cake?"

He looked up from his onion chopping. "Instead of the crème caramel for pudding?"

I winced, feeling bad about my demand. "To go with the crème caramel." I felt Robert's stare of disapproval, but ignored it. "It's Andrew's birthday. I'm about to buy him a T-shirt from the curio shop, but I think a cake is also needed." I was throwing myself on Matanta's mercy, but I added, "Please don't tell him I only remembered now." I could only hope I wouldn't become the butt of a retaliatory prank to make up for the last one we had pulled on him.

But it seemed Robert was the greater threat. "The Chief's birthday?" he bellowed with about as much subtlety as an axe in the head. If Andrew hadn't heard that yell, then age must have affected his ears. "Of course we'll make him a cake. The best one he's ever had."

I patted Robert on the arm to say thank you, and we both grimaced—him from the heat radiating off my hand, and me from the sweat streaming down his arm. Oh, I wished it would rain. A vain hope because a brilliant blue sky continued to mock us.

It was time to find somewhere cool.

I plodded over to reception to read the latest letter from my mother. A photo of Woodie dropped out of the envelope. Painfully thin, at least the hair had started to reclaim her face. She lived with my parents, and their three Siamese cats. Apparently, Woodie was being a real witch, constantly beating up on them, leaving them gibbering idiots. Why couldn't she have done that with Tom? Although I'd spent precious little time with her, I missed the comforting feel of her furry body pressed against mine at night.

Shouts coming from the river pulled me out of my musing.

Not knowing what to expect, I trotted down to the bay to see what was happening. I was greeted by a traffic jam, Okavango style.

Our bachelor herd of elephant had taken to the river just up from the camp. Hidden by the reeds and the curve of the channel, the guides had almost poled right into them. With a burst of speed, which belied the heat, the guides did a quick reverse, parking their *mekoro* in the reeds a few yards from the elephant.

A smile spread across my face. Our South African guests and their guides were laughing together at the elephant frolicking in the water. Thanks to Human Relations 110—Elephant Encounters, the South Africans and their guides were late in for lunch. No one complained.

* * *

That evening, Petso shyly placed a crabmeat and avocado starter before Andrew. I plunked his birthday present down, too.

"What's this?" Andrew asked, pointing to the brown paper parcel.

"A T-shirt."

"Oh. How original. What for?" He had yet to lift his spoon to eat his starter.

"Your birthday."

"My birthday? I thought you'd forgotten."

"Forgotten?" I said indignantly. "Really, what do you take me for?"

"Someone who forgets her husband's birthday."

"Like I ever would." I could see our whispered conversation was attracting some attention, but ignored it. As soon as we served the birthday cake, the guests would discover that it was the most important day of Andrew's year.

"Then why am I eating this?" Andrew prodded his starter—or more specifically, the avocado part—with his spoon. "Or, correction, not eating this?"

Damn. My story was blown. Avocados. Yet another thing Andrew didn't eat. We both knew I'd never have scheduled avocados for his birthday dinner. I blasted him with my most ingratiating smile.

He ignored it.

Turning to Bram, one of the Canadian guests, he asked loudly, "Has Sharon ever forgotten your birthday?"

Sharon answered for Bram. "Of course not." She winked at me. "But if I had, this is what I'd do." She stood up and started singing—yup, singing. *Skinnamarink*, to be exact. Complete with crazy hand gestures. Bram also leapt to his feet, and, before we knew what was happening, both of them were crooning, "I love you in the morning, and in the afternoon, I love you in the evening, underneath the moon."

Blooming red, Andrew buried his face in his hands.

When the clapping and cheering from the other guests had finally stopped, Andrew looked up. "Thank you. I've always wanted to be serenaded with children's songs on my thirty-second birthday."

George, an English chap sitting at the far end of the table, called out to the singers, "I *thought* I recognised you both. You're Bram and Sharon, the Canadian children's singers! My kids love your songs."

Bram and Sharon took a stage bow, and then Sharon said, "But what we do best is getting people to sing along." She waved her arms at us. "Up. On your feet, everyone." We all groaned, but Sharon was having none of it. "Come, people, it's Andrew's birthday. The least we can do is sing him a happy birthday."

Everyone joined in and the song went like this:
"Hi,
My name is Joe, and I work, in, a button factory,
I got a wife, and a dog, and a family.
One day, my boss comes up to me.
He says
"Hi Joe, are you busy?"
I says, "No!"
He says—turn the button with your right hand."

Bram and Sharon had us all laughing uncontrollably as we moved our body parts in time with our signing—left hand, right leg, left leg, neck, knee, elbow—until every conceivable part of our anatomies were simultaneously involved in turning that button. Try doing that after a few glasses of wine.

Later, much later, Matanta and Robert served Andrew's cake. It came complete with the thirty-two brightly burning birthday candles.

Birthday candles were not something any of the stores in Maun stocked. As his gift to Andrew, Matanta had spent his afternoon hand-whittling ordinary domestic candles into birthday treats. He'd depleted our entire stock, but it was worth it just to see the delight on Andrew's face. Robert and Matanta joined us round the table as we carried on singing children's songs.

Andrew's forgotten birthday turned out to be the latest night we'd spent at Tau Camp. But even at three in the morning, no one, including Robert and Matanta, wanted to leave the party.

I took a moment to step back, to watch us all through my third eye as jokes, songs, and hilarity flowed. Andrew and Matanta goofed around together, doing silly hand gestures to even sillier songs. It struck me that this moment, with these people, at this place, was probably the closest we would get to paradise on Earth.

That almost made me sad.

Transient as I knew the moment would be, I lodged the joy deep into my memory banks. I would live off this party for many years to come. Smell being such an important part of memory, I took a wild sage-filled breath, drinking in the scents of the night. A ripple of cool air wafting in from the river caressed my skin. Soak it all in, I told myself, determined to never forget.

I suppose, deep inside, I knew Andrew and I were on the downward curve of our Tau adventure. Although neither of us had voiced any thoughts about life beyond here, I guessed, like me, Andrew was beginning to feel the tug of a world of Land Rovers, freedom to travel more than a mile from our front door, and easy communications with the friends and family left back home. Not to mention Woodie.

But for tonight? I said a silent prayer of thanks to Robert, Matanta, and the Canadian singers who had not only rescued Andrew's forgotten birthday, but had made it eternally memorable.

CHAPTER 49

For some weeks, as spring turned to summer, Gwynn and I seemed to have more baboons and elephants in camp than guests. There was little we could do about the baboons, but the elephants were another matter. With the right mental attitude and enough noise, they could—almost—be discouraged from wrecking the camp. Elephant patrol became an important part of the maintenance team's job descriptions.

The first time I'd asked them to undertake this assignment, Olutuswe clicked his tongue disapprovingly, muttering something in Setswana. Matanta translated it to mean that the men from the insane asylum must come take me away.

But, crazy or not, for the safety of our guests, not to mention our last remaining palm trees, the elephants had to be made to leave. That meant Thekiso or Olutuswe spent their days beating metal dustbin lids together while running after elephants. If I'm honest, all the activity really achieved was to tire out the maintenance team, give everyone else a headache, and annoy the elephants. It also put a nasty drag on the completion of my maintenance projects.

I was therefore more than a little proud the day we put the final touches on my new donkey boiler. I considered it a small miracle that we built it under the feet of four belligerent male elephants. Not to mention the months it had taken to assemble the building materials. Now, while Thekiso kept a lookout for elephants, Olutuswe and I gave the donkey boiler a final coat of mud plaster. Unlike the many reed walls and ceilings I had commissioned and installed at Tau, this boiler would be here for years to come. I even signed and dated my initials in the concrete.

Tonight it would be christened.

Brimming with satisfaction, I stood back that afternoon and watched Alfred build a fire in the belly of the boiler. That evening I hurried my shower, and dashed down to the pre-drinks fire to ask the guests in number four, the cottage my new boiler served, how they'd found the hot water. I skidded to a halt just inside of earshot, unable to believe what I was hearing. Agatha and Yvonne moaned loudly to everyone about the cold shower they'd been forced to endure.

"But you have a brand new donkey boiler all to yourselves," I objected.

Agatha turned steely eyes on me. "If I said there was no hot water, then there was no hot water."

The customer is always right. Except when they're wrong. Anyway, the ambient temperature was so hot, a cold shower couldn't have been the torture she claimed.

Or so I comforted myself.

Still, I was troubled by her claims. Sean's boiler blueprint had been cut out of *Farmer's Weekly* magazine. I had always had my doubts about the design, but without building it first, there was no way to test it. Sean hadn't bothered with such niceties before commanding me to construct one.

I sighed. Oh well. It still looked great.

Drink in hand, I slumped down into a chair and left it to Gwynn to entertain the guests. Although I may have looked vacant as I stared out over the bay, my mind was scheming on how to improve an inefficient boiler without having to rebuild the damn thing.

My pensive mood continued through an excellent meal of garlic mushrooms, followed by fillet steak, and then a chocolate mousse. Despite frowns from Gwynn, I contributed little to the conversation.

No that it mattered. I was no closer to a solution when I finally collapsed into bed that night.

As Gwynn and I leaned over to share our chaste goodnight kiss, I heard a deep cracking coming from the centre of the camp. A bang followed. Then silence. My heart sank. I knew exactly what it was.

"Sounds like elephant," Gwynn said unnecessarily.

"Don't bother waiting up," I replied. I didn't wait for Gwynn's answer. After the hyena's late night visitation, we both knew she'd be leaving this to me.

Groaning like a very old man, I flicked on my torch. Then a spurt of adrenalin kicked in and I casually, almost calmly, pulled on my trousers, donned a shirt, grabbed my Maglite, and walked out into a night as black as coal.

I made my way to the kitchen for vital elephant chasing equipment. Meanwhile, my treacherous mind conjured pictures of broken cottages, dead guests, and Sean in a fearsome rage at his manager's ineptitude. I quickened my pace. Once in the kitchen, I couldn't find the dustbin lids, so I settled for a large stainless mixing bowl.

I stopped to listen.

From what I could make out, this was one, maybe two elephants. They must have entered the camp from the runway end, passed our cottage unnoticed, before settling down to some concentrated chewing and tree pushing near number four, the cottage where the frosty Agatha and her partner were sleeping.

Then again, sleeping was being optimistic. Above the rumbling of elephant stomachs, whooshing trunks, and creaking palm trees, I heard the unmistakable sound of women squealing—and not in delight either. The guests were scared and, as manager, it was my job to protect them. Or so I told myself.

I scratched my beard, plotting my attack strategy. At this point, I should have felt some sympathy for Thekiso and Olutuswe who did this every day. In truth, I felt nothing. It was daylight when they chased elephant around the camp. They could see things like snakes, and cottages, and tree roots, and, well. . .elephants, before they tripped over them.

Elephants can't see very well. Even so, I couldn't risk lighting my torch. Not that the darkness helped me because they more than made up for poor eyesight with an acute sense of smell. Considering the garlic I'd eaten at dinner, I didn't give myself good odds at remaining undetected should things go wrong. That meant I needed an escape route where they could neither see nor smell me. But where?

Then I remembered my new donkey boiler with its extra wide mouth

Surely, the acrid smelling ash would mask me and my breath? All I needed was to hide in its belly should things go wrong.

I heard the elephants shake fruit from the palms. It wouldn't be long before they got frustrated and brought a tree down. Definitely time to move.

I set off into the dark, soundless night. And tripped over a log. Grunting, I dropped the bowl and the torch at the same moment a spider's web wrapped itself around my face. Cursing inwardly while trying not to imagine the size, or current location, of the spider, I felt along the leaf litter for my stuff. My hand brushed something hard and cold.

Ah ha. The torch. Then the bowl.

I scrambled to pick them up, then stood—and bumped my head on an overhanging branch. The bowl fell out of my hands again, clattering to the ground.

This was the stupidest day ever. So much for my element of surprise.

I took in a deep breath and, weapons held securely, prepared for another attempt. As I moved forward, I pictured myself in my mind's eye. In a strange way, this was a realisation of a dream, a dream I didn't even know I had—until now.

I, the great white hunter, had been sent to frighten away huge, fierce creatures threatening my home. I was experiencing Africa at its rawest, alone, with only my ignorance to protect me from abject fear and borderline incontinence.

Still, firm in the belief that my game plan was sound, I stalked my quarry. Not wanting to fall again, I occasionally flashed the torch against the sky, hoping to simulate distant lightening, something elephants would be familiar with. Each flash briefly illuminated the path. A few more steps and I reckoned to be about twenty paces from the elephants. They were still way too far off for me to see their dark bodies, in the dark wood, in the dark night.

I did however see a faint orange glow from the dying embers deep inside the donkey boiler. I crouched, my torso tense with excitement. Then, with three swift movements, I struck the bowl as hard as I could with the torch.

For a few seconds, nothing happened.

Then a scream rent the night like an express train screeching to a halt after the emergency stop chord is pulled.

All hell broke loose.

I don't know how many there were, but six, eight, twenty elephant charged through the bush towards me. The ground beneath my feet shook, branches cracked and fell, and two women screamed, and screamed, and screamed some more.

No second to waste.

I sprinted in the pitch dark towards the orange glow in the boiler. Diving in head first, I was vaguely aware of the hot coals charring my hands. Nothing for it but to suck it up. Weirdly, I felt no fear; the entire event was just surreal. Ash stirred by my feet wafted to my nose and I stifled a cough. How long could I hold it?

Trumpeting and the rumble of feet passed around me.

Then silence.

My plan had worked.

Sneezing, I crawled out, gasping for air. I turned on the torch, and stumbled towards cottage four. "It's safe now." My voice sounded like someone was strangling me. "You can sleep peacefully."

The next morning over breakfast, I waited for Agatha and Yvonne to boast about my braveness. Surely, they would recount my heroic deed to the other guests? But then I heard Agatha say, "And then, just before the elephants took off, Andrew tripped over the fire bucket!"

"What?" I spluttered.

"You know, that red bucket next to the cottage? I assume it's for putting out fires. We heard you fall over it." She turned to her audience. "Not once, not twice, but three times, he fell. That's how frightened he was."

I looked to Gwynn to redeem my flagging honour, but she merely patted me on the arm. "Tripped over a fire bucket, huh? And you told me you'd driven the elephants out of the camp."

I buried my face in my blistered hands, ready to cry.

CHAPTER 50

Andrew and I had just seen Agatha, Yvonne, and our other guests out on a plane that had brought us in nothing, not even a roll of toilet paper. Grinning with excitement, we watched as Morag, who was helping at Scops while Kyle and Milly were on their ten-day break, met her guests and started the trek down the runway with them.

An empty camp awaited our pleasure.

Even better, the heat had finally been broken by a week of cloudy weather. That meant the batteries attached to our solar panels were dead. We were completely cut off from the outside world. It was so bad, Joan had stopped calling, choosing instead to send messages in the mail. For the first time in the almost ten months we had been here, we were free to do exactly as we pleased. It was as if the universe itself had conspired to help us in the rebellion Matanta, Robert, Andrew and I planned.

Today we were going to Jugujugu in the motorboat Sean had sent up two months ago at the time of our short-lived guide strike. A mode of transport Sean had expressly forbidden we use, except in the direst of emergencies.

But a craving for sautéed bream, fresh from the river, constituted an emergency, didn't it?

As soon as the departing plane cleared the trees at the end of the runway, Andrew and Matanta ran down to the lagoon at the far end of the strip to retrieve the carefully hidden boat.

I dashed into the CIM room to grab the fishing rods, while Robert manhandled two cooler boxes filled with food and drink. Heart skipping with delight, I loped to the bay, ready for our adventure.

I've never really appreciated motorboats. They're too noisy and smelly for my tastes, but today the dulcet scream of that Yamaha was music to my ears. An operetta promising a broadening of horizons, grand new vistas, and freedom from the same endless questions asked daily by an ever-changing flow of people.

Who cared how deep the river was?

Or what the dining room chairs were made from?

I was so ready for this trip.

Matanta at the helm, Andrew waving and cheering, the motorboat roared into the bay. The jacana squawked, seeking cover. Matanta shot the boat up the bank. He moored the stern on the grass, just like the guys from Wildlife did every time they visited the camp.

Today I didn't complain.

"Cool driving," I said, as Andrew hopped off to help Robert heave our drinks on board. "Where do I sit?"

"Next to me." Andrew claimed a bench in the middle of the boat.

Robert plunked down onto a spot at the prow, slapped on his sunglasses, and stretched out. "Me. I am a rich *lekgoa* today."

Our staff gathered to see us off. They laughed, making derisive comments about Robert's ludicrous bright green shorts, blazoned with black and orange palm trees.

Arms held open wide, Matanta shouted, "When we see you again, we'll have fish this big."

Uproarious laughter punctuated his brazen speech. The sound soon fell away, lost under the howling engine.

"Where did you learn to motorboat?" Andrew shouted, as Matanta steered us expertly into the main channel.

"Before I came to Tau, I worked in Maun as a motorboat guide. It doesn't pay as well as feeding *lekgoa*." Matanta grinned. "Especially for a man like me with so many mouths to feed." Apart from one little boy whom he occasionally brought to camp, Matanta didn't often mention his various offspring. But when he did, he always got a rakish look in his eye. It seemed fitting.

Skimming effortlessly over the water, we soon passed the swimming hole, the only place outside of Noga Island I regularly got to visit. I threw my head back, face basking in the sunlight, conscious of how small my world had become.

I knew Andrew felt it, too, the closing down of his life, as he called it. We still hadn't spoken much about our plans after our contract expired in February, but I knew Andrew well enough to recognise his restlessness. Playing hooky today was a sign that things were changing.

"How far is Jugujugu?" Andrew shouted as he handed around some drinks.

"Less than an hour now," Robert replied. We had been on the river for at least thirty minutes. "When another river, a big one, meets up from the right, then we know we are near."

I was glad I didn't need to navigate by those vague directions. A smile split my face. Today, it wasn't my problem. I happily handed my life over to them. I was headed north, and that was all that mattered.

It wasn't long before the familiar channel, so narrow near the camp, widened considerably. We roared around a corner and our wake washed up onto a little reed island. It swamped a resting crocodile. If you can imagine a crocodile spluttering, then this one did. Sean was right; motorboats were not the best way to see the Okavango. Still, this was fun.

Unexpectedly, Matanta slowed the boat, and then idled to a stop. I looked around, wondering at the holdup. Then I noticed Robert rubbing his hands together. "This is Jugujugu," he said. "Let's scare some fish."

I don't quite know what I was expecting, but whatever it was, it definitely wasn't this. Apart from the confluence of the rivers, there was nothing—no signboard, no human habitation—to indicate that we'd even arrived at a place with a name. Where Matanta had found all the nubile girls he boasted of after his leave, well, that was anybody's guess.

I didn't care.

It was fantastic just being here.

While the boys fished, I pulled out a book and settled back to get lost in some fantasy world, far, far away from the Okavango.

Every so often, when my sun-baked body threatened to spontaneously ignite, I dropped my book, and rolled out into the river. But swims in Jugujugu were not for pleasure: a quick splash to cool off and then back into the boat because more than one crocodile glided past us as the sun slipped across the sky.

Fish filled the bowels of the boat when Andrew finally reeled in his line. He looked at his watch. "Four o'clock. I didn't realise it was so late. We should probably be getting back before the hippo start moving."

"There's no rush, *Rra*," Matanta answered, casting his line wide. "This time we go with the stream. We'll be home in an hour. Long before the hippo will be a *matata*."

Deferring to Matanta's superior knowledge, Andrew cracked open another drink, and settled down next to me. "Enjoying the freedom?" He offered me a sip of tepid Coke.

I waved the can away. "I could do this every day."

He peeked at me from the corner of his eye. "Getting tired of chasing after guests?"

I glanced up at Robert and Matanta, not wanting to have this conversation in front of them. "I think I'll feel more settled after Christmas when Jonty and Sarah visit." Our friends, Jonty and Sarah, were coming for a short visit over New Year.

Andrew sighed. "I never thought I'd miss friends so much. Even Jonty."

It was my turn to eyeball him. "You do realise that a year ago we were biting our fingernails to the nubs about getting this job?"

"True. And I don't regret it for one second. . ." But—that unspoken word hung in the air between us.

"I guess I just didn't consider how exhausting it would be." I was about to nod in agreement when he added, "Being cut off from the world. I never thought I'd actually crave a telephone. And hardware shops. And flying. And my car."

There was nothing I could say. He had zeroed a thousand-watt lamp onto the basic problem tugging at us: we both loved our jobs, the people we worked with, and met—most of them anyway—but should a *job* be one's life? Working nine to five, and often way past it, back in Johannesburg hadn't been much of life, either. That's why we'd come here. But hadn't we merely replaced one extreme with another? Surely there was a balance somewhere? If there was, I didn't know how to find it.

Matanta's fishing rod landed at our feet, pulling us out of our private chat. "Time to go," he announced, shuffling into his spot at the engine. "Or it will be dark when we are cooking our fish."

The sun lay low on the horizon as Matanta angled the boat downstream toward the camp. He opened the throttle and we set off, now doing twice the speed we had before.

We had not gone more than fifty yards when a squadron of midges dived to attack. Robert, sitting in the prow, was the first to be face-splattered. He was still coughing up bugs when Andrew and I ploughed through the swarm. We didn't even have time to cover our eyes.

"*Eish*," Robert spluttered, 'this is a *matata*."

"We will soon be through them," Matanta shouted with the confidence of a man who had done this route before.

Turns out he was wrong. The bugs just kept on coming.

Without warning, the boat veered to the left, grazed the reeds, and then slewed across to the other side of the river.

"Got a problem?" Andrew shouted to Matanta, waving his arm to clear the bug-infested air around his face.

"Can't see a bloody thing," Matanta yelled back, fighting to bring the boat under control with one hand, while his other swatted bugs.

"Here, take these." Andrew passed Matanta his bug-splattered sunglasses. "Should at least keep your eyes clear until we're through this swarm."

Through this swarm. If only. It was as if every midge in the Okavango had chosen that moment to dive bomb the river.

I squinted, spitting out bugs as Matanta popped on the glasses.

"These are great, *Rra*," he shouted. "Only one problem. Now I can't see where I'm going."

"Then slow down," Robert yelled, fanning his face.

"Then we'll still be on the river when the hippos start moving," Matanta yelled back, powering the motor to make his point.

The prow hit a log.

Or I think it was a log.

Could have been a croc, but we were going too fast to know for sure.

The engine spluttered and then died.

"*Matata*." Matanta sighed, peering over the edge at the motor. "I didn't see that with the sunglasses on."

No blood bloomed in the water, so I guessed it was a log. But the warning was clear: with sunglasses, Matanta would not be belting the boat back to camp. Without them, he couldn't open his eyes. We'd be limping home.

Andrew and Matanta got the engine going. Even with the current in our favour, we set off at a plodding pace. All thoughts of reaching the camp before dark were dashed. As *matatas* went, this was pretty serious. A week ago, a Scops guide had been attacked by the hippo on the river near Tau. It hadn't been nearly as dark that day as it was now. The guide had been lucky to survive. He was still in hospital, fighting to save his arm and his leg.

To add to our worries, the bugs worsened. Now they were a cloud of black, hovering over the river as far as the eye could see, which, granted, given the conditions, wasn't very far.

If asked what's worse—bugs doing breaststroke in my eyes or bugs boring up my nose—I'd be hard-pressed to answer. Amazing how nothing in life—even the most perfect of days—was ever truly perfect.

The sun dipped below the horizon.

We heard the first grunts of moving hippo.

My insides turned to water and I huddled low in the boat—as if that would offer me any protection from Africa's most dangerous mammal. My hands gripped my seat as the grunts turned into snorts, and then bellows as the motorboat glided into their haunt.

Honking like a deranged locomotive, one of them surged away from the herd and lunged for us. A tidal wave crashed into the side of the boat. Even in my panic to stay on board, I instantly sympathised with that poor croc we had almost drowned. The thought was swamped away as a second wave hit us. The hippo rapidly closed the distance between us.

Swearing, Matanta opened the throttle wide, powering the boat over the wave, inches past the hippo's nose. Mouth gaping, it taunted us with its tusks as we surged by. Laughing hysterically, a combination of fear, relief, and possibly sunstroke, we roared into the bay with the hippo on our heels.

Thank all the saints who protect naughty employees playing hooky, it stopped at the entrance to the camp, snorted a couple of times, and then swam back up river. Too grateful to care about the reason for our reprieve, I leapt out the boat.

Then I saw what the hippo must have seen—an unexpected fire twinkling in the hearth at the sitting out area. Around it waited four chairs. On the ground sat our entire complement of staff. As one, they stood and cheered.

"What are you all doing here?" I had given them the day off. "The hippo! How will you get back to the village?"

Seatla bowed, and then gestured to a table decked with salad, condiments, and a jug of lemon butter sauce. "We are here for the fish *braai*, Mma. We will spend the night at Honey Camp."

"How did you know we'd catch any?" I asked in astonishment.

A knowing smile spread across her face. "You cannot go to Jugujugu and not catch fish, *Mma*."

While Seatla and Kekgebele barbecued sixteen of the fattest, juiciest bream I had ever seen, Andrew, Robert, Matanta and I sat under the stars (not used for getting anyone to bed) and traded fishing stories with our staff.

Perfection.

CHAPTER 51

Christmas was almost upon us. To my delight, I had just completed the fastest Christmas shopping I had ever done. In Maun to renew our work waivers, (our promised work permits were still to arrive) I dropped into a convenient curio shop and bought Gwynn a necklace and a small duck broach that I called Florence.

I guessed she'd bought me yet another T-shirt from our own curio shop, so I was glad to get her something different. At Maun airport, I helped load the Cessna, making sure every square inch of packing space was utilised. We arrived back at camp in time for lunch.

Stomach rumbling, I made my way into the dining room. Being low season, the camp was almost empty with only a couple of Germans and a small group of Norwegians visiting. The Norwegians were already seated at the table.

"Got a letter from my Dad," I told Gwynn after greeting everyone. I sat and opened the envelope. It read:

*"G'day and howzit in the bush, then? Evie (*my mother*) said the other day: 'Have you written to Droonie and Gwynn?'*

'Does the elephant knock down trees in the Savuti?' I replied, in my usual evasive manner. 'Is the Sitatunga quiet and retiring? Does the boat beat the bike as a means of urban transport in the Okavango CBD? Does the fish eagle use sonar buoys?'

'OK, OK, OK,' she stopped me. (Just like the guy in 'Local Hero')

'Does the dung beetle...'

'OH-KAY!'

A thought for the day:

Roses are red
Violets are Blue
I am a schizophrenic,
And so am I."

And that was it. His way of telling us everything at home was normal. I wished I was there to share the joke with him.

I put my letter away and noticed two empty place settings where our German guests should have been. "Where are Fritz and Ursula?"

"Good point." Gwynn frowned. "You know, I haven't seen them since breakfast. I better go and check—"

I squeezed her arm. "Sit, I'll go." I wanted to hide her Christmas present anyway, so I could swing past number three on my way home.

The camp was quiet with all the off-duty staff lying low because of the December heat. Not nearly as bad as spring, it was still easily a 100 degrees under the trees. Even the birds seemed lethargic. I figured Fritz and Ursula were enjoying an extended post-breakfast, pre-lunch nap.

I stopped at the back of their cottage and called. Early morning wake-up calls had taught us that the most effective way of waking people was to use their names.

I had no sooner finished speaking when I heard an agitated voice reply, "*Mein Gott!* At last! Get these foul creatures out of here before we have heart attacks."

Foul creatures?

Not knowing what to expect, I bolted around the chalet, into the front door.

And froze.

Then my nose crinkled against the smell—a malodorous one I knew too well. I took a step closer. The mosquito net, once white and pristine, hung in ragged loops over a faeces-smeared duvet cover. The crap continued across the floor. The water flask and glasses lay shattered amid piles of clothing, ripped from an open suitcase. But in all this chaos, there was no sign of our guests.

Then I heard desperate sobbing coming from the bathroom. I darted across the room, skidded on the filth, and lunged for the bathroom doorframe to stop myself falling. As my hand gripped the frame, my face burst through the reed curtain, giving me an uninterrupted view of the room.

Trousers around her ankles, Ursula sat on the toilet, her face buried in her hands. Fritz, naked as the day he was born, cowered in the shower. Strangely, neither of them showed any reaction to my appearance.

Then I understood why.

Standing in front of them was the alpha, the same baboon who'd out-stared me when I'd first arrived at the camp. Robert had named him Idi Amin, after the African dictator who ravaged Uganda some decades before. Idi Amin now turned to look at me, cunning eyes devoid of fear.

"We've been here the whole morning with this thing," Ursula finally moaned, looking up for the first time. "Every time we try to move or shout—"

Idi Amin lunged at her, barking. She shrank back, collapsing into herself. Fritz huddled deeper into the corner of the shower until his blotchy white flesh was almost one with the *letaka* wall. I could see the baboon getting high on the fear pheromones swamping the air.

But I hadn't braved black mambas, and hippos, stared down a hyena, and scared off thirty six elephants to now be frightened by a mere baboon—no matter how big his incisors or dangerous his name sounded.

Arms held high, shouting at the top of my lungs, I leapt into the room. Idi Amin hesitated, clearly loath to give up his dominance. I shouted louder, right into his face. Barking raucously, he fled through the opening between the reed wall and the ceiling.

We both knew who had won that round.

But there was no time for triumphant chest thumbing. I had guests to attend to.

Crying like a baby, Fritz crumpled into a heap in the shower. Ursula rocked back and forth on the toilet, also keening.

I tossed a towel over Fritz. "I'm going to call Gwynn to help you. And the housekeeping ladies to clean up this mess." Fritz mumbled something, but I couldn't make out what it was, and I didn't stop to find out.

"Get down to number three, now," I panted into Gwynn's ear when I reached the dining room.

She looked at me questioningly, but must have seen my anger and frustration because she excused herself from the table without comment.

Morag looked up from her lunch. "Find Thekiso," I commanded her. "Now. Tell him to bring his *ngashi* to reception."

Perhaps it was my imperious tone, but she didn't even murmur. She put down her glass, dropped her napkin on the table, and followed Gwynn from the room.

So *that* was how to control Morag.

By the time Gwynn and Morag calmed Fritz and Ursula down, Thekiso was on his way up stream to the Wildlife department with a hastily drafted letter demanding action.

It was time to shoot some baboons.

CHAPTER 52

Rifle in hand, Mishak and two of his cronies arrived at camp the next morning. The weapon was an ancient-looking thing that had probably been around since the Anglo-Boer war. For the first time ever, their uniforms were clean and pressed. Pressed? Mishak was obviously taking this cull very seriously. I must admit, it inspired confidence, convincing me I'd done the right thing by calling in the law.

Mishak pulled a piece of paper out of his pocket and waved it at Matanta, on hand to translate. Matanta listened and then moved to grab the paper. Mishak deflected, rattling something off in Setswana.

Rolling his eyes, Matanta turned to me. "This is the permit to kill two baboons, but he won't give it to you until he's checked your story with the *lekgoa*."

I couldn't fault that. So, aided by Matanta's translation skills, Fritz and Ursula were called over to recount their trial. Face hard, clearly looking for revenge, Fritz seemed only too happy to retell their story.

Finally, Mishak nodded. "Bad, bad *matata* for the tourism." He turned to Matanta and spoke in rapid-fire Setswana.

Matanta translated. "Andrew *Rra*, he says we must fetch all the *lekgoa* to the front of the camp. All the staff must hide in the laundry. Everyone must stay still while they're shooting the baboons."

That made sense. The last thing we needed was for our guests to witness this cull. And the staff? Well, with our luck one of them would be mistaken for a baboon. My mind stuttered, not wanting to pursue that line of thought.

"What about breakfast for the *lekgoa*?" Gwynn asked.

Matanta didn't bother conferring with Mishak. "Of course the kitchen staff will prepare and serve breakfast, *Mma*. This is Tau Camp, after all."

Typical Matanta.

So, while Gwynn rounded up the guests for breakfast, I herded the rest of the staff into the laundry with instructions to stay put until Mishak gave the signal. I needn't have bothered with the warning. Any Motswanan worth his salt would be only too happy to be told by the boss to goof off when he should have been working. I made my way to the radio to alert Kyle and Milly to keep their staff and guests away from the camp.

I knew Gwynn would have no interest in watching animals, even if they were baboons, being shot, so I wasn't surprised when she joined the guests at breakfast.

Matanta wasn't so reticent.

Leaving Seatla to cook the eggs, he set off with me towards the runway. Mishak and his two cronies stood in the centre of the strip, deep in conversation. To me the whole thing was simple: all we had to do was creep under the trees where the baboons lived, take aim, and pull the trigger. Twice. Two baboons, that's all I wanted to kill. The rest would quickly get the message that they weren't welcome.

I set my jaw in a hard line and pointed to the closest tree. "Let's go."

Mishak turned to face me. "No, *Rra*." His chest puffed out with self-importance. "This is official Wildlife business." He gestured to Matanta. "You must both wait with the *lekgoa*."

I wanted to protest, but it was hot, and he did look like he meant it. Also, he was holding a gun.

Matanta was having none of it. He opened his mouth to complain.

I grabbed his arm and dragged him back to the kitchen. "Stay. Cook eggs." His laughter ringing in my ears, I went to breakfast. Gwynn dished me up a plate of food even though I wasn't hungry.

Neither was anyone else it seemed because no one was eating. We sat in heavy silence, punctuated by gunshots. These were followed by panicked screams of baboons.

Just how many of the damn things was Mishak killing?

Gwynn and I exchanged looks and I could read on her face that she was as unhappy about this as I was.

Fritz was less subdued. "This is good, *ja*. The more he kills the better."

Perhaps if I had been trapped in the bathroom for hours by an arrogant alpha baboon, I may have understood the sentiment, but right now I just felt heavy with regret. It was because of the camp with its easy pickings of food that the baboons had become problematic. As much as I disliked them, it wasn't their fault. I guess it wasn't anyone's fault, really.

Closer at hand, the bush and trees in which the camp huddled, usually alive with the raucous sound of squabbling babblers and starlings, was ominously silent. All living things, other than Mishak and the few surviving baboons, seemed to have gone to ground. It was only once the waiters were clearing away the tea and coffee cups that the firing finally stopped.

I braced myself for Mishak's report.

Like Rambo with a rifle slung over his shoulder, Mishak and his two sidekicks marched through the camp, coming to a halt at reception. Every eye at the breakfast table turned to me. I dropped my napkin and left.

Grinning like a maniac, Matanta darted out of the kitchen and loped over to join us. He slapped Mishak on the shoulder. Clearly, he had no problems with the wholesale slaughter of a troop of baboons. The result of almost-daily post-baboon invasion clean ups, perhaps?

Despite Matanta's joyous assault, Mishak stood to attention at reception, rifle held proudly in front of him as if he were one of the President's guard.

"*Er, Rra*, well done for solving this *matata*," Matanta gushed at Mishak.

I wasn't so effusive. "Are there any baboons left of the island?"

Mishak cleared his throat and then looked down at his feet. After what seemed like an eternity, he muttered something in Setswana. Matanta leaned in closer, holding his hands up in a typical what-was-that gesture. Mishak cleared his throat again and picked at the black insulation tape wrapped round the rifle's hilt.

Something was definitely wrong here.

My jaw dropped. "Don't tell me you've shot someone."

Mishak's head jerked up, his eyes wide and tortured.

"Who was it?" I demanded. "Someone from Scops Camp? A guide who didn't know we were shooting today?"

Mishak turned to Matanta and started sprouting in Setswana, words tumbling out a dozen a second. Eyes boring into Matanta, I waited impatiently for a translation.

Finally, Matanta threw up his hands and, in a voice brimming with disgust, declared, "He says he can't shoot moving targets."

"What? Was the guide running?" I tried to stop myself from laughing at the bizarre comment. "He can't . . ." I shook my head, trying to process that. "What the hell does that mean?"

Matanta rolled his eyes. "All those shots we heard? He says he didn't even hit the trees. The gun was jumping around in his hands so much, he almost shot his assistants. He says his shoulder is now very sore."

I took in a long, deep breath and tried not to laugh. No doubt, the baboons knew very well who had won that round.

Face scorched with shame, Mishak pulled the shooting permit out of his pocket. Like his uniform, it now looked decidedly crumpled. He laid it on the table, together with a pen, which appeared like the hyena had been chewing the end. Painstakingly, he jotted my name onto the permit, next to a sentence of Setswana words underlined in black ink. Then he spoke to Matanta.

Matanta translated. "This is a permit to shoot two baboons. But he has something very important to tell you."

In very broken English, Mishak said, "Two baboons only. Bury on same day." I nodded agreement. "And you must shoot. Only you. Not Matanta. He cannot shoot anything."

Matanta yelled something at him, but Mishak merely said, very loudly, "*Gagona*. No. Mister Andrew, only. Understand?" He looked sternly at Matanta.

I think that was Mishak's English vocabulary used up.

Ignoring Matanta's outraged disappointment, I asked, "What gun am I supposed to use?" It was clear from the way Mishak was hugging his rifle, that he had no intention of handing the old relic over.

"Ask Sean to send his gun," Matanta suggested glumly. He shooed Mishak out of reception, back to the Wildlife motorboat.

So, that was it. I, who had never held a rifle in my life, let alone killed anything bigger than a fly, was now responsible for culling two baboons.

"So, what's the baboon plan now?" Gwynn asked, joining me at reception after seeing Mishak off the island.

"I'll get me a gun and shoot the bastards."

She didn't smile. Neither did I.

Sighing, I scribbled a quick note to Sean, asking for a big gun with big bullets. I popped it in the mailbag. But first we had to get through Christmas."

CHAPTER 53

I love Christmas. I always have. Being with family. The twinkling lights. The decorations. The tree. The whole *ho ho ho* that is Christmas. Maybe it was because our families were so far away, with not even a telephone to call them, that I intended to make our Tau Camp Christmas as memorable as possible.

My planning had started in October, probably around the same time as the Christmas decorations appeared in the shops and malls back in Johannesburg. First off, I'd written to my mother, asking for the recipe for her traditional Christmas pudding. Sepei had balked a bit when she'd seen my order for candied peel and glacé cherries but, give her her due, she'd rallied to the cause, and had rustled up all the ingredients we needed.

Then, in the scorching October heat, Matanta and Robert had made me my pudding. So intent on humouring me, they had even agreed to allow the staff, at least those who wanted to engage in my madness, to line up for a chance to stir the pudding batter for luck.

"*Lekgoa* magic." Andrew winked to Matanta and Robert by way of explanation as he too prodded the mix with a sticky wooden spoon.

That raised a smile, but not nearly as broad, or as incredulous, as the ones that greeted me when I started boiling a handful of coins to add to the batter.

"You waste money on a pudding?" Robert demanded.

"It's tradition," was my only answer. After all, what was Christmas without a pudding no one wanted to eat, other than to dig through to find the money? Or at least, that's how it always worked in my home.

Once prepared, I stashed my pudding in the deepest, darkest recess of the pantry, far from hyena and baboon deprivations.

Come November, I'd pulled out Tau Camp's Christmas

decorations and found nothing but a few limp pieces of tinsel. Another order sheet went off. Sepei did her best, but there was nary a bauble to be found in Maun. I would have to make do with my ragged tinsel. She did at least find a couple of boxes of Christmas crackers, complete with party hats.

In early December, I'd ordered the turkey and a ham, which, astonishingly, arrived a few days later. Sepei also managed to squeeze in some chocolates and nuts.

Now, on Christmas Eve, I was set.

All I needed was my fresh fruit, vegetables, cold cuts of meat, and cheeses. Sepei promised to send them in on today's plane. Given our lackluster fridges, and the shop closures accompanying the holiday season, the timing of the fresh order was critical. Arrive too early, and it would all rot in the summer heat. Arrive too late, and, well . . . I didn't want to think about that.

I had just crossed off the last item on my Christmas to-do list when I heard the roar of an airplane on final approach. Apart from our Christmas fresh, we were meeting the last few guests who'd grace our Christmas table. I hoped they'd be as pleasant as the quiet Botswanan couple we had in camp. Our day-to-day happiness depended largely on the guests. Some were wonderful, some plain dull, and a few truly awful. All we hoped for were people who would enjoy the festivities with us. Christians, of one sort or another, would be good.

As I neared the strip, a raindrop the size of a coin splattered my face. Then another hit my arm. I peered through the canopy of trees and blinked. A grey sky peered down at me.

Grey?

How was that possible after two months of brilliant sunshine? As if to mock me, a blast of cold air gusted past, pebbling my skin with goosebumps.

"What's with the weather?" I shouted to Andrew who joined me from his work shed.

"I've been watching it roll in all morning. It looks pretty ominous."

"It better just be passing through because this wind is really cold."

Another gust hit as we stepped out onto the runway. It almost bowled me over. Thunder rumbled across the now purple sky, followed by a crack of lightning. Someone in the heavens opened the sluices and a deluge of water gushed from the sky. We broke into a run towards the plane just as Wes threw the cockpit door open and jumped out.

"Andrew, Gwynn," he shouted, handing Andrew a shotgun. Sean must have accepted Wildlife's instruction to kill two baboons. "We've got to make this a quick turn-around."

As if we needed to be told that.

"Maun has closed the tower to all traffic, other than the planes already in the air." He wrenched the passenger door open and started ushering everyone out.

"Closed the tower? Why?" Andrew demanded, barely noticing the guests cowering in the wind, hands covering their heads against the driving rain.

"The cloud base is two hundred feet. Too dangerous to fly." Wes started dragging stock out of the pod. "According to the Met office, this bugger is here to stay until New Year. If it is, you won't be seeing me, or any other planes until the clouds lift." He chucked the last piece of luggage into the rapidly forming lake next to the plane, leapt back into the pilot seat, and slammed the door shut. Just before starting the engine, he shouted out, "Happy Christmas."

The words were almost lost in the wind. How he was going to take off in this was anybody's guess. I suppose that was another reason the tower had closed Maun airport. Getting in and out of these bush strips was challenging enough at the best of times, let alone in the driving wind and rain. So, despite the miserable conditions, the guests, Andrew and I watched the take-off like spectators at a gladiatorial fight to the death.

Wes turned the Cessna's nose. Engine roaring, he trundled down the waterlogged strip. Water sprayed up on either side of the plane as the wheels dug into the rapidly forming mud.

My breath hitched. He had reached the take-off point but the Cessna wasn't flying nearly fast enough to make it over the trees. If Wes didn't pull up, he'd smash right into them.

Someone clutched my hand. Andrew. I dug my fingers into his as Wes coaxed the plane out of inches of muddy water sloshing on the strip. Inexorably, the plane inched into the air. There it hung, a few feet above the ground, hardly moving against the wind. Then, as if spurred on by angels, it lurched upward. In a brilliant piece of precision flying, Wes aimed for the narrow gap between the clouds and the top of the palm trees. A whoop of joy broke out on the runway as he cleared the tree tops and sped low across the horizon towards Maun. He had no sooner vanished from view when the clouds settled, blanking out the end of the runway.

So much for a sunshine-filled African Christmas.

While I quickly sorted out through the rain-drenched stock, Andrew rounded up our guests. Our Christmas additions consisted of a bedraggled-looking Japanese man, and an African couple with three young children. Andrew shepherded them down to reception. From their swarthy complexions and French accents, I guessed the black family were from somewhere in West Africa. I hoped they all enjoyed celebrating Christmas.

It was still pelting rain half an hour later when I left the pantry and made my way back to my cottage to change my sodden clothes. Andrew was already there, pulling on a dry shirt. I opened my mouth to tell him something of great importance, but he cut me off.

"Joan forgot to mention on the flight sheets that the Nigerian family are vegetarians."

"What?" I slumped down onto a wicker chair. "Can't be."

"Fraid it is. They don't eat meat, so it looks like it will just be us two, Morag, Sipho, Thembi, and the Japanese guy eating all that turkey and ham."

My hands clutched my face, knowing my despair bled into my eyes. "My fresh order never made it onto the plane."

Andrew slumped down into the chair next to me. "And now?"

"And now what? I've got a wilted cabbage, some butternut and gem squash, a handful of over-ripe tomatoes, a few potatoes, and a couple of onions with green things sprouting out of them. Tinned peas, tinned corn, tinned tomatoes, and tinned mushrooms. That's it." I rubbed my face. "Oh, and no cheese worth mentioning."

"Scops?" Andrew asked.

"I've already radioed them. Their fresh didn't arrive, either. They have even less than we do, so I'm lending them a couple of trays of tinned stuff."

"We'll just have to ply the guests with booze."

"The kids as well?"

He smiled. "It is Christmas."

Not seeing the funny side, I lumbered to my feet to change. Teeth chattering from the cold, I muttered, "I better get the housekeeping ladies to give everyone hot water bottles tonight."

Andrew threw a wet towel at me. "You're just grumpy because the fresh didn't arrive."

I glared at him. "Correction: I'm just grumpy because the fresh didn't arrive *and* it's bloody freezing in here."

Andrew pulled me into his arms. "I get it. You're homesick. You're missing Woodie. I am, too. And the weather isn't helping. The thermometer at reception says its nine degrees." That was a rosy 48 degrees. "But we've handled far worse, so we'll manage this little challenge, too."

As much as it burned me to let go of my self-pity, he was right. The show must go on. "I think we should make an effort to decorate the table, seeing we don't have a Christmas tree."

"As soon as the rains breaks, we can cut some palm fronds," Andrew said, clearly humouring me.

Then he smiled, the boyish one I loved so much. "At least the rain is keeping the baboons out of the camp. That means I have a reprieve from shooting them."

* * *

As soon as the rain breaks we'll cut some palm fronds. . .now there's a laugh.

It rained all through dinner.

Thanks to the lack of fresh veg and cheese, it was the first time I'd seen curried eggs and rice come out of our kitchen. Still, our vegetarian guests seemed to like it.

Christmas morning dawned gloomy and wet. The visibility was so bad the guides couldn't have taken the guests out even if anyone was foolish enough to want to go walking. The pretty paths threaded through the camp were mud. There wasn't a dry sheet on the island. To add to everyone's miseries, it was a bitter forty-two degrees—exacerbated by the airy reed huts, patently not designed for weather like this. The lack of hot water didn't help either. Not for the want of trying, Alfred had been unable to find dry wood, so the donkey boilers smoked and stuttered, producing no heat to warm the water. Andrew tried to assist by adding petrol, but all that did was produce small explosions, followed by great clouds of smoke.

Still, we tried to keep up the Christmas cheer, even sneaking off to listen to our short-wave radio in the hope of hearing a couple of Christmas carols. But the BBC World Service failed us. Not one carol broke through the mire of Middle Eastern conflict and politics.

Just before lunch, I cornered Andrew in the kitchen. He was stealing chocolates intended to supplement the Christmas pudding. I ignored the infringement, even helping myself to a handful of Quality Streets. I shoved a toffee into my mouth, and said, while chewing, "I'm tired of bolstering our *lekgoa's* sagging spirits. Let's steal a minute to go and exchange presents."

In the past we'd always torn into the present pile on Christmas Eve, with more left for Christmas morning. Given our limited gifts, this would be it. It was a testament to the strangeness of the day that the tradition had failed.

Andrew tossed a packet of chocolates at Matanta and Robert. "Share." He grabbed my hand and we skittered out of the room. We raced through the rain to our cottage. Laughing and giggling, we dived under the mosquito net and collapsed onto our bed. I reached for

Andrew's present first.

"Let me guess," he said, taking in the very obviously T-shirt-shaped parcel. "It's a house plant."

"Nah. It's a fishing rod."

"Could have fooled me." He tore off the brown wrapping paper. "Oh, look, how thoughtful of you. Yet another Tau Camp T-shirt to add to my collection."

"Be thankful you got anything, given that I haven't left this camp in months." I took the parcel he was holding out to me. It was small, wrapped in a zebra striped print paper. I shook it, and then poked it, trying to figure out what it was.

"Get on with it," Andrew said, with an expectant smile. Clearly, he was well-pleased with his present choice.

I ripped the paper open.

A very boring necklace, made from brown, black, and cream-coloured beads fell out. I recognised it immediately, having sold the last one in this line a few weeks ago in our own curio shop.

"I know brown isn't really your colour," Andrew said, "but I hope you like it. I went all the way to Maun to get it for you."

Brown most certainly wasn't my colour. But, as I told myself, it was the thought that counted. And I didn't have to wear it. Not really. I couldn't resist saying, "The only reason you went to Maun for it was because our stock of them had already sold out."

"True," Andrew admitted. "I had meant to buy one before the last one went, but I forgot." He grabbed the wrapping paper. "There's more."

This time I gave the paper a good shake. A bright yellow duck with an orange beak and feet tumbled out onto my lap. I pounced on it, squealing with delight.

"It's a brooch," Andrew said, unnecessarily because I was already pinning it to my shirt.

"The best gift ever." I hugged him, knowing this was his real gift for me. "You've made my Christmas."

"Yeah, well, if it carries on raining like this, we're all going to need webbed feet." Andrew tossed his boring new T-shirt aside and leaned back against his pillow, as if he didn't have half a dozen listless guests waiting to be entertained. "Come cuddle."

We *finally* got to have sex. Those stolen moments in the rain, under our mosquito net, were perhaps amongst the most memorable at Tau Camp.

Around three in the afternoon, the rain let up enough for me to grab Andrew's hand and a pair of garden shears. "Come, let's go foraging for Christmas finery."

We dashed through the soggy camp. Water dripped down our necks as we made our way to a spray of palm fronds growing next to our vegetable garden.

"How many do you want?" Andrew asked, shears poised to cut.

"Enough to cover the length of the table. I'm going to wreath them in tinsel. I'm using chillies as baubles, so it should look quite festive."

"Consider it done." Andrew pulled the closest fan down to eye level to snip the stem. Leaving him to it, I sloshed through the mud to the chilli bush. I was about to start picking, when Andrew let rip with an ear-shattering scream.

"What?" I shouted, slipping and sliding across the mud in my haste to get back to him.

He tugged at his shirt, trying to undo the buttons, looking more desperate to be rid of it than he had a few hours ago. Giving up the unequal struggle, he finally yanked it apart, caveman style. The fabric tore along the button line.

My mouth dropped. It was his favourite shirt. A colourful patterned one, I always hoped he wouldn't wear on special days. He shrugged it off and flung it around his head in some sort of manic dance. I had almost reached him, when he yelled, "Get back. Wasps. Hundreds of the bloody things."

It was then I heard the angry buzzing and saw a swarm of mud wasps. They surged around a nest, hanging from the frond Andrew had been about to cut. I grabbed his arm, dragging him, moaning—this time in pain—back to our cottage.

He slumped down on the chair. "Bastards. Check my back. Tell me how many got me."

I counted nine angry stings on his neck and shoulders. "Wait here." I dashed into the bathroom and grabbed a tube of antihistamine, which I daubed liberally on each welt. Foraging for Christmas finery was now clearly off the table—if you'll excuse the very poor pun. I was about to suggest to Andrew that he lie down, when he stood up, looking determined.

"And now?" I asked.

"It's Christmas, and I'll be damned if something as insignificant as a few wasp stings stop us from decorating the table." The second time in one day he'd been my hero.

He stomped back outside and I wondered if the wasp venom had addled his brain. It could, couldn't it? What else would explain the insanity of going back to the same bush, dangling the same nest?

Muttering under his breath about bruised egos and confounded insects, Andrew opened the blade on his Swiss Army knife and, in one quick swipe, levelled the branch. He then hacked off an armful of palm fronds, all before the wasp could react. We then beat a hasty retreat to the dining room.

* * *

Our Christmas dinner was served promptly at seven-thirty.

Morag joined us, smiling at our festive table. "Very nice."

Our guests weren't so effusive. To a man, they stopped and stared, mouths gaping. Finding no fault with my tinsel and chilli-covered palm fronds, paper hats, and Christmas crackers, I guessed the blankets draped on the back of each chair puzzled them.

"I figured we could all do with the warmth," I said by way of explanation.

"The blankets are wonderful," Miriam, one of our Nigerian guests, said, throwing hers over her shoulders. "But what's that stuff on the table?"

My heart sank. The words *Christmas Philistines* flashed through my mind. I pasted a smile. "It's . . . you know, Christmas decorations. Make the place look cheerful. Get into the spirit, and all that?"

"We don't celebrate Christmas," Miriam said, wrapping her kids in their blankets, as if the cuddly fabric would protect them from an evil cult threatening to ensnare them.

"Us neither," Thembi added, speaking for both herself and her husband Sipho. They had been our best hope.

Naoki the Japanese man, who spoke very little English, looked bemused.

Morag smiled at me, an oh-what-the-hell kind of look. She was right. On the one hand, my instinct was to serve my guests. But, on the other hand, I felt wronged. Why shouldn't I celebrate my ancestry, my culture, and my religion in my own home? Why should I let this lot of ungrateful sods ruin my day? I'll show them Christianity! I unrolled a yellow paper hat, and put it on my head.

Andrew immediately followed, and, pleasingly, so did Morag.

Andrew then announced, "We celebrate Christmas with good food, good talking, and coloured hats. I welcome you to join us in any part of the festivities you wish."

Naoki's eyes widened even further at the three of us wearing our absurd crowns. "Camera," he declared, and dashed out.

Undeterred, Andrew opened a bottle of wine. "We begin with a very good South African wine."

Not one of them wanted any.

But Morag said, "Yes, please."

Andrew went over to do the honours. By the time he had finished pouring, Naoki had returned. He snapped off a dozen or so shots of the three of us in our hats.

The rest of the guests, looking uncomfortable, would have to put up with it. I went into the kitchen to order all the waiters to wear silly hats. But I needn't have. They were already brightly decked. Even the scullery staff, Matanta, and Robert had joined in. Matanta wore his hat upside down. Robert, who was molesting the Christmas pudding, wore his on his sleeve, probably because his head was too large.

Back at the table, everyone began to settle. Even the Nigerians seemed to relax a bit.

Suddenly Naoki yelled, "Film." He dashed out again, just as Andrew and I were about to pull our second cracker.

Naoki was the best part of Christmas that year. His smile stretched across his round face as, again and again, he reloaded his Pentax.

"Do we have film stock in the shop?" I asked Andrew, sure Naoki must be running out of supplies.

"Oh yes. Out of business hours, with limited stock and a mad Japanese photographer on the loose, we'll make a killing."

The Nigerians, who had been mostly keeping to themselves, laughed. They were human after all.

Naoki rushed back, pointed at me, and smiled at Andrew. "Bang. Again."

"Didn't we do that earlier?" Andrew smirked, holding a fresh cracker.

As we pulled it for him to photograph, I made sure I didn't look over at Morag. Years later, I wish I had, because, for the first time ever, I heard her guffaw with laughter.

Andrew then took a huge risk by reading the appallingly lame jokes sprinkled onto the table from the crackers. "Who hides in the bakery at Christmas?" he asked no one in particular. Without waiting for an answer, he said, "A mince spy."

"Andrew!" I laughed, holding my side.

Morag was laughing out loud now.

"Maybe that's a bit too on the nose. Let's try another one." Andrew found another joke amongst the litter. "On which side do chickens have the most feathers? The Outside."

He was embarrassing me now, so I kicked him under the table.

"But that wasn't even Christmassy," he said, feigning obliviousness. "Don't worry, I'll try another." He waded through more scraps. "Ah. This is really lame. One that everyone will understand.

What do you call a penguin in the Sahara Desert? Lost."

Not a smile for a thousand miles. At least, not from our African guests. Our Japanese friend's grin hadn't changed one jot since he sat down, got up, sat down, got up, and sat down again.

For all that, the carnivores amongst our guests seemed to appreciate the meal, if not the silliness. They polished off an entire turkey and ham before the night was done. Aside from the vegetarians, no one seemed to notice the tinned vegetables on the side.

Needless to say, it wasn't a late night. It seems traditional English Christmases are definitely an acquired taste.

CHAPTER 54

The Met office had been right about the foul weather. It only started to lift a few days after Christmas. Getting planes in and out of the camp over the past week on the rare occasions the Maun runway opened had been a challenge. On more than one occasion, Gwynn and I joined the maintenance guys and the kitchen staff out on the runway with brooms and rakes, clearing great puddles of water in advance of an incoming plane. Landings were hair-raising and take-offs spectacular.

Now the sun was beginning to break through enough to evaporate the sodden ground. But despite the rain, with the Okavango's unique contradiction, the water level continued to drop. Our little bay began to look a little sad. The depressing spectacle of cracking mud and brown water lilies stood in sharp contrast to the air of excitement that buzzed around us as New Year approached.

Our good friends, Jonty and Sarah, were in camp with us. Wonderful as it was to have them, their presence was unsettling. It reminded us both of what we missed back in Johannesburg.

January the first dawned. Exactly one year had passed since we first visited the camp. With our contract due at the end of February, we had to decide whether to renew or not.

I was torn. I loved being here, but I missed 'real' life with telephones, working with film, my car, and shops, although I loathed shopping. Most of my limited free time had been spent writing my very first book—*A Complete Guide to Four Wheel drive in Southern Africa*—and I was close to completing the first draft. I wanted to find a publisher.

Added to that, I knew Gwynn was keen to start a family that didn't include just a Siamese cat. The prospect filled me with dread. If a cat was a challenge, then what would real babies be like? Thus far, we had skirted around these issues, neither of us ready to broach the subjects. So, it was with conflicted thoughts that I set out to attend to my early morning chores on New Year's Day.

The whole camp, including Gwynn, was sleeping. Glad to have the morning to myself, I breathed in the wonderful, fragrant air, sweet after the rains.

A sudden crashing above my head broke into my musings.

Surprise, surprise, the baboons were cavorting in the canopy. This was the first time they'd breached the camp since the rains. My mind dashed to Sean's shotgun, waiting in the CIM room. I had to kill a couple of them. Dread plummeted like a rock through my chest. I hated baboons, but I hated killing things more.

My head jerked around in time to see three baboons bolting straight up the pathway towards me. One of them was the troop beta. Robert had named him Saddam Hussein. He was only marginally smaller than Idi Amin, the alpha. The other two baboons were not small either, each easily as tall as my waist. Fangs glaring, they darted closer, stopping a couple of feet away from me.

One baboon I could handle, maybe two, but three? Especially with the rest of the troop waiting in the trees behind me? Those didn't feel like comfortable odds.

Heart racing, I stood my ground. Then, realizing I had to show no fear, I ran at them. This was almost as scary as my encounter with the hyena. The three bolted up trees, barking hysterically.

And then it happened.

Baboon crap. Foul, stinking, stringy, disgusting shit hit me on the head, splattering in my hair, on my arms, my shoulders, my back, my face. It was everywhere, flying thick and fast. I ran. And so did they, tracking me as I weaved along the paths.

Then I understood.

The bastards had ambushed me! This was payback for sending that idiot Mishak after them. Idi Amin, the master strategist, had used three of his meanest henchman to literally herd me under the trees, where the rest of the troop waited to pelt me with faeces.

He had just declared war. I was going to learn how to shoot Sean's shotgun if it killed me.

Retching in disgust, dodging fistfuls of the stuff, I charged for the CIM room. Seconds later, shotgun and ammo in hand, I tore back up the camp, waving the weapon at the baboons.

That got them.

Shrieking like banshees, they scarpered, flying across the tree canopy out of the camp. But I knew they'd be back. I sprinted to my cottage to plan my counter-offensive.

Gwynn lay awake, her face expectant. "Ooh, what is that *disgusting* smell?"

"They crapped on me, the bastards! They waited and attacked me." I bolted for the shower, stripping off before I even got there.

Gwynn's head peered around the door. "Jonty. Jonty can shoot anything with anything."

What genius! Why didn't I think of it? Jonty armour-plated cash-in-transit vehicles for a living. He had been playing with guns when other kids his age were vrooming around the playground with their Dinky cars. If anyone could shoot them, he could. Dead they'd be. Dead and buried. Desperate to get him awake and shooting, I sloshed great fistfuls of shampoo on my head. It didn't seem to help much. I still retched from the smell.

Then I heard Gwynn laughing. *Laughing?* How was that possible? Whose side was she on, anyway?

"What the hell is so funny about being crapped at on New Year's Day?" I raged.

"Comfort yourself," Gwynn said through her mirth. "Your year can hardly get any worse."

* * *

Ten minutes later, I handed Jonty the gun and ammo. He read the label on the ammo box and nodded his approval. "This will do fine."

I agreed, although I had no idea what it said that was so was vital to killing baboons.

He broke the barrel, ready for loading. Although outwardly serious, I could see that if he tried any harder not to laugh, he'd have a hernia. What was the matter with these people? Didn't they understand the affront I had just borne?

Jonty wedged two cartridges between his fingers and pushed another into the barrel. With the gun still broken, he said, "Let's go." Then he started humming *Danny Boy*.

That raised a smile despite my fury. Yesterday, he'd watched me and Thekiso unblocking the toilet in number one, serenading us with an endless refrain of, "Oh Danny boy, the pipes, the pipes are calling."

I punched his arm. "Take this seriously because if Wildlife find out, they'll probably have us both—"

"Shot?" Jonty's eyebrow quirked. "They'd probably miss."

"Jonty, no one can know you were responsible for the massacre.

And if we can, Idi Amin and Saddam are the first prizes."

"Relax, Andrew," he said. "I'm all over this problem. Your crappy honour will be avenged."

I led him to the anthill next to the runway.

We crouched low to reconnoitre. Just down the way, our bachelor herd of elephant cavorted around like kids, but I didn't spare them a moment's notice. All my attention was on the baboons sunning themselves across the strip.

Then we saw and heard *them*.

The patter of feet scampering across the runway towards us.

Idi and Saddam were on the move. They loped purposefully across the runway, headed our way. Saddam stopped, but Idi continued forward, skirting to the left of us. Sensing another ambush, I nudged Jonty. He nodded, slid in a cartridge, and gingerly closed the weapon.

Although he made no sound, the baboons bolted.

Jonty sprang, aimed, fired, reloaded, and then relaxed—all in less time than it took me to blink.

Saddam hit the ground in a ball of dust.

Jonty swung around to find Idi, but he was gone. He handed me the shotgun. Only then did I notice that he had already broken the barrel, removed the cartridges, and closed it. I admit to being a bit stunned at how quickly it had all happened.

Saying nothing, we walked over to inspect the corpse. A small, round entrance wound penetrated Saddam's temple, with a thin line of blood leading from it. The baboon never knew what hit him.

"I knew you were good, but this is ridiculous," I said, knowing my words would go straight to Jonty's head.

He grinned down at the corpse. "Payback's a bitch, huh?"

"He's just a henchman," I said. "An important one, but he didn't call the shots. For real payback we need Idi."

I didn't add that this wasn't just about revenge because I didn't need to. Jonty knew very well there was more was at stake here than my pride. It was only a matter of time before these fearless animals mauled someone.

He turned to me and grinned. "Idi's toast. But we will have to change tactics first because he's also smart."

I nodded. How Idi heard the soundless click of the shotgun remained a mystery. Also, I realised, shooting outside the camp would not get the message through that Tau was not a safe place for baboons. Idi and his troop still had a vital lesson to learn.

And so our plans were laid.

Climb Mount Niitaka—tomorrow at sunrise.

We had just finished scheming when we heard shouting. The morning shift ran toward us, cheering and clapping. Matanta and Dylos reached us first, skidding to a halt at the fallen baboon.

Matanta knelt down and poked the hole in Saddam's temple. "What a shot! Chief Andrew, you are incredible." He gazed at me standing nonchalantly, holding the smoking gun as if I had just sprouted a halo and wings. The Chief had done something all the local camps, the village, the next village, and probably half of Maun would hear about before Saddam even got a decent burial. I reckon I went up eight million percent in their eyes. But, as much as I wanted to give Jonty the credit, it was out of the question. Not even Matanta could know what we had done.

"Lucky shot," I said. "Let's leave Saddam here until Alfred arrives. He can bury him on the other side of the runway."

The rest of the morning staff had reached us. As one, they threw up their hands in shock at my words. I looked at them expectantly, but as usual, it was left to Matanta to explain.

"Alfred won't touch a baboon, *Rra*. Bad juju. Evil spirits. I'll get Letabo to do it. He doesn't take notice of the spirits."

Letabo was a very slow-witted chap who had been helping with the runway sweeping during the rain.

I nodded. "Get him on it as soon as he gets to work or else we'll have the hyena back before we know what happened." Already vultures circled the sky. The other scavengers would quickly follow.

Matanta gave me an oversized grin. "I can't wait for Robert to come on shift. We had a bet. Twenty bucks. He said you would never shoot a baboon. That you were too kind. I said he was wrong. That you could do it." He rubbed his hands together, gloating. "Twenty bucks! And, even better, now I can tell him that he can't read people as well as he says he can."

Guilt bit. Twenty bucks was a lot of money for Robert to lose over Jonty and my deceit, but I could say nothing other than, "Still, Robert is a very smart man."

"No, he's not. He's a poor man."

* * *

Not surprisingly, at a little after five in the morning, the sun was about to rise. It was January the second. A day of infamy was about to unfold. Mount Niitaka was about to be scaled. This time we would stalk the baboons in the camp.

Jonty, holding the shotgun, and I crouched behind the curio shop next to reception, waiting for Idi and his raiding party. I admit to being a bit doubtful whether they would come back after the loss of Saddam, but Jonty was leaving that afternoon, so this was our last chance.

I needn't have worried.

Barking and squealing as if nothing had happened, the baboons strolled into the camp. I ignored them, waiting for Idi.

Finally, swaggering like he owned the world, Idi loped down the path towards us.

I felt Jonty tense next to me. Idi must have sensed something because he spun to the left, and bolted up the sycamore fig tree that dwarfed the kitchen. In the same moment, Jonty stood, snapped the weapon closed, and fired.

Before I even knew if he'd hit anything, the shotgun was in my hands.

An instant later, there was the crash of a very large body falling through branches. It tumbled until the fork in the tree stopped the free-fall.

A stab of triumph jabbed me. A hit. Idi, who had plagued and tormented me for almost a year, was finally gone. The surviving baboons shrieked their protest, and bolted out of the camp.

Next thing I heard were running feet. Kekgebele and Matanta sprinting down the path towards the kitchen.

Kekgebele clambered up the tree and pushed the baboon down with his foot. As nonchalantly as I was able, I trotted over with Jonty to check the damage.

A mix of admiration and disappointment made me gasp.

It wasn't Idi. My adversary had survived. Even now, he was probably in his hideout, plotting his next assault.

Still, it was a baboon, and it was dead. Very dead. A single round hole penetrated right between its black eyes. Like his friend Saddam, he never knew what hit him.

Forget halo and wings, Matanta and Kekgebele now looked at me as if I were Zeus's more dextrous younger brother—but with a big gun.

"Nice shot, Andrew," Jonty said, patting me on the back. "That's very good. Even I am surprised. . .at you."

In truth, I tried to feel okay about what I had done—or rather, what Jonty had done in my name—but no matter what kind of a hero I was thought to be, the whole thing left me empty inside. I could only pray the raids would finally let up. If they didn't, then the whole exercise had been pointless.

Matanta broke my introspection by calling to Letabo. He had turned his sweeping skills to tending to the paths. Letabo dropped his rake and chugged over to join us. I was struck again by how slow he looked. Not simple or backward, but just not very bright, like the elevator never made it to the top floor.

Matanta spoke slowly to him in Setswana. Letabo's face fell, and then blanched. His eyes widened as he looked down at the baboon. Matanta shoved his shoulder, sending him lumbering towards the kitchen.

"And that?" I asked.

Letabo looked back at us with a mixture of despair and disgust.

Matanta grinned at me. "He's bringing a knife so he can cut off the baboon's right index finger."

Jonty and I raised eyebrows at each other, and then I asked Matanta, "Do I even want to know the reason for that?"

An air of saintly innocence settled on him, which I recognised as his prank facade. I would get nothing more out of him until the joke had run its course. I turned on Kekgebele. "You've seen how well I can shoot. Tell me what Matanta is planning."

Kekgebele looked first at me and then at Matanta. But instead of the usual hero-worship blazed across his face when he was with Matanta, he now looked anguished. The kid was torn between betraying his mentor or obeying the Chief with the gun. Matanta gave him a rakish smile, clearly eager to see how Kekgebele would respond under pressure.

Just then, Letabo returned from the kitchen with a carving knife. Face puckered with abject horror, he bent down to comply with Matanta's instruction.

This I couldn't watch. The baboon had been a menace, but I could not let his body be desecrated for a prank. "No! Stop." I grabbed Letabo's shoulder.

He fell back on his haunches, letting out a strangled sob—relief, I think, at the reprieve. Matanta grinned, and then said something in Setswana. Letabo dropped the knife, scrambled to his feet, and stumbled away.

Matanta chuckled. "I told him we needed the finger to put in a stew for the *lekgoa's* supper."

My stomach roiled like a ship on a high sea. "Why on Earth would you say that?"

Matanta winked. "Don't you know, *Rra*? It's an old Bushman recipe. If the *lekgoa* eat the finger of a baboon, it will make them clever, solving all the *matatas* of being stupid."

"Right," I said, choosing not to be offended that he had called me—and every white man—stupid. "A Bushman recipe. A bit like your oxtail aardvark bones."

Matanta raised his hand for a high five. "*Er, Rra*, and it almost worked. But you are too smart for me."

CHAPTER 55

My mother had a saying about Africa: it was always famine or feast. She was right. New Year celebrations a distant memory, our little bay continued to dry up as the water level dropped. Now, to get to the water in the main channel, we had to tread a path of rotting lily pads, lying on cracking mud. Beyond the river, the reeds and grasses on the floodplains had also withered and dried, exposing the muddy flats to the baking sun.

It was a sorry sight.

Worse, with the water level so low, it lost the benefit of being filtered through a thousand miles of reeds and sands. It was now no longer safe to drink without boiling.

Added to this was the January summer heat. The last rains had fallen around Christmas. The burning air, dusty and dry, hung heavy over the camp, doing little to encourage activity.

Once again, Andrew and I were due for leave, and we were tired. Tired of guests, tired of smiling, tired of eating huge meals three times a day, every day. In a word, tired of being camp managers. More and more, the prospect of going home and resuming a 'normal' life played on my mind. I missed Woodie, my parents, my friends, hot chocolate and cake at my favourite coffee shop. Life. Real life.

My ingratitude wasn't lost on me. Oh, how fleeting was my attention span. This time last year, I had been hankering to be here. But, such is life. I could not camp forever.

It was such gloomy thoughts that occupied my mind one evening out on the runway. Andrew worked at sending the guests to sleep with some stargazing. I heard his voice take on a sharper tone than usual as he tried to show off the Coal Sack—impossibly difficult to see because one is essentially looking for blackness in a black sky.

"How do you hope to see anything?" he snapped at one of the

hapless guests trying to locate it with a torch beam. "Turn off your light." The guest got such a fright he dropped his Maglite and popped the bulb.

I snorted back a laugh. Yes, Andrew was tired and thin on patience, too.

Amid all this star gazing, and torch dropping, I suddenly noticed something far more interesting in the sky—a faint orange glow just above the horizon.

The next morning, I radioed Morag down at Scops. She had finally gotten one of the things she had wanted—to manage a camp. Sadly, Kyle and Milly had moved on because the Department of Labour had refused to renew their work permits. Ours had yet to come.

"110, 638."

"Gwynn," came Morag's clipped voice. "What do you want?" I missed Milly.

"Late last night, we saw signs of fire towards the south. It was too far away to worry you then, but have you seen anything today?"

"Yes. It's coming fast. It might be here tonight or tomorrow." I detected concern in her voice. The low water level meant fire was our biggest threat, living, as we did, on a grassy island in reed huts.

There was no point in trying to discuss strategy with Morag. She'd never listen to me. Andrew was another matter. I tracked him down and broke the bad news. "Morag says the fire could reach us tonight."

He tossed down his monkey wrench with a clank, and looked up from the toilet pipe he was repairing. "Things always look worse on the ground. Radio Maun. Ask them to get the incoming pilot to check it out for us." He wiped the sweat off his face with his sleeve. "We better hope it bypasses because I doubt we have anything on this island to fight a fire with."

On that cheery note, I went to make the call.

That afternoon, Andrew and I waited with tense anticipation for Wes to land. Thankfully, due to the low season, we were not expecting guests on this plane.

"Bad news, guys," Wes announced as he hopped out the cockpit. "I took the scenic route. The fire's burning across a sixty mile front. Measured it. Only torrential rain will stop it. Like the stuff we had over Christmas."

My teeth found my lip, chewing it as if my life depended on it.

"When will it reach us?" Andrew asked.

"Three, maybe four days. No more than that."

"Maybe we can order some firefighting gear," I said, rubbing my arms for comfort.

Both Andrew and Wes looked at me as if I had just sprouted a second head. Andrew flung his arm around my shoulders and said, somewhat patronisingly, "Wes, ignore her. It's the heat talking."

I elbowed him in the ribs and snapped, "What? My reasonable comment is met with some nasty remark?" I guess it was fear, not heat that had control of my mouth because I didn't usually snarl at Andrew. And he wasn't usually demeaning.

Wes smiled at me. "Gwynn, the only way you're gonna fight this monster is with aerial bombardment, like we do with fires back home in Aus. But, I can't see the authorities paying for a lark like that. Best you guys can do is to have some boats ready to take you up north before it reaches you."

Joy. Just what I needed to hear as our world shrivelled up.

"If you need me to bring you some petrol for that motorboat you've got hidden in the reeds," Wes added, "just shout and I'll squeeze it on board the next flight."

"Might be a plan," Andrew said, his smug, patronising tone long gone. "We better hope we don't have to evacuate at night. The hippos sure as hell won't like that." He tugged at his beard, eyes darting around the runway.

Would this tiny ribbon serve as any kind of firebreak for us? I doubted it. Our only hope lay in the narrow river that flanked the south-eastern side of the island. But if the fire jumped that barrier. . .

I didn't even want to contemplate that. The reality was that we had no escape. If the fire came onto the island, we would be trapped.

Still, life goes on. Meals had to be prepared, guests entertained, and cottages cleaned. Toilets still broke and needed to be repaired.

Nights were different. With the southern sky a brilliant orange, it was harder to pretend the fire wasn't raging towards us. In the evenings, we took our guests to the runway, not to view the stars, but to watch the advance of the inferno. With each passing night, the thorn and palms trees on the horizon stood brighter against the ever more livid sky. By the third night, the horizon had shifted close enough for us to see—and hear—the flashes of exploding palm trees.

When a palm tree caught fire, it smouldered first. Once the sap began to boil, the tree roared like a jet engine. When the temperature reached boiling point, flames burst from its heart. Each little inferno lasted less than a minute before the palm's flammable gasses were spent. If a large clump of palms were struck, the roar was truly frightening

The fire was now a mere twelve hours away.

CHAPTER 56

D-Day.

A roll call at both camps revealed a total of forty-one people on the island. We would never all fit in the motorboat. Like it or not, we had to make a stand.

Trouble was, everyone looked at me to make the tough decisions. I think my success at shooting those blasted baboon had something to do with that. Then, at least, I had a shotgun, some ammo, and a friend with a lethal aim.

Now I had nothing except for nine tiny fire buckets at Tau Camp, and six down at Scops. That, and four rubber fire beaters were the sum total of my firefighting gear.

I thought back to my snide comment when Gwynn had suggested we order equipment. I laughed. Even if every person on the island was kitted out in asbestos suits and gas tanks, and wielded the most high-tech fire beaters in the world, we stood no hope against the coming inferno. I prayed for a shift in the prevailing wind that drove the flames towards us.

Both Morag and I suggested to our respective guests that they move on to their next destinations. For reasons I will never understand, they all opted to brave out the coming firestorm. One of them even called it, "A great adventure. Something to tell my grandchildren." If the idiot survived that long.

Feeling the crushing weight of responsibility for all the lives on Noga Island, I sought out Matanta in the kitchen. A tense atmosphere greeted me. Somehow, preparing breakfast lost some of its urgency when lives were at stake.

"Call the staff. We're having a *kgotla*. Except at this one, I am the only person who gets to speak."

Matanta's eyebrows shot up but he didn't argue.

Soon, everyone, guests included, gathered at the sandy patch outside reception. I studied their faces. Everyone was scared and it showed in the tightness around their eyes, and in the intense conversations.

I called them to order.

"The pilots say the fire will reach us tonight. We have to be prepared. Everyone who doesn't have family in the staff village will stay on here." A ripple of concern greeted my announcement. "This camp, and these *lekgoa*," I pointed to the idiot guests, "are what feed you. If we don't save the camps, you have no jobs. If we all split up, some of you at the village, some at Honey Camp, Robert at Romance Island, then we stand no chance of saving anything. We must work together."

I expected someone to say something but all was silent. They were taking me at my word that I was the only one to speak.

"You will all stay at Otter Lodge. If the fire comes, you get your butts over to Tau as quickly as you can. We will use the duvets off the beds to fight the flames if we have to." That would be as effective as trying to kill an elephant with a rolled up newspaper, but what else could we do?

I turned to the guests. "I wish I could offer you safe passage out of here, but you've all elected to stay. Therefore, I am enlisting you in the firefighting corps. If you hear this sound—" I clanged two dustbin lids together, "please come to the runway with your blankets." I heard the bright spark who had spoken about his grandkids snigger. I ignored him, and instead divided everyone up into teams with fire captains.

That left nothing else for the staff and guests to do but wait.

Not good at waiting, I headed over to the mic to call Englishman. "I'm bringing the motorboat down, do you want me to pick you up so we can see where the fire is?" I asked as soon as he answered.

"*Er Rra*," came his enthusiastic reply.

Twenty minutes downstream from Scops, Englishman and I hit a wall of smoke. Coughing and spluttering, E'man, who had the controls, slammed on anchors, bringing the boat to a rapid stop. There was no possible way we would break through that pall without oxygen tanks. I was helping him negotiate a reverse manoeuvre in the narrow channel when a head popped up in the water in front of us.

"Hippo!"

Eyes the size of a hippo's butt, Englishman opened the throttle as wide as it would go. The motorboat ripped through the reeds, and shot back into open water, missing the hippo by no more than a couple of feet. It reared up angrily behind the boat, clearly incensed by us, the low water level, the smoke, and who knew what else. It doesn't take much to piss off a hippo.

Eyes streaming from the smoke, we retreated a short distance and waited for the hippo to settle. After a few irritable snorts and much bubble blowing, it sank back into the river. We waited a few more minutes to ensure it didn't have murderous intentions, and then turned our attention to the fire.

I hissed in an acrid breath. Fear-induced nausea threatened to empty my stomach. In the drifting smoke, flames licked over the main channel, grazing the tree tips on Noga Island. Jaws tense, saying nothing, Englishman and I waited helplessly for the terrifying moment that a branch on our side of the river ignited.

Then I realised how pointless our vigil was. The fire had the island flanked. Who knew where the jump would occur? It could have already happened.

Seeing the threat up front, in person, honed my thoughts. "I've got this all wrong. I was going to throw everything I have at Tau. But if the fire jumps down at Scops—"

"*Er Rra*, then it would be better to fight first at Scops," E'man interrupted.

"Let's get back. I need to speak to Morag."

We returned to Scops to find Morag waiting for us. She looked pale, with dark rings around her eyes. I felt for her. I, at least, had Gwynn. Morag had no partner to bounce her ideas and issues off. Still, she had what she wanted—the title of camp manger.

"So what's happening?" she asked.

"The fire could jump at any time. I suggest we both keep staff on the lookout. At the first sign of danger, radio us and we will come and help. If it hits us first, you come to Tau. Neither camp turns off the radio tonight. We'll deal with flat batteries in the morning."

I didn't bother mentioning the possibility of the fire splitting the island in two. If that happened, we would be fighting it on two fronts.

* * *

Dinner was a nervous affair. As far as the eye could see, dancing towers of flames marred the view across the floodplain. Every few minutes, a clump of palm trees exploded with a roar. The painted reed frogs were silent. Smoke hung heavy in the air, causing noses and eyes to stream, making breathing difficult. Added to that, a layer of airborne soot

282

covered everything.

Only the thin band of river stood between us and destruction. I shuddered, wondering how I ever thought I could contain that inferno with a handful of fire buckets, a couple of rubber beaters, and a collection of duvets. It was laughable. In a sick, distressing way.

I wasn't the only one who couldn't keep still. With shock etched on their faces, every few minutes someone grabbed the binoculars to see if the fire had jumped.

My biggest fear lay in the fire sneaking around the back of camp, trapping us under the trees between it and the river. There would be no escape. I leaned over to whisper to Gwynn, "Let's check what's happening on the airstrip."

She nodded, and we quietly slipped away while our guests absorbed the pyrotechnic display on the other side of the bay. We stopped on the runway. Eyes fixed on the sky, we turned a full circle. In every direction, the sky was livid and red. Flames, high as the tallest palm trees, leapt into the air both left and right of the island.

Gwynn clutched my hand. "We're surrounded by fire."

"Maybe this is what Dante meant," I murmured, unable to believe we could be spared. "You know I love you, don't you?"

Gwynn laughed nervously. "That's what you say to people who are about to die." She looked at me through strained green eyes. "Faith. We have to have faith." Almost as an afterthought, she added, "And yes, I love you, too."

We returned to our guests. Driven by fear, we all huddled around the dining table long after the staff left for the night.

It was about midnight when the radio squawked into life. The desultory conversation around the dining table stopped and everyone looked at me. Fighting to portray a calm I didn't feel, I headed for the mic.

It was Englishman. "Andy, it's here."

My heart sank. "Be more specific."

"We need the motorboat," came his panicked reply. "The fire has reached the Y-junction right opposite the camp." That was about hundred yards from the Scops jetty. "We want to attack it before it crosses."

"I'll gather a team." I dropped the mic and was about to head off to Otter to get a group together, when E'man called back. "No need, *Rra*, we have a bunch of guys here. Just bring the boat."

"I'm on my way."

I suddenly saw the flaw in all my planning. The staff had gone, and I didn't have the knowledge of the river to power a boat in pitch darkness down to Scops. I sprinted to Otter Lodge.

It was deserted.

I shouted and swore but no one came. Time was of the essence, so I ran to Romance Island, but again, no one was there.

"Where the hell are they," I raged.

I was out of time. Panting hard, I bolted back into camp, meeting Gwynn at the bay.

"I'll go to Scops alone."

She gave a sick laugh. "No you won't. Get Matanta."

"They've gone. Nobody's here." I ran to the motorboat.

Gwynn grabbed my arm. "Andrew, don't make me hurt you."

"Every minute we waste could see the fire jump. Once it crosses . . ." My voice trailed off. She knew exactly what that meant.

Her hands found her hips. "So, you're taking a motorboat out, alone, past hippos that will try and kill you?"

I swallowed hard, but Gwynn wasn't finished. "Past the fire burning along a channel? And with the water level so low, it's difficult to see the sand banks during the day?"

Gwynn didn't need to tell me this. I knew it was madness. At no time since being on the island—or during my tenure on planet Earth—had I been this scared. But what choice did I have?

I kissed Gwynn on the cheek. "Hold that thought." I was halfway to the boat when the radio crackled again.

"638. 638. 110."

Gwynn raced to the mic.

I stopped to listen as Morag's excited voice broke through. "The wind's changed!" I straightened up, suddenly aware of the breeze shifting the smoke over the camp. It had indeed turned. "The fire's burning back on itself," Morag half-sobbed, half-laughed. "We're saved."

Relief ploughed through me. I wouldn't have to do this impossible thing. I sagged to the ground. All I wanted was a drink—something strong.

But the danger hadn't passed.

The wind could change again just as easily. While the fire surrounded our tiny island, sleep would be impossible.

It was past two when the guests crawled off to bed with promises that we would wake them the minute anything dangerous happened.

Gwynn and I grabbed a few blankets from the CIM room and curled up on the lounge chairs, waiting for radio calls. It was a strange time, talking about the important things in life. It's not very often that such an opportunity presents itself. Every now and again, we strolled, hand in hand, through the camp onto the runway to see if the halo from the fire had grown. It remained unchanged. As the night slipped away and dawn crept across the sky, I knew for sure that we had been spared—at least for that night.

* * *

That morning, the staff arrived in camp in their usual happy dispositions. The same could not be said for me.

In the kitchen, Matanta, Robert, Kegkebele and Petso were getting the day started. I barged in and demanded, "Where the hell were you last night?"

They looked at me as if I had lost my mind.

"I told you to stay at Otter Lodge. I needed you last night, urgently."

"What did you need us for, *Rra*," Matanta asked, looking genuinely concerned, but also a bit confused.

"I needed to take the boat down to Scops."

"But the boat is still here," Matanta replied, with annoying logic.

"Yes. I know. But Englishman needed it to stop the fire jumping the channel."

"But it didn't jump the channel."

This was getting me nowhere. "Yes. I know that, too. The wind changed."

"Yes, we know. The wind changed." Matanta looked at me as if I needed help—of the psychiatric kind.

What was the matter with him? Couldn't he see how infuriating he was being? "But before the wind changed, I needed someone to help me get the boat down to Scops."

"You needed help to drive the motorboat on the river?"

"Yes," I almost shouted.

At that moment, I realised that to continue arguing threatened the four hundred quintillion points I'd scored during the baboon shooting. They would drop to less than 25 in an instant.

"Well. The company would have been nice," I said lamely, almost hearing the reverse-beeping noise as I backed up. "I told you all to stay at Otter. You weren't there. So where were you?"

"At Honey Camp," Matanta said, as if that was the most logical thing in the world. "It's closer to Scops. We thought it best to be in the middle."

I rolled my eyes. Didn't it occur to anyone to mention this during our *kgotla*? Then I remembered saying that I was the only one who would be speaking. Man, what a time to take me literally.

"I get that, but how would you know if you were needed? Honey

Camp is too far from both camps to be of any use."

Silence. They all stared at me. None of the brainiacs had considered that.

Matanta picked up a pot and dropped it noisily. He was never ham-fisted.

Saved! I kept most of my points. I couldn't be too cross. Everyone was alive and no harm done.

After breakfast, Gwynn and I went out alone with the motorboat to view the fire damage. As far as the eye could see, reeds, islands, and floodplains were black and desolate.

I could only imagine how the game and birds had suffered.

"At least it was a quick burn," Gwynn murmured, obviously thinking along similar lines. "The bigger game and birds will probably have survived."

The quick burn had spared the two palms that stood sentinel in front of the camp. Their silhouettes were a vital part of the visual composition when looking out from the bay across the floodplains. They had graced every Tau Camp T-shirt ever printed, most of which now resided in my wardrobe.

As I stared out at this scorched Earth, it was hard to believe that fire triggered new life in so much of the Kalahari. The seeds from the palm trees we mourned would never germinate unless doused by fire or the heat of an elephant gut.

There was some comfort to be had in that, I suppose. They, too, were torn trousers.

CHAPTER 57

January turned into February, as it always does. The fires burned
themselves out, and the water level continued to drop. With it, our
stamina. Like the walking wounded, we stumbled onto the plane that
would take us back to Johannesburg for our ten days leave.

We had serious decisions to make about our future. Should we
renew our contract? Or did we tender our resignation when we returned
to Maun?

Our discussions only started about half way into our leave because
we used the other half to catch up on sleep. Truth was, we were
exhausted.

It was a hot day in Johannesburg with towers of cumulous clouds
threatening an afternoon thunderstorm. Perched on the swing in
Andrew's parents' garden, we barely noticed the darkening of the sky.

"I'm tired of working someone else's business," Andrew said.

I understood what he meant. While we had escaped our own
businesses by selling up, relieving ourselves of the stresses of making a
living, the results were far from paradise. Actually, it was mostly
geography. I wondered if it was possible to truly escape on planet Earth.
I had my doubts. Both good and bad stress, I was coming to realise, were
the human condition.

I bit my lip, suddenly conscious of a chill in the air. The wind
picked up as the storm approached. Perhaps it reflected the change
coming in our lives. I wasn't sure if I was quite ready for it.

"How about we stay for another six months?" I ventured.

Andrew's eyebrows knotted and his hand tugged at his beard.
"We've seen all four seasons. Done stuff no tourist will ever do. Met
some of the best and some of the dullest people the planet has to offer.
Been bitten by every known insect."

I snorted. "Your point?"

"How can we top that? Is there a magic we haven't experienced yet? Would we remember it more by staying another six months?"

I hated it when he was right.

The first drops of rain started to fall.

* * *

We drove to Maun in our Land Rover with yet another letter for Sean. Again, as we had done so many months ago, we parked in the patchy shade outside his Maun offices.

Sean was in his cave. Andrew handed the letter over and we waited. He looked up after reading it, and said. "I accept. With regret."

And that was it. We had just resigned from Tau Camp. We would work out a month's notice and then it would all be over.

I must admit to butterflies in my stomach, squadrons of them, as we flew into camp that afternoon.

I could not help channelling Karen Blixen, of *Out of Africa* fame. Would the birds that squawked and squabbled around the camp pause in their capers to acknowledge our decision? Would the lechwe and impala look up from their grazing to mark the change? Or would the ripples of our influence dissipate, unnoticed?

We took Matanta aside as soon as we landed. He waited, a quizzical expression on his face. I left it to Andrew to break the news.

"We're leaving."

"But you just got back."

"No. I mean, leaving. For good."

Matanta's mouth dropped and he stepped back, looking as if he had been struck. "No, *Rra*. Don't joke with me like that."

I placed my hand on his shoulder. "I'm sorry. But it's time. We need to move on. Get on with our lives."

Matanta buried his face in his hands, saying nothing.

I hugged him. He hugged me. Then he hugged Andrew.

When they parted, tears sparkled in Matanta's eyes. "For a year, *one* year, I have been the deputy manager at Tau Camp. The new managers," he spat on a nearby bush, "to them, I will just be another stupid black man."

Guilt bit at me. "It doesn't have to be like that, Matanta."

He snorted. "It does. And it will. I know how things work." He studied each of us in turn. "Why? I thought you liked it here. Liked my jokes."

I smiled. "We love your jokes. But I'm kind of ready to have a family. You know, settle down." I could see he wasn't buying that. But then, why should he? If the rumours were true, he had bits of families scattered all over the delta. "I want a home of my own again."

He sighed. "I can tell the other staff?"

We nodded.

And that was how the month-long procession of well-wishers started.

Impeleng was the first to appear. I was sorting through some paperwork at reception when I noticed her, impatiently tapping her fingers on the desk. I looked up and smiled. Without uttering a word, she shoved a large, colourful basket at me, and then scampered off to the laundry. Tears filled my eyes.

Hers was the first of many gifts we received.

Strange thing, though, I didn't recognise some of the bearers who came toting baskets, woven bread trays, animals carved from palm wood, and seed bracelets and necklaces. Matanta and Robert said they were people who lived in the village. People I didn't even know.

It was humbling.

Every day Matanta came to work armed with his camera. He kept sneaking up, capturing shots of me doing the most mundane things, like packing away stock, writing menus, or arguing with Morag.

Yes, Morag and I continued our hostilities right up until the end. I never really figured out her case, though. I knew she wanted my job, but it all seemed so pointless. Life was too short and these precious interludes so fleeting.

CHAPTER 58

We had only a couple of days left when Joan called me up on the radio.

"Your Land Rover has been broken into. They took the bonnet off and broke the back window."

My stomach plummeted. "Is the bonnet still there?"

"Yes. I think they might have tried to steal the engine or something. But they were disturbed. They didn't get much by the look of it."

The Land Rover had been parked at Joan's home, hidden under some trees. Protected by a low fence and locked gate, it was easily accessible to passers-by.

It could no longer remain there. But what would I do now?

Assuming it was okay to drive, I could bring it to Tau. That would solve the problem of getting all our stuff to Maun by plane at the end of the month. But as no vehicles were allowed on the island, I'd have to keep the whole expedition quiet from Sean. Just like we had the Jugugugu trip he still knew nothing about.

The camps had once been served by vehicles, the two wrecks in the bushes attested to that. But would the track still be visible enough to follow? I had my doubts, so I went and asked Matanta.

"The village does sometimes get trucks with supplies," he explained. "So driving there should be okay because the water is low. Only between the village and here, it could be difficult."

I saw an instant solution to my problem. "Why don't you come with me?"

Matanta's face beamed and he even did that twisty jive thing with

290

his hips.

The next challenge was to secure two seats on an outgoing plane—without Sean knowing about it. For once, the gods smiled on me. Two empty seats were up for grabs on tomorrow's outgoing flight.

I grabbed the radio. When Joan answered, I asked, "Is Sean around?"

"He's out for the day."

Could this get any better?

"The two seats on tomorrow plane....they're mine. I'm collecting the car. Please don't say anything."

"Roger that." I could hear the smile in her voice. "Let's pray the thieves leave it alone for another twenty-four hours." If ever there was a woman whose outward appearance belied what went on in her heart, it was Joan.

Mid-morning, the next day, Matanta and I arrived in Maun. Sepei happily ferried us to Joan's house. I rushed to my car. The thieves had smashed one of the small back windows, but the bonnet was there. Its hinges lay in the dust. Inside, most of our camping gear was present, save for two Maglites missing from their clamps. In the engine bay, it was clear that something had been going on.

"I think they tried to steal the carburettors," Matanta said.

One had been unbolted and its connections removed. But the repair was easy and the two of us had the engine running in an hour.

"How long is the drive to the camp?"

Matanta frowned. "Four. Maybe five hours."

I grinned at him. "Four if it goes well. Five if we get lost?"

"Get lost? This is me, *Rra*. How can you even suggest that?"

"Okay. Four if we don't get stuck in the mud."

"As driver, that's your problem."

"No. *You* are going on look out duty. If anything goes wrong, the problem is all yours."

Matanta laughed. "Nothing will go wrong, *Rra*. You'll see."

Wishing I shared his confidence, (I'd been around too long), we fuelled up in Maun. I bought us some biltong (similar, but much better than beef jerky) and Cokes for the road. We set off.

Within an hour of Maun, the road narrowed into a side-scraping bush track, the type Gwynn and I loved to explore. Alone, I would never have found my way but, as promised, Matanta knew which way to turn on the dozens of intersections we encountered.

We reached our first hurdle, the Buffalo Fence rimming the delta. We stopped at the veterinary check-point. The official knew Matanta and waved us through. Ordinarily, without a special permit, access to the delta would have been denied. To say Matanta was smug would be an understatement.

Four uneventful hours later, we arrived at our staff village. A horde of people came running out to meet us. After a cheery welcome, we looked for the track to Tau.

There was none.

We both knew which direction the camp lay, so it wasn't a major problem. But, between it and us, lay an obstacle course of rivers, dried flood plains pitted with foot-deep elephant footprints, mopane tree stumps waiting to rip through a tyre, and, of course, aardvark holes by the thousand.

It was thrilling.

Matanta seemed to think so too. I had him perched on the window sill of the passenger door so he could look out for hazards. He leaned out further than necessary, obviously having a blast.

"Left. Straight. Right," his voice called above the grind of the engine.

And then there was a loud bang, a lurch, a thump, and silence. The car stopped moving.

I swore. Partly at him.

"I thought you saw it." Matanta pulled his head and torso into the car. "You didn't see it?"

"No. I seem to recall that looking for things was your job."

"I saw you swing the wheel. I thought you had seen it."

Eyes rolling, I climbed out to look at the damage—and discovered that your average aardvark burrow measures almost exactly the same diameter as a General 7.00 x 16 radial tyre. The kind my Landy was shod with. We were stuck. And this kind of stuck could only be solved by lifting the vehicle out of the hole with a jack.

"*Eish*," Matanta moaned. "Sorry, *Rra*."

I smiled. "Relax. I've got this one." Eager to show off more of my skills, I trotted around to the back door where my hi-lift jack was mounted.

My heart sank.

"Bugger! They stole it." Bravado shattered, my hand reached for my beard. It was time for some serious tugging while I pondered the impossibility of getting my car out of the hole without a hi-lift jack, or a winch with a second vehicle. We could be here for days.

"It's not a problem," Matanta said, cheerily. "They are coming."

"Who are coming?"

"The guides. They would have heard the engine for a long time. They'll come and find us."

I shrugged and we sat down in the shade of the car with a couple to Cokes to wait. Ordinarily, a mishap like this would have infuriated me, but not today. Maybe I had finally caught some of the stuff that made Matanta great. "Man, I love this continent." I grinned as I cracked the tab on my can. "No problem. Why stress? Help will come. Chill out."

Matanta grinned. "Finally, you get it *Rra*."

Less than twenty minutes later, four Scops' guides appeared through the bush.

Laughing and joking, they strode over to the car and, without prompting, instruction, or persuasion, lifted the entire back end. They parked it on level ground.

I handed out the last of the Coke and biltong and we drove on.

The staff at Tau also heard us coming. Every single person lined the runway. They waved and laughed as we took a slow drive past, almost like a victory lap.

A Land Rover One-Ten V8 station-wagon was a particularly cool looking 4x4 when it came to bush travel, so the points I'd lost over the fire boat incident were quickly regained. I could imagine, years from now, folk singing songs about the great chief, with the big gun, and cool 4x4.

The adoration didn't stop there. They showed their appreciation by immediately cleaning my dusty, mud-splattered car. Even Matanta got his hands wet.

I might have been their hero, but in every way I could think of, they were mine, too.

* * *

The next day, Gwynn and I packed up all our worldly treasures and drove Darien out to the runway. This time, the waves of the waiting crowds were subdued, the laughter stilled. I noticed more than a few tears in Gwynn's eyes.

Heart in my throat, I drove the Landy down the airstrip for the very last time. The bush at the end swallowed us whole, and the camp and our staff disappeared from view.

EPILOGUE

Gwynn was pregnant with our first child when we next visited Tau
Camp. Exactly two years to the day that we had started our Tau
adventure, we returned. We left Woodie (who made a full recovery and
had forgiven us for her troubles) in the care of Gwynn's mother and
departed from Johannesburg in Andrew's twin-seater Grob motor-glider.
The motor-glider's 17-metre wingspan made it too hazardous to land on
Tau's narrow airstrip, so we camped the night in Maun.

Joan, Verity, and Sepei were pleased to see us, but Sean was cool.
He didn't offer us a free night in the camp as we had hoped he might.
How could we have forgotten so soon about that tight wallet of his?

We did manage to scrounge a discount at Scops, though. We were
writing a 4x4 travellers' adventure book and promised to feature the
camps. The article was eventually published in three editions of that
book.

Our first night on Noga Island was spent at Scops. The next
morning, we walked the familiar path back to our old home. We might
have left the island, but the elephants certainly hadn't. Not many palms
remained standing.

As we walked the length of the runway, we noticed that most of
the sprinkler heads were missing or broken. We shared a warm chuckle.

The hippos were still around, too.

So were the baboons, sunning themselves on the runway opposite the camp. Bold as ever, they were fat and healthy, no doubt from regular kitchen raids. The shooting of Saddam and the other baboon had made no dent in the raids when we were at the camp. It was unlikely anything had changed in our absence.

Close to the camp entrance waited a small bachelor herd of elephant. They looked familiar. Had they come back to greet us? Or hadn't they moved since the day we left?

There were two new signs nailed to a tree next to the anthill. The first one read, 'Private Camp.' That seemed like a good idea. The second, 'No Elephant Allowed'. We both thought that very cheesy.

In the camp, everything was quiet. There were no guests, no manager, and few staff.

We found Robert in the kitchen.

He greeted us warmly with a traditional handshake. "*Rra en Mma,* when you left, everything changed. Sean hired a Zimbabwean lady. She was a *matata*. The worst racist you can imagine. She drove us all to rebellion."

We listened with sadness as Robert recounted the details of the ensuing strike. Matanta and all the guides had been fired.

Robert shook his head, as if still unable to believe the carnage. "Three weeks later, Sean fired the Zimbabwean woman who caused all the trouble."

Leaving Robert to his quiche-making, we ambled to the bay.

Thoughts of happy times nudged away our sorrow at Matanta's loss. Being autumn, the water had filled the floodplain. Only one of the palms that created the camp's picture-postcard composition remained standing.

Sean had built a raised platform between the lounge and the dining room. We thought it an ugly addition that spoiled the open feel of the guest area. But then we would have preferred to return and see it just how we had left it—a happy, vibrant place, filled with the spirit of friendship and laughter, with bits of chewed plastic lying around.

Before saying our good-byes, we stepped into the curio shop and bought a beautiful bream, carved from palm-heart. It remains a treasured possession.

After our first two daughters were born, we escaped Johannesburg again, this time to settle in Cape Town. Sadly, Woodie didn't join us, having succumbed to kidney failure the year before. With a third daughter added to the family, we built a book and documentary film production business. The 4x4 book Andrew wrote at Tau Camp was the very first we published.

In August 2010, we visited Tau Camp for the second time.

Andrew was making an adventure travel program and had embarked on an expedition to find the source of the Okavango River in Angola. He followed its course through the delta, past Tau Camp, onto its end in the Boteti River at Rakops.

Gwynn met him on Noga Island.

Tau Camp had changed so much that it was unrecognisable. In fact, the two camps had swapped places. We walked around Scops, which now occupied Tau Camp's side of the island. Our old home had gone, as had the ugly raised platform Sean had built. Half of the cottages had vanished, too. An air of disrepair hung about the place.

Down at the new Tau Camp, the famous *mokoro* bar and its skulls had gone. The camp itself was as beautiful and, if anything, more luxurious than when we had left it.

Even better, a Motswanan man was in charge. Despite Sandy's greatest fears, he was an excellent host. Turns out he remembered us, but we didn't remember him.

We learned from him that Kamanga, the venerable man who had not approved of Sam's strike, had been taken by a crocodile. He had fought to save his guests after a croc upturned his *mokoro*. While they scrambled to safety on the bank, Kamanga was dragged under and never seen again.

Most of the guides we knew were still in the Okavango.

But the person we were most interested in was Matanta.

He, too, had moved on to manage a camp in Savuti. We still have to meet up with him again.

Back in Maun, we bumped into Robert. He had become a successful businessman. We joined him for dinner at the lodge and restaurant he managed. He shared the sad news that Thekiso, Olututswe, Seatla, and Alfred had all passed on.

It reminded us of how fragile this mortal life really was. Following one's dreams is important, regardless of the outcome.

Like everyone, we have regrets, but the year spent on Noga Island wasn't one of them.

As we write this final chapter in late 2014, we still feel the indescribable urge to do it all over again.

Dear Reader,

Thank you for reading our story. We hope you enjoyed it as much as we enjoyed writing it. Please help others to find it by leaving a review on Amazon or Goodreads. Thank you.

* * *

ABOUT ANDREW AND GWYNN

Andrew and Gwynn live in England with two of their daughters, a golden Labrador, a yapping Toy Pomeranian, and a fantastic farm cat called Pixel. Like Woodie, Pixel rules them all with a sharp claw in a velvet paw.

Andrew is a published author of fifteen 4x4 books, and countless travel and 4x4 magazine articles. He also produces and directs adventure travel TV shows. These have been broadcast on three continents. You can stalk him at:

http://4xforum.com/

and

https://www.youtube.com/user/4xforum

Gwynn began her publishing career writing travel books. She now devotes her creative energy to fantasy and science fiction.

You can find her at: http://gwynnwhite.blogspot.co.uk/

and

https://www.facebook.com/pages/Gwynn-White/1424220634521068?ref=bookma